TROUBLEMAKERS

Troublemakers

Students' Rights and Racial Justice in the Long 1960s

Kathryn Schumaker

NEW YORK UNIVERSITY PRESS

New York

NEW YORK UNIVERSITY PRESS
New York
www.nyupress.org

References to Internet websites (URLs) were accurate at the time of writing. Neither the author nor New York University Press is responsible for URLs that may have expired or changed since the manuscript was prepared.

Library of Congress Cataloging-in-Publication Data
Names: Schumaker, Kathryn, author.
Title: Troublemakers : students' rights and racial justice in the long 1960s /
Kathryn Schumaker.
Description: New York : New York University Press, 2019. |
Includes bibliographical references and index.
Identifiers: LCCN 2018042919 | ISBN 9781479875139 (cl : alk. paper) |
ISBN 9781479820498 (paperback) | ISBN 9781479801138 (ebook) |
ISBN 9781479821365 (ebook)
Subjects: LCSH: Students—Civil rights—United States—History—20th century. |
Nineteen sixties—Social aspects.
Classification: LCC KF4150 .S36 2019 | DDC 344.73/07909046—dc23
LC record available at https://lccn.loc.gov/2018042919

New York University Press books are printed on acid-free paper, and their binding materials are chosen for strength and durability. We strive to use environmentally responsible suppliers and materials to the greatest extent possible in publishing our books.

Manufactured in the United States of America

10 9 8 7 6 5 4 3 2

Also available as an ebook

For my students, past and present

CONTENTS

List of Figures   ix

Introduction   1

1. The Right to Free Speech: Students and the Black Freedom
   Struggle in Mississippi   11

2. The Right to Equal Protection: Segregation and Inequality
   in the Denver Public Schools   51

3. The Right to Due Process: Student Discipline and
   Civil Rights in Columbus, Ohio   92

4. A Right to Equal Education: The Fourteenth Amendment
   and American Schools   131

5. *Tinker's* Troubled Legacy: Discipline, Disorder, and Race
   in the Schools, 1968–1985   171

Epilogue   209

Acknowledgments   215

Notes   219

Index   269

About the Author   283

LIST OF FIGURES

Figure 1.1. Freedom school students listen to folksinger
Pete Seeger at the Palmers Crossing Community
Center, 1964, Hattiesburg, Mississippi.   16

Figure 1.2. A group sings freedom songs at the Freedom Schools
Convention during Freedom Summer, 1964,
Meridian, Mississippi.   31

Figure 2.1. Map of Denver public high schools and attendance
boundaries in 1962.   56

Figure 2.2. Black men and women demonstrate in favor of
passage of the Noel Resolution in Denver, Colorado,
May 16, 1968.   63

Figure 2.3. Members of the Black Berets stand guard in front
of Corky Gonzales as he delivers a speech during a
demonstration at the Colorado State Capitol Building,
Denver, on November 3, 1968.   67

Introduction

In the late 1960s, teenagers rebelled in public schools across the United States. From the Mississippi Delta to East Los Angeles and Columbus, Ohio, young people spoke out against injustices they witnessed at school and in American society. This was also the moment in which school districts around the nation began implementing desegregation plans to comply at long last with the Supreme Court's 1954 *Brown v. Board of Education* decision, which declared laws requiring the segregation of students by race unconstitutional. Amid this ferment of social protest and educational reform, black and Latino students seized the moment to speak out against other forms of racial discrimination at school and advocate for practices and policies that would make education more equitable for students of all races and ethnicities.[1] Students sometimes conducted peaceful, silent protests and, at other times, disrupted classes with walkouts, picket lines, sit-ins, marches, and rebel assemblies. Predictably, school administrators often punished them in response.[2]

High school students, however, had no right to protest at school. Until the mid-1960s, elementary and secondary students were generally not considered to be protected by the Constitution, including the First Amendment right to free expression. The constitutional claims a young person could make in a public park were entirely different from those that could be made in a public school classroom just across the street. Merely wearing a button or a T-shirt with an unpopular message could be enough to warrant suspension or expulsion in the eyes of disapproving adults. Principals suspended or expelled students for their words and actions, and state laws generally deferred to the authority of school officials to punish students at will.[3] And students and their families had no constitutional recourse to challenge administrators or teachers who disciplined them, including cases involving the suppression of free speech.

Undeterred by suspensions and expulsions and assisted by sympathetic lawyers, the parents and guardians of some of these teenaged protesters sued their schools and claimed for all public school students the protections of the federal Constitution. In doing so, they asked federal courts to tread on new legal ground and recognize that certain constitutional rights should protect young people in public schools. In this respect, students' rights litigation was a great success. Between 1969 and 1985, the Supreme Court issued a series of rulings that defined and limited the constitutional rights of students in public elementary and secondary schools, beginning with the 1969 landmark *Tinker v. Des Moines* decision, in which the Court declared that students and teachers do not "shed their constitutional rights to freedom of speech or expression at the schoolhouse gate."[4] *Tinker's* broad language about students and the Constitution opened the floodgates for lawsuits concerning the constitutional rights of students. In the following decade and a half, the nation's high court similarly established students' rights to due process of law and privacy and considered cases involving a range of other rights.

Many historians and legal scholars have written extensively on *Tinker* and its progeny of free speech cases, noting how the Supreme Court has since narrowed the scope of students' rights to free expression.[5] At the same time, other scholars have offered detailed histories of the path that led to *Brown v. Board of Education* and the consequences of the decision's later implementation, while others have debated the merits of the focus on dismantling school segregation through the courts.[6] Justin Driver, in his book, *The Schoolhouse Gate: Public Education, the Supreme Court, and the Battle for the American Mind*, argues that schools have been central battlegrounds in conflicts over the meaning of the American Constitution. At the same time, Driver demonstrates how, through school cases, the Court has shaped American society.[7] This book, in contrast, provides a new history of the development of students' constitutional rights, focusing on lawsuits that emerged out of the efforts of students to secure racial justice at school. By foregrounding students' concerns and reading the history of students' rights through the lens of race, this book reveals the wider stakes of implementing racial reform in public schools. Students do not understand their rights in the narrow way that lawyers or judges approach legal doctrine. Instead, young people often view their legal claims to free expression and fair disciplinary practices as interlocking parts of a broader struggle against racial discrimination and segregation in American public education. Yet this book also demonstrates how, even as students secured certain constitutional rights, this litigation often did little to strengthen the ability of young people to challenge persistent racial discrimination at school through the courts.

Student protesters of the 1960s and early 1970s followed in the footsteps of previous generations of young people who participated in acts of protest against racial inequities in American public education. Even the *Brown* decision had roots in the political activity of young people at school. A 1951 student strike at Robert Russa Moton High School in Farmville, Virginia, which targeted the shabby conditions at the school, set off a chain of events that would end with the filing of *Davis v. County School Board of Prince Edward County*, one of the three cases that were combined with *Brown* by the Supreme Court.[8] And in the years following the *Brown* decision, young people put their bodies on the line across the South from Little Rock to Atlanta as they became the first students to desegregate previously all-white schools in the 1950s. Offered as symbols of racial injustice while also serving as actors in the challenge to white supremacy, the involvement of students in the struggle for racial justice reflected a broader increase in political participation by young people that peaked in the 1960s. High school and college-aged students staged sit-ins at lunch counters, marched with Martin Luther King, Jr., in Birmingham, and rode across state lines during the Freedom Rides.[9] They often worked side by side with white activists, cross-pollinating ideas about participatory democracy, individual rights, and grassroots organizing among New Left organizations in the early 1960s.[10] Students at high schools and colleges often faced discipline from administrators, and these shared concerns were perhaps best exemplified by the clashes between students and administrators that sparked the 1964 Berkeley Free Speech Movement.[11] The rise of youth protest during the 1960s also marked an important turning point in Mexican American history, as self-identified Chicanos claimed a "brown" racial identity.[12] The emergence of a robust Chicano movement during the latter part of the decade and its central focus on schools as sites of protest against discrimination and exclusion brought parallel yet distinct challenges to the inequities in American education. Indeed, it was the East Los Angeles "blowouts"—a string of walkouts, boycotts, and protests that took place in the city's public schools in March 1968—that first garnered national attention and introduced Americans to the nascent Chicano Movement.[13]

Despite—or perhaps because of—the increased involvement of young people in social movements in the 1960s, students frequently faced resistance to the idea that their protest activity was legitimate. Condemnation came from everyone from President Nixon to legislators, mayors, school board members, teachers, parents, and other students. Many judges and some Supreme Court justices were similarly skeptical of their political activity. Nonetheless, they continued to organize and air grievances that ranged from curricula to disciplinary policies to the hiring of teachers of color. That high school students had the right to be heard was patently absurd to many and deeply disturbing to others who worried that the disruptions of the era jeopardized the ability of schools to carry out their mission to educate all young people. Their claims were frivolous, their methods crude, and their efforts the result of youthful immaturity. Why should anyone care what teenagers think?

This disregard for the political beliefs and actions of young people is rooted in a linked set of beliefs and assumptions, all of which were contested during this historical moment. The first assumption is that the ability to participate in the political sphere rests upon a person reaching the age of majority, a moment that is often accompanied by the extension of political privileges such as voting and obligations like military service. But American history is peopled with actors who participated in political activism even as they were members of groups who were denied formal participation in the political sphere, including those who were excluded owing to their status as enslaved persons, women, or immigrants. The second assumption, which distinguishes the young from other historically marginalized groups, is that young people cannot or do not have the competence to form their own political beliefs. The age of majority, which is set by state law, determines a distinct range of competencies and associated ages that reflect the judgment of legislators about when individuals are old enough to shoulder certain kinds of rights and responsibilities. The age of consent for sex or marriage, for example, often differs from the age at which a person can vote, which is distinct from the age at which a person can legally purchase alcohol.[14] Laws determining the age of majority demonstrate, therefore, significant differences in community beliefs about when and why age discrimination is reasonable or unreasonable. Conceptions about children and childhood itself have been made and remade throughout American history, and the creation of a separate category of "adolescents"—distinct from "children"—is a recent phenomenon that reflects discomfort with a bright line between childhood and adulthood.[15] Rather, as teenagers approach the threshold of adulthood, so, too, do they gain the competency that leads to independence and justifies political participation.

The third assumption, and the one with which this book primarily engages, is the idea that young people in school should be primarily passive actors whose role is to receive the accumulated wisdom of educators. Until the 1960s, the law largely conformed to this view of the relationship between students and teachers, analogizing it to the relationship between parents and their children. But this idea was historically a contested one, as education experts argued for the radical reform of pedagogy in the 1960s.[16] The condition of being a student insulated young people from rights protections they had outside the schoolhouse gate and justified the authority that teachers and school administrators had to discipline students who were seen as unruly. This is a belief that many Americans still hold, and it is the one that high school students most visibly rebelled against during the 1960s and 1970s. It has also been the expressed belief of several Supreme Court justices, one of whom—as of the writing of this book—remains on the Court. As recently as 2007, Justice Clarence Thomas argued in a concurring Supreme Court opinion that high school students have no rights that the law is bound to respect.[17]

The legal scholar Barbara Bennett Woodhouse describes this kind of rejection of children's rights as a result of a "lack of imagination."[18] Thinking of the extension of the rights of young people as inherently restrictive of the rights of adults assumes that all such litigation is a zero-sum game, with adults suffering losses as young people gain rights protections. It also positions the struggle for students' rights as one founded in a desire to rebel rather than in meaningful grievances. In *Hidden in Plain Sight: The Tragedy of Children's Rights from Ben Franklin to Lionel Tate*, Woodhouse emphasizes how it is necessary to study the subject of children's rights from the perspective of young people.[19] In taking this approach to the student protests of the late 1960s and early 1970s, we can see that this litigation arose from arguments that protecting the rights of students would improve education for all. Young people were not merely rebelling against principals and teachers; instead, they claimed to be resisting a system of education that perpetuated racial discrimination.

Why did young people mobilize so forcefully around concerns about racial discrimination in education in the late 1960s and early 1970s? A confluence of outside factors contributed to the rise in student protest and the resulting wave of litigation that transformed the landscape of students' rights. The first decades of the twentieth century witnessed the rise and bureaucratization of public education in Northern cities, making high school attendance and completion a new expectation for young people.[20] But was not until the 1940s and 1950s that Southern states—which, historically, lagged behind other regions in the schooling of its children, both white and black—began making sincere efforts to equalize education for black children and teenagers, in large part owing to pressure from lawyers with the National Association for the Advancement of Colored People (NAACP) Legal Defense Fund (LDF).[21] In contrast, Mexican American children in the Southwest were far less likely to attend and complete high school than their peers elsewhere, creating a legacy of exclusion that carried through the generations.[22] But by the 1960s, American secondary education was more universal than ever before, drawing in the most diverse swath of students in history just as movements for racial equality swelled at the grassroots.

As high school education became expected and protest movements emerged, the presence of politically conscious young people in American public schools increased. Certainly not all young people who attended high schools in the late 1960s were involved with protest at school or even aware of the wider political currents in which they lived. But many did become politically engaged and, in doing so, clashed with school rules, cultural expectations, and a legal tradition that marked them as apolitical children rather than as persons who could or should express political beliefs. Furthermore, schools became focal points of the struggle for racial justice in the public eye through the implementation of *Brown v. Board of Education* and the 1964 Civil Rights Act. As Ansley Erickson's study of Nashville demonstrates, even in the midst of desegregation officials made and remade schools and their curricula to perpetuate the inequities that the policy was supposedly intended to ameliorate, which often generated further conflict in the schools.[23]

Developments in law and lawyering also played important roles in the establishment and development of students' constitutional rights. As students expressed dissent at school, advocates for young people mobilized on their behalf. Lawyers sent to the South by the LDF took up students' cases as part and parcel of their work defending civil rights activists in state and federal court. The establishment of the Mexican American Legal Defense Fund in 1968 and the Puerto Rican Legal Defense Fund in 1972 brought funds and attention to student rebellions over English-only policies, bilingual education, and school desegregation.[24] The Children's Defense Fund's creation in 1973 brought attention and resources to issues that primarily affected young people—especially racial disparities in schooling.[25] At the same time, much of the litigation brought on behalf of students originated with local lawyers whom parents and guardians persuaded to join the cause of advancing students' rights. Although national organizations did work on the cause of students' rights during the 1960s and 1970s, local activists and lawyers often made crucial contributions to this litigation.

Lawsuits challenging the constitutional rights of students were part of a historical moment in which American courts reconsidered the rights of children more broadly. Juvenile courts, which arose in the early twentieth century, treated young offenders in a separate system that ostensibly sought to reform young people through legal paternalism. This mission justified insulating young people from constitutional rights, giving judges virtually unlimited authority that was often abused.[26] But in 1967, in its decision in *In re Gault*, the U.S. Supreme Court ruled that young people in juvenile courts do have some constitutional protections, thereby breaching the wall that historically separated young people from the Constitution.[27] *In re Gault* represented a crucial moment of transition in which changing conceptions of children and childhood justified the extension of limited rights. The cases studied in this book are part of this constitutional moment in which courts reconsidered and redefined long-standing legal doctrines that governed the relationship between young people and the state.

The students' rights revolution began with the cases that preceded *Tinker v. Des Moines* and was hastened in the courts by litigation that challenged the authority of school administrators. It was dominated not by the Warren Court—often identified as the catalyst of the twentieth-century rights revolution—but instead by the years in which Warren Burger served as Chief Justice of the U.S. Supreme Court.[28] Beginning in the late 1960s and concluding by the mid-1980s, the justices of the

Burger Court identified and defined the most important constitutional rights that extended to students. Students successfully claimed rights to free speech, due process in suspensions and expulsions, and privacy in relation to searches of their belongings. Yet when it came to many of the constitutional rights that were most relevant to the racial justice claims of black, Chicano, and other minority student activists—the rights to substantially equal educational opportunities, to bilingual education, to not be corporally punished, and to education itself—the courts hedged and deferred to the authority of legislatures. This pattern of extending some rights while limiting those that were essential to making substantive rights claims in the face of racial discrimination led, ultimately, to a student rights' regime that privileged orderly schools over ones that demanded equal educational opportunities to all. In this sense, the success of the student rights revolution ultimately enshrined in law many of the inequities that student activists challenged in the first place.

Because this book takes seriously students' rights claims while also considering the legal doctrines developed by lawyers and judges, the first three chapters begin with grassroots efforts of students to create change at school before pivoting to examine how those rights claims fared in federal court. The book therefore employs social history methodology to recover the roots of student discontent as well as an examination of the legal doctrine of students' rights as it was created and employed on behalf of students in courtrooms across the country, including at the U.S. Supreme Court.

This story is both national and intensely local. The first three chapters are composed of case studies that are geographically diverse and cover distinct sets of rights claims made on behalf of students in court to free speech, equal protection, and due process, respectively. The geographic range covered by the book accounts for important regional differences while revealing foundational similarities in the complaints at the heart of students' protest activity. While no single story can accurately portray all facets of student protests for racial justice, these case studies demonstrate shared concerns about school discipline, leadership, and curricula despite stark differences in place and circumstance. The first chapter begins at the height of the Black Freedom Struggle in Mississippi in 1964, revealing how free speech concerns were central to civil rights activism in the state's segregated black schools. The second chapter travels west to Denver, where the Chicano Movement rose in the midst of school desegregation litigation, and focuses on equal protection as a distinct right that all students could claim. The third and final case study examines black student protest and disciplinary authority in Columbus, Ohio, through a Supreme Court case that laid the foundation for students' constitutional rights in the realm of school discipline.

The book's final two chapters take a national view, examining how the court decisions of the late 1960s and early 1970s shaped efforts to secure students' rights in relation to equal opportunity and school discipline, which I argue had important consequences for the ability of students to make headway through the courts against persistent racial discrimination at school. The fourth chapter focuses on the concept of equal protection, exploring how minority groups sought to leverage the Fourteenth Amendment to make claims for more equal schooling. Finally, the fifth chapter looks at students' rights in regard to school discipline, particularly in relation to conflict over the use of corporal punishment in schools and students' rights to privacy. These chapters bring together related cases that reveal how the extension of certain rights to students both expanded and constricted the kinds of constitutional claims that young people could make at school. By the early 1980s, the formative period of students' constitutional rights came to a close. Later courts would narrow and refine the extent of students' rights, but they did not fundamentally alter the terms that dictated why and when students in public schools received constitutional protections. The modern legal terrain therefore remains largely reflective of the cases that shaped students' constitutional rights between the 1960s and the early 1980s.

While the first three chapters of the book foreground student movements and the last two chapters focus more on national developments and the way lawyers and judges talked about students' rights, read together they reveal a perpetual conflict at the heart of these cases. Those who looked to litigation over students' rights often did so out of a conviction that public schooling perpetuated racial discrimination. Yet the ways in which the courts eventually articulated students' rights worked to reinforce rather than unmake that phenomenon. This is not to say that the goals of maintaining order and enforcing robust civil rights reforms are antithetical. Instead, this book identifies how the narrowed conceptions of other rights—in particular, the right to equal protection of the law and the right to education—constrained the means by which those who challenged racial discrimination in education could do so through constitutional law.

* * *

Given the attention paid to the social history of the rights movements of the twentieth century, it should come as no surprise to us that students in public secondary schools offered and acted on their own criticisms of educational institutions. As the historian and sociologist Charles Payne explains, histories of local people generate "a faith that ordinary people who learn to believe in themselves are capable of extraordinary acts, or better, of acts that seem extraordinary to us precisely because we have such an impoverished sense of the capabilities of ordinary people."[29] Looking to the teenaged protestors produces a new narrative on the way students' rights were articulated by courts in the last third of the twentieth century and the meanings of those decisions. The legal legacy produced by the student protests of the late 1960s and early 1970s transformed the relationship between public school students and the Constitution. Even as activists did not achieve all of their desired aims, they left their imprint on American public education, and their stories serve as continual reminders that young people can and do shape the course of history.

1

The Right to Free Speech

Students and the Black Freedom Struggle in Mississippi

In October 1964, a black teenager stepped up to the witness stand to offer her testimony in a Mississippi courtroom. Her name was Canzetta Burnside, and she was fifteen years old. The judge had to instruct her to speak up so that the court reporter could hear her testimony. The school district's lawyer spoke to the young woman condescendingly, calling Burnside by her first name despite the protestations of her attorney. Just moments before, the lawyer had prodded Burnside's mother about her older daughter Martha's out-of-wedlock pregnancy, making a pointed dig at the family's reputation.[1] Even in the courtroom, it was difficult for black men and women to demand respect from white people in Mississippi. Another student offering testimony, Neva Louise English, was just fourteen years old. Both students attended the segregated high school for black students in Philadelphia, Mississippi.[2] Burnside, English, and dozens of other students had been suspended from school two weeks earlier for wearing "freedom buttons" that expressed support for voter registration.[3] They were in court to protest the suspensions and claim the protection of the First Amendment's free speech clause. Burnside and English insisted that the buttons, which were inscribed with the Student Nonviolent Coordinating Committee (SNCC) slogan "One Man, One Vote," mattered a great deal to the students. Her lawyer prodded English: What did the buttons represent, and why did she and so many other students insist on wearing them to school, risking suspension and possible expulsion? "The reason we were wearing them is for our rights. . . . Our rights to speech and to do the things we would like to do," English responded. Upon further questioning, she added, "And to register and vote without being beat up and killed."[4]

In the autumn of 1964, when the judge initially heard the button case, the decade-old *Brown v. Board of Education* decision had not yet been brought to bear upon Mississippi's segregated system of education. Canzetta Burnside's principal was black, as were all of the teachers at her school. Concerned for his livelihood, the principal swiftly disciplined the students for their silent display of support for voter registration. Those who challenged Jim Crow did so at their own peril, as anyone present in the courtroom when Canzetta Burnside and Neva Louise English testified would know. English's reference to people being "beat up and killed" for attempting to register to vote invoked the horrific crime that attracted the national spotlight to Philadelphia months earlier: the kidnapping and murder of civil rights workers Andrew Goodman, James Chaney, and Michael Schwerner. This chapter explores the two button cases that emerged from Mississippi schools in the months after Freedom Summer, which marked an important turning point in the development of students' free speech rights. Yet the button cases were about far more than the First Amendment. The protests that spurred litigation and the harsh responses of school administrators revealed internal conflicts over the extent of administrators' authority and the provision of separate and unequal education to the state's black students. The treatment of black students in public schools and the inferior education they received became a focal point of protest as teenagers emerged as historical actors, inspired by the activism of others but bearing grievances and agendas of their own.

Education and Freedom in Mississippi

The button cases emerged from a historical moment in which young people were politicized, with many participating in direct action protests during Freedom Summer, a voter registration and education campaign launched in June 1964 by the Council of Federated Organizations (COFO). The council coordinated the efforts of several civil rights organizations, making it possible for hundreds of black and white college students from outside the Deep South to travel to Mississippi to join local people in challenging the legitimacy and legality of Jim Crow.

Freedom Summer was certainly not the first effort to register voters and fight white supremacy in Mississippi, and by the time SNCC arrived, youth organizing was already a tradition in the state. While the threat of violence or the loss of a job kept many African Americans reluctant to join civil rights organizations and publicize their support in the process, many young people joined the anti-white supremacy efforts spearheaded by adults. In the late 1950s, intrepid local teenagers organized National Association for the Advancement of Colored People (NAACP) Youth Councils in several Mississippi cities.[5] Their activism, like that of Canzetta Burnside and Neva Louise English, often resulted in consequences at school. Black administrators in segregated schools straddled two worlds. They served black students and families while being perpetually conscious of the control whites held over their jobs and livelihoods.[6] And so, when black students brought their protests to school, black administrators responded by punishing them with suspensions or expulsions. In Meridian, Youth Council members were suspended by school administrators for wearing badges to school stating "U.S. Supreme Court Decision, May 17, 1954," in reference to *Brown v. Board of Education* and in protest of continuing racial segregation in the city's schools.[7]

In the spring of 1961, the Freedom Riders rolled across state lines to test the enforcement of federal lawsuits that struck down racial segregation in interstate bus terminals, garnering a bloody response from local police officers and the Ku Klux Klan.[8] A few months after the Freedom Rides, a group of SNCC workers began voter registration work in the southwestern city of McComb, where violence and threats forced the NAACP chapter to go underground during the increase in white violence after *Brown*.[9] During the voter registration drive, organizers in McComb were arrested and brutalized by police, and in late September, a white Mississippi state legislator shot and killed local black NAACP member Herbert Lee, bringing a violent end to SNCC's work.[10]

Amid the effort to register voters in McComb before Lee's murder, more than 100 high school students staged a walkout at Burgland High School to demonstrate solidarity for their classmates Brenda Travis and Ike Lewis, who had been arrested and thrown in jail for attempting to desegregate the local Greyhound station.[11] When the school's principal expelled Travis and Lewis, Burgland students left the school and marched down to city hall. While the sole white SNCC worker was beaten by angry whites, police arrested more than 100 of the student protesters as well as the SNCC workers. After her expulsion, Travis was declared delinquent by a local judge and sent to a reformatory school, where she remained until May 1962.[12] The students' protests divided local black adults, and some furious parents publicly whipped their children once they were released from jail.[13] Students were required to sign a pledge vowing they would not participate in any direct action protests in order to return to school; those who refused were expelled and attended an alternative school, Nonviolent High. The school offered courses taught by SNCC organizers, including Robert Moses, a former teacher at New York City's Horace Mann School.[14] The use of alternative schools as forums for teaching black history in tandem with raising the political consciousness of young people was one that flowered during Freedom Summer and was later used in other instances when young people were excluded from school for their protest activity.[15]

In 1963, the sit-in movement came to Woolworth's in Jackson when three black students and their white teacher from Tougaloo College sat at the whites-only lunch counter as whites jeered, dumped ketchup on them, and physically assaulted the peaceful protesters.[16] Black students in Jackson likewise put their bodies on the line during a walkout in 1963. Gene Young testified in 1964 before Congress that he had been a part of the peaceful protest, during which policemen brutalized children as they marched to the state capitol. They were rounded up, and because there were too many students and too few jail cells, the children were forced into animal pens at the state fairgrounds where, Young testified, they were fed food cooked in garbage bins and stirred with mops.[17] Months before Freedom Summer began, thousands of public school students in Canton staged a walkout and day-long boycott of their schools in protest of the poor conditions.[18]

These teenagers joined college-aged men and women in a generation that was more politically active than any other since the 1930s.[19] In planning the Mississippi Project, COFO organizers identified education and voting rights as interlocking parts of the challenge to white supremacy. The voter registration drive of Freedom Summer culminated with the establishment of the Mississippi Freedom Democratic Party, which challenged the legitimacy of the segregationist Southern delegation from the state at the August 1964 Democratic National Convention in Atlantic City, New Jersey.[20] It also contributed to a wave of national support for meaningful voting reforms that crested with the passage of the 1965 Voting Rights Act.

In addition to its voter registration work, COFO founded "freedom schools," which mostly catered to children and teenagers. Just as the voter registration efforts necessitated teaching black Mississippians to ace the literacy tests required for voter registration, the freedom schools sought to create an analogous role as the incubators of future voters and activists by allowing students to study black history and the political systems of the state. Historians have shown how transformative the experience of attending a freedom school was for many black children and teenagers.[21] Although most college-aged volunteers stayed only for the muggy months of July and August, Freedom Summer's impact rippled outward in the following months, rocking other facets of Mississippi life long after it ended—especially public education.

The ideas undergirding the freedom schools and their role in undermining racial subordination were embodied by SNCC organizer Charles Cobb's initial pitch, which he circulated during winter of 1963–1964. The prospectus emphasized the basic inequities of Mississippi's public education system and how it was "burdened with virtually a complete lack of academic freedom." Cobb concluded that the state and its "classrooms remain intellectual wastelands."[22] With a focus on young people, COFO could cultivate a new generation of leaders in the Black Freedom Struggle who would carry on movement work long after Freedom Summer ended. From the very beginning, Cobb conceived of the summer freedom schools as being deeply connected to and potentially transformative of the everyday experiences of black children in Mississippi's segregated public schools. One of the main goals was to meet "the responsibility to fill an intellectual and creative vacuum in the lives of young Negro Mississippians, and to get them to articulate their own desires, demands and questions." In sum, as Cobb put it, "More students need to stand up in classrooms around the state and ask their teachers a real question."[23]

Cobb proposed a program in which high school-aged students would spend only part of their time in the classroom; the rest would be out on the streets and in organizing meetings with COFO volunteers.[24] Students who attended freedom schools would learn to help potential voters prepare for registration and get their first taste of direct action campaigns. The council's recruiting letter for college volunteers described the purpose of freedom schools as to "provide politically emerging communities

Figure 1.1. Freedom school students listen to folksinger Pete Seeger at the Palmers Crossing Community Center, 1964, Hattiesburg, Mississippi. Source: Herbert Randall Freedom Summer Photographs, box 6, folder 4, McCain Library and Archives, University of Southern Mississippi, Hattiesburg.

with new young leadership, and constitute a real attack on the presently stifling system of education in the state." Ideally, then, "the basis will have been laid for a cadre of student leadership around the state of Mississippi committed to critical thinking and social action."[25] The freedom schools would constitute one part of Freedom Summer's "program of social and political education," opening the eyes of children and teenagers to their own ability to challenge the state's racial caste system.[26]

The freedom schools did not all live up to the lofty expectations organizers had for them; many of the teachers were underprepared (and themselves uneducated in black history), and the donated books were often either too few or did not cover a useful subject.[27] But a rigid curriculum did not fit the idea of freedom schools, and years later, many freedom school participants recalled the sessions as crucial moments of political awakening.[28] One freedom school teacher in Hattiesburg observed that the students did not learn in a "point-by-point, organized, 'logical' manner" but that they instead "learn[ed] by talking, by conversation, by rambling around and beating the nearby bushes."[29] The schools were less focused on rigid lesson plans and learning objectives and more concerned with teaching students to acquire political consciousness—to see the inadequacy of their schools, the leadership of their state, the economic subjugation of their families as strange. Charles Cobb described the education black Mississippians received in the public schools as "parochial," and, in contrast, described the mission of the freedom schools as centered on introducing students to new people and new ideas, regardless of the subject matter. "You would get some kind of payoff without thinking—just from the fact you had a student from Yale talking to a Mississippi ninth grader about Asia," Cobb later recalled.[30] The council workers wanted to use the freedom schools to nurture the political consciousness of young people and prime them for later activism.

Within his original prospectus, Cobb floated the idea of a statewide school boycott to occur after the summer ended, which would be spearheaded by student leaders who had been cultivated in freedom schools.[31] Students and volunteers in Hattiesburg discussed planning a walkout to support the registration of their teachers as voters.[32] But taking direct action to school could result in disciplinary action by school administrators. In Holmes County, just north of Jackson and Yazoo City, a SNCC fieldworker reported that a rumor circulated around town that any students who attended freedom schools would not be permitted to return to the public schools in the autumn. No such ban was issued, but after the school year began, a report surfaced that two black students at one school were suspended for singing freedom songs at lunch. When one was expelled for refusing to promise not to sing the songs in school, a COFO fieldworker reported that he called the Jackson office of the NAACP Legal Defense Fund and was told that nothing could be done to reinstate the student.[33] Elsewhere, students who had participated in the freedom schools joined efforts to desegregate all-white schools, restaurants, barbershops, and theaters.[34]

So when black students in Mississippi rebelled against school authority figures, they did so out of concerns that ranged beyond the issue of free speech itself. They also challenged the edifice of Jim Crow. Freedom Summer embodied a kind of radical pedagogy—interchangeable in the parts of student and teacher, local people and organizers taught each other and learned from one another. This included the children and teenagers who witnessed their parents' activism and experienced it first-hand in the freedom schools. This radical pedagogy was primarily about seeing the world in a new way. It meant seeing Jim Crow as vulnerable and imagining change as possible. When school began in the autumn of 1964 and black students returned to their classrooms, they took some of these lessons with them.

Free Speech and School Segregation

Canzetta Burnside, Martha Burnside, and Ajatha Morris, whose parents filed the initial complaint in the first button case, staged their protests at Booker T. Washington High School, the town's segregated high school for black students. The months before classes resumed were especially tense in Philadelphia, given the disappearance of the three civil rights workers in June and the discovery of their bodies in August. Before their abduction, Schwerner and Chaney traveled to Neshoba County and gave a speech at Mt. Zion Church, encouraging the congregation to host a freedom school. The Klan later burned the church to the ground in retaliation. When they returned with Goodman to investigate the arson, the three men were arrested on trumped-up charges and jailed until just before midnight. They then disappeared into the night.[35] Their burned-out car was discovered on an Indian reservation a week later, but their bodies were not found until early August, buried in an earthen dam. The gruesome discovery marked the end of Freedom Summer, but it did not end civil rights activity by local people or COFO, even in a dangerous place like Philadelphia.[36]

The abduction and murder of the three men put a damper on the COFO activity in Neshoba County over the summer, but a staff worker hastily set up an office in the wake of the discovery of Chaney, Goodman, and Schwerner's bodies. Local white resident Florence Mars, who was sympathetic to the cause of civil rights and later published a memoir recounting the summer's events, wrote that Philadelphia's whites boasted of the town's "good race relations" and took pride in its "'good Negroes,' those who worked hard but knew their place." On the other hand, Mars observed, "Any Negro who wasn't appreciative" of white benevolence "was considered a troublemaker."[37] Mars noted that the mood among white Philadelphians was "jovial" after the three men disappeared, as many declared that it was certainly a publicity stunt staged by COFO. Such claims to harmonious interracial relationships withered after the confirmation that the three men had, in fact, been tortured and murdered. Fearful of the dangerous climate for COFO workers, the organization did not establish an office in Philadelphia until August 13. When COFO finally sent someone to Philadelphia, they chose black SNCC worker Ralph Featherstone. Featherstone had been present during SNCC's voter registration efforts in McComb, where he directed Nonviolent High, and so he had a history of working closely with local teenagers.[38] He had also proven himself to be willing to organize in a place with a history of white violence toward black civil rights workers. Local Ku Klux Klan leaders immediately planned meetings to drive COFO out of town. The workers were threatened with eviction and by nighttime displays of intimidation by Klan members who drove slowly past the office, firearms on display.[39] It was clear to anyone who associated with COFO that many local whites found local black cooperation with COFO to violate the rules of expected behavior they held for the town's black population. Demonstrating an interest in registering to vote led a person across the line that demarcated "good Negroes" from "troublemakers."

While voting and education were linked in the mission of Freedom Summer, they were also intertwined in Philadelphia as adults attempted to register to vote and teenagers brought their support for voting rights to school. The council's first efforts at voter registration in Neshoba County in September 1964 inspired the student protests that took place at Booker T. Washington High School and resulted in the suspensions of Canzetta Burnside and Neva Louise English. On September 14, a group of eighteen black men and women set out to register to vote. Concerned about Klan violence—even in broad daylight—the COFO office had previously informed local police of the group's intent. Word spread quickly, and by the time the black men and women arrived at the courthouse, curious and angry whites lined the street to jeer at the would-be voters and witness the spectacle of black defiance. In response, Judge O. H. Barnett ordered the county clerk to close the voter registration office for two weeks and reopen after October 3. The registration moratorium coincided with the state's deadline for voter registration for the upcoming presidential election on November 3. On September 20, Sheriff Lee Rainey informed COFO workers that if anyone turned up hoping to register, he or she would be promptly arrested.[40] The following day, six prospective black voters arrived at the courthouse anyway. Sheriff Rainey met them on the steps and refused to allow them to enter the building. When the potential registrants asked to see a copy of Judge Barnett's order, Rainey refused and told them if they did not leave, he would arrest them.[41]

As a show of support for the voter registration efforts, a small group of black teenagers, including children of two of the prospective voters, affixed freedom buttons to their clothing before school. Like their parents, the students received nearly immediate threats for their actions. The school's history teacher reported the students to Principal Montgomery Moore, who demanded that the students take off the pins. When they refused, they were sent home and were told to return to school the following day without the pins. On Wednesday evening, the suspended students regrouped at the COFO office, where dozens more students joined them, grabbing their own freedom pins, which they wore to school on Thursday. Predictably they, too, were suspended. This time, the number of students the principal sent home numbered closer to 50.[42] Principal Moore sent letters to the parents of suspended students, notifying them their children could not return to school unless they agreed not to wear the pins. The letter announced a school policy prohibiting students from bringing in materials that were "not educational," warning that "all students will be suspended for wearing freedom pins in school. The school has the right to set the policy for what students should wear."[43] Moore saw the students and their buttons as troubling, and so he invoked his authority to exclude students for engaging in behaviors that he termed "non-educational."

As James D. Anderson has noted, white Southerners structured the segregated system of education in order to exert control over black administrators, teachers, and children, socializing students to accept the racial caste system and its attendant political economy.[44] When black students asked their teachers and principals to take a side in the Black Freedom Struggle, their precarious position put school administrators and staff in a difficult spot, further motivating students and their parents to demand more reforms. This complicated relationship of black educators to their students means there is no simple narrative that fully explains their role in the Black Freedom Struggle.[45] But in the button cases, black students and their parents clearly saw black principals as antagonistic toward the movement and their teachers as, at best, agnostic. In Philadelphia, Montgomery Moore wasted no time in stamping out protest activity at the school, sending a clear message to students that they would not be allowed back to class with the buttons.

Embedded in the idea behind the freedom schools and, therefore, the entire Mississippi Project was an impulse toward the reform of public education. Materials geared toward recruiting volunteers to staff schools and raising cash to fund them focused on the idea that Mississippi's schools were the worst in the nation and its segregated black schools were the worst in the state. Despite the efforts of white moderates to equalize public education in order to sidestep compliance with the desegregation mandate of *Brown v. Board of Education*, educational opportunities for African American children remained abysmal in the early 1960s.[46] Furthermore, the structure of segregated education made schools into spaces that were simultaneously black-centered and white-controlled. While the principals and teachers at the schools in places like Philadelphia belonged to the educated black middle class, white school boards and white superintendents determined hiring, firing, and school policy. Their position meant that black teachers and administrators had to either disavow any challenge to white supremacy or, if they were sympathetic, maintain the veneer of disapproval.

Ajatha Morris was one of the students who first wore a button to school, and she later explained her decision to defy Moore's authority as one rooted in her own developing political consciousness. The same day as her silent protest, her mother had been one of the would-be voters threatened by Rainey on the courthouse steps. Morris later recalled how her mother's activism drew her into the movement. She recalled, in particular, being largely unaware of civil rights activity in the state until Chaney, Goodman, and Schwerner disappeared in June. Ajatha's mother Ola Morris labored as a domestic during the day but dedicated her spare time to voter registration efforts in Neshoba County, mastering the literacy test and teaching it to others.[47] The Morris family lived just a quarter mile from their kin, the Burnsides, who were also involved in civil rights work. Margaret Burnside was Ola Morris's sister.[48] Margaret's daughter, Martha, also participated in the protest. Martha was older than the other students: At age nineteen, she received special permission to leave school early each day to work as a domestic.[49] When the local newspaper reported on the voter registration attempt and the button protests and named the Burnsides as participants, Martha's employer promptly fired her. "That's just like your mother to be mixed up in a thing like this," she reportedly told Martha.[50] Margaret Burnside had crossed the boundary, marking herself as a troublemaker. In her comments, her employer sent a clear warning sign to Martha that her involvement in the button protests jeopardized her income as well as her standing in white eyes.

After Moore suspended the young women, Margaret Burnside went to the COFO office to ask Ralph Featherstone for help.[51] The NAACP Legal Defense Fund (LDF), which employed lawyers in Mississippi to manage the many arrests of Freedom Summer protesters, stepped in to take on the case. Ola Morris traveled to Jackson the day after the students were suspended for the second time, where she sought assistance from LDF lawyers, including Henry Aronson, who would later argue the case in court. The students' parents and guardians filed a lawsuit, *Burnside v. Byars*, on their behalf, asking the judge for a preliminary injunction to allow the students to return to school while the case was litigated. The LDF also filed a lawsuit on behalf of the prospective voters, charging that the sheriff and judge "entered into a conspiracy in order to deprive the above defined class of their right to vote."[52] The original complaint noted that the young people had been suspended "because of said children's advocacy of the abolition of racial segregation in the state of Mississippi in a lawful and peaceful manner fully protected by the First, Fifth, Thirteenth, Fourteenth and Fifteenth Amendments to the Constitution of the United States."[53] By invoking several constitutional amendments, the complaint made a forceful case that it was outside Moore's authority to ban the buttons by relying upon the constitutional rights that students supposedly had. Whether these constitutional protections actually applied to students in public schools was another question entirely.

"A Philadelphia Teen-Age Movement"

While on its surface *Burnside v. Byars* was clearly about the freedom of expression, the law was less clear about whether this was something with which schools had to concern themselves. In 1964, when the Philadelphia protest occurred and the first button case was filed, the First

Amendment had not been interpreted specifically to protect the right to free expression of secondary students in public schools anywhere in the nation. As these cases reveal, the participation of black students in protests at school tested the limits of the authority of school administrators and the existence of students' constitutional rights at schools. Previous decisions from the early and mid-twentieth century indicated that school officials' authority to make policy affecting schools was not absolute, but they also did not establish a clear sense of students' individual rights.[54]

An old common-law doctrine, *in loco parentis*, stood in the way of the Constitution. According to the common law as described by William Blackstone in his *Commentaries on the Laws of England*, nature granted parents with certain rights over their children. When parents sent their children to school, they temporarily transferred those rights to school administrators and teachers, who stood "in the place of the parent"—or in Latin, *in loco parentis*.[55] The parent's right to discipline, teach, and treat his child in nearly any way he saw fit became the privilege of teachers in the domain of the school as the public education system developed in the nineteenth century.[56] Over the course of the nation's first century, public education shifted from being a primarily local affair to one that was guaranteed by each state.[57] Massachusetts and New Hampshire were the first to encourage the provision of education as a means of developing an informed, virtuous citizenry in the 1780s.[58] During the nineteenth century, many states incorporated education clauses into their state constitutions. Indiana's constitution was the first to explicitly guarantee free public education in 1816, and other Northern states followed.[59] During Reconstruction, Southern states adopted similar education provisions into their constitutions as black politicians sought to secure universal education for future generations in order to ensure full citizenship rights for African Americans.[60] State constitutional provisions related to education did not necessarily ensure that public schooling was universal; it sometimes took decades for legislatures to establish a statewide system of education.[61]

The theory of *in loco parentis* was complicated by changes in the law, especially as new ideas and structures of modern education developed during the Progressive Era. In particular, the passage of compulsory attendance laws strained the theory of *in loco parentis*, as they gave the state, rather than the parent, the choice about whether to even educate the child.[62] Compulsory education circumscribed the natural rights of parents as the education of children became obligatory in the service of civic duty. As the idea of education changed, the power of the state expanded while limiting the rights of parents under law.

Despite public education's historical character as a creature of state and local law, some Supreme Court cases established that school officials were not exempt from the demands of the Constitution. The pressures of wartime and, in particular, the patriotic zeal of state legislatures generated litigation over whether schools could require students to stand and recite the Pledge of Allegiance while saluting the Flag. A case brought on behalf of students expelled for refusing to participate in the mandatory flag salute in Pennsylvania, *Minersville v. Gobitis*, reached the U.S. Supreme Court in 1940. The students were Jehovah's Witnesses, and their religious tenets forbade swearing loyalty to any authority but God, including the United States. In an 8-1 decision, the Supreme Court upheld the school's authority to discipline the students, deferring to the authority of school officials to determine appropriate policy. "The wisdom of training children in patriotic impulses by those compulsions which necessarily pervade so much of the educational process is not for our independent judgment," wrote Justice Felix Frankfurter for the majority.[63] The lone dissenter, Justice Harlan Fiske Stone, rejected the idea that the Court could disregard concerns about civil liberties, even though the case involved children. Stone declared,

> I am not prepared to say that the right of this small and helpless minority, including children having strong religious conviction, whether they understand its nature or not, to refrain from an expression obnoxious to their religion, is to be overborne by the interest of the state in maintaining discipline in the schools.[64]

State and local authority over education did not immunize school officials from taking into consideration the "guarantees of freedom of the human mind and spirit" that the Constitution intended to protect.[65]

Just three years later, the Court reversed itself on the issue when a majority of justices sided with students in another nearly identical case involving Jehovah's Witnesses who refused to participate in the flag salute.

In *West Virginia v. Barnette*, the Supreme Court held that West Virginia's state law requiring that students participate in a flag salute during each school day was unconstitutional per the First and Fourteenth Amendments. In response to the accusation that such a ruling would make the courts the "school board for the country," needlessly interfering in what were purely local matters, the majority decision declared that the Fourteenth Amendment "protects the citizen against the State itself and all of its creatures—Boards of Education not excepted."[66] School officials were not exempted from the requirements of the Constitution simply because they worked in education. But the Court in *Barnette* was primarily concerned with the idea that the flag salute was compelled speech, and the majority opinion did not address whether students had a positive individual right to free expression at school.

So school officials, despite having a large degree of control over education policy, did not have the power to do whatever they liked. But the limits of their authority as determined by the Constitution was an undecided issue in 1964 when students in Philadelphia, Mississippi, wore their freedom buttons to school. It was not even clear, for instance, whether the actions of teachers and administrators within schools were subject to judicial scrutiny. The decision to file the lawsuit in federal court, however, was a conscious one on the part of LDF lawyers who understood that the state courts were almost certain to be hostile to the rights claims of black children and teenagers. Furthermore, the young people who wore buttons to school were (with the exception of Martha Burnside) minors. Even Martha was too young to register to vote, as Mississippi set the age threshold at twenty-one. At the heart of both button cases was the question of whether secondary school students could even be considered to have legitimate political opinions. Surely, not all young people in school cared about the right to wear the buttons or the voter registration battle that played out in the town's streets and on its courthouse steps. But what about those, like Neva Louise English, who made forceful statements that the buttons represented their support of the broader struggle against Jim Crow? This was a central point of contention throughout the hearings in both *Burnside v. Byars* and *Blackwell v. Issaquena County* (which is discussed later in this chapter).

The hearing, at which Canzetta Burnside and other students testified, was held on October 8 before Judge Sidney Mize at the federal courthouse in Jackson, and it put on display the full range of arguments adults used to dismiss the protest activity of young people. An assistant attorney general for the state of Mississippi, Will S. Wells, argued the case on behalf of the school board and Principal Moore. Wells peppered the students with questions, insisting on calling the teenaged witnesses by their first names to underscore their relative youth. In a display of defiance, one student, Linda Jordan, insisted that Wells call her "Miss."[67] Wells repeatedly emphasized that the young women were not old enough to vote, implying that they could not understand or have a stake in the battle over voter registration in the state. He also played up the ignorance of the young women, asking them if they knew what SNCC was (they did not).[68] The responses of Burnside and English instead revealed local understandings of outsiders involved in the movement, as they—like many other black Mississippians—identified the COFO workers as "freedom riders," linking their work with the 1961 effort to desegregate interstate bus stations.[69] Wells, in turn, attempted to draw a bright line between the "freedoms" the young women claimed were the point of their protest and the right to vote as relayed by the "One Man, One Vote" buttons. As if to make his point, Wells asked Canzetta Burnside, "Is there anything on [that pin] that talks about freedom?"[70]

But the young women were insistent that it was their decision alone to wear the buttons and that they did so as a show of support for voter registration and the end of racial segregation. They also repeatedly asserted that they each decided on their own volition to procure and wear the pins to school as a statement in support of civil rights. As Linda Jordan explained, "The people in the community that are children, we decided we wanted a Philadelphia teen-age movement."[71] Legal Defense Fund lawyer Henry Aronson also asked Jordan whether students did, in fact, bring other "non-educational" materials into the school in order to underscore the fact that it was the message of the buttons that led to the suspensions. Jordan explained that students often wore buttons to school. Couples who were "going steady" wore "his" and "hers" buttons, while others sported "Beatle" pins. None of these students faced suspension or expulsion because of their pins.[72] The point that LDF lawyers hoped to make was that the students were engaged in political speech, no matter how rudimentary, and that it was that kind of speech that the principal and school board targeted for punishment.

In addition to arguing that the buttons were "non-educational," Moore testified that he believed the SNCC buttons might have been disruptive of the school day. In his cross-examination, LDF lawyer Henry Aronson posed the question of whether the denial of basic rights and privileges to black Mississippians might in fact be worthy of study and discussion in a classroom. Aronson asked Moore directly, "Do you think it is part of the learning process to integrate, to require for the Negroes, the Negro race, those rights which are guaranteed in the constitution and the law decisions and administrative rulings of the higher authorities in this country[?]"[73] The principal managed to dodge the question as the judge interrupted Aronson and labeled the question "incompetent," but Aronson's point opened up an important line of interrogation. Who got to decide whether or not a particular topic was educational? And was it not strange that a discussion of democracy was considered inappropriate for black schoolchildren in Mississippi? A crucial detail of the case, as it turned out, was the fact that the principal was not actually at school to witness what happened between students.[74] He testified at the hearing that he was home that day caring for his sick wife. Once the case left the district court and ended up in the Fifth Circuit, this helped the judges demarcate the scope of school officials' authority and the limits of students' rights to free speech. The principal's insistence that the buttons caused a disturbance was not particularly persuasive if he had not even been in the building to witness it.

Furthermore, the importance of the buttons and whether they constituted political speech were downplayed by the school district's lawyers. Their strategy framed the students' actions as trivial and their desire to wear buttons the product of ignorance and the pressure of COFO workers. Several parents of suspended students served as witnesses for the district, insisting that they did not much care about the buttons but did care whether their children followed school rules.[75] "I didn't have no part to say about the buttons," one parent testified, "a boy sixteen years old and out of school and me and his mother both working. What would he do without a school? That was all I was concerned—him getting an education."[76] When pressed, the man admitted that he had been asked to testify by his (presumably white) employer, who gave him the day off to go to court. The testimony of these parents, most of whom defended the principal's actions, exposed fault lines within black families. Like teachers, the parents of students were often at the whims of white employers who disapproved of protests. This put them in a difficult position. Whether these men truly wanted to testify for the district or whether they felt coerced into doing so is impossible to discern. Their feelings about the participation of young people in such a brazen protest so close to where the three COFO workers were abducted and murdered just a few months earlier were likewise opaque. The value of a job, an education, their own dignity—all of these had to be weighed by the parents caught in the middle by the actions of their children.

During the hearing, the school district's lawyers repeatedly asked the students whether COFO volunteers were behind the school protest, persistently implying that the young people were not truly engaged in any kind of meaningful political movement. Judge Sidney Mize seemed open to the suggestion that the students had not come up with the idea themselves but were under the control of outsiders with their own agendas. This was a claim that was often made by critics of the Black Freedom Struggle, who attributed the actions of local African Americans to communist influence or other nefarious "outside agitators." At the *Burnside* hearing, the judge declared that "the final decision in this court will depend upon whether or not [the button prohibition] is a reasonable rule and . . . to see whether or not some foreign element had come into this state and created a situation that would cause such confusion in the school as would make a rule like that reasonable."[77] Mize stressed the importance of discipline to schooling and noted the disruptive character of the students' actions. "There was laughing and, I imagine it could be inferred, giggling" as students passed out buttons, and Mize repeatedly praised Principal Montgomery Moore's actions, calling them "fair" and a "wonderful solution" to the problem.[78] The judge clearly accepted the idea that the buttons had caused a disruption, even though no one testified to significant disruptions at the hearing. Furthermore, Mize's comments that the ruling relied on whether some "foreign" element caused the students to wear buttons reinforced the idea that such behavior was not likely to stem from the beliefs of local black teenagers. The inference, of course, was that Philadelphia's black residents were otherwise happy with their lot. At the same time, this assertion put the impetus for button wearing on anyone except the students themselves, which supported the idea that young people could not and did not have their own political opinions that might be protected by the First Amendment.

Unsurprisingly, Judge Mize denied the request for a preliminary injunction. He declared that, "if children are permitted to go through the lower grades running the school, rather than the teachers running the children, it will probably wind up in a lot of juvenile delinquency."[79] The students could return to school, but they could not wear the buttons. Nonetheless, some in Philadelphia were undeterred. The following Sunday, the Burnsides held a "freedom rally" at their farm that drew COFO workers from as far away as Meridian. Charles Evers, the brother of slain NAACP fieldworker Medgar Evers, and COFO worker Annie Devine spoke to the crowd.[80] A few weeks later, the LDF appealed the case to the Fifth Circuit.[81]

The Delta Student Strike

The following winter, another group of students rebelled in one of the poorest parts of the Delta. The other button case, *Blackwell v. Issaquena County*, came from far western Mississippi, and the facts of the case bore a striking similarity to those in *Burnside v. Byars*. Deep in the Delta region, the Mississippi River snakes between Louisiana and Arkansas to the west and the cotton-rich but cash-poor Mississippi counties of Issaquena and Sharkey to the east. With only 3,500 inhabitants in 1960, Issaquena was the least-populated county in the entire state.[82] Unita Blackwell, a sharecropper and local civil rights activist who lived in Mayersville, described the place as the "boondocks"—a town so sleepy that outsiders could be identified by the fast pace of their gait.[83] In fact, in the 1960s, Issaquena County was so small that it had no schools at all for black children. The region had so few residents and education was so poorly funded that black students from both counties attended the same segregated high school in Sharkey County, which was more populous and had 10,000 residents.[84] Some black students traveled as far as forty miles to get to Henry Weathers High School, the site of the freedom button protests, in Rolling Fork.[85]

In Issaquena County, COFO workers operated out of Unita Blackwell's home in Mayersville, registering voters and leading organizing meetings.[86] Blackwell worked in the cotton fields and had only an eighth-grade education, but she was a savvy and fearless organizer who jumped at the chance to be involved with SNCC when volunteers first came to town.[87] That summer, residents hosted small freedom schools in churches and homes, even though the area had a reputation for being a dangerous and difficult place to organize.[88] In COFO organizational notes on the freedom schools, it is noted that between two and four teachers should be assigned to the two-county area and, in an indication that the organizers understood the potential for trouble, that the teachers "must have (fast) car."[89] Like Philadelphia, Sharkey and Issaquena Counties were not nodes of Freedom Summer protest activity, but they did have a COFO presence despite the threat of white retaliation.

The protests at Henry Weathers High School in Sharkey County were sparked by the involvement of members of a statewide union of black students. As the summer session neared its end, freedom school students from across the state traveled to a convention in Meridian. Meridian, the hometown of murdered civil rights worker James Chaney, was chosen in part due to "the symbolic association with Philadelphia" and the disappearance of the three men.[90] The freedom schools convention was led by Joyce Brown, a sixteen-year-old from McComb, where the local freedom school had been bombed. Students drafted a platform modeled on the Declaration of Independence that drew connections between the political, economic, and social repression of African Americans in Mississippi.[91] The platform included stances on school segregation and access to decent housing and jobs for all African Americans in the state.[92] Later, the students listened to a lecture by A. Philip Randolph, the head of the Brotherhood of Sleeping Car Porters, who famously pressured President Franklin Roosevelt into creating the Fair Employment Practices Committee by threatening a March on Washington during World War II. Bob Moses also addressed the students, as did other freedom school workers who discussed college admissions processes and scholarships.[93]

At the convention, many freedom school students joined the Mississippi Student Union (MSU), a loose organization of high school students that predated Freedom Summer and found new recruits among freedom school attendees. The MSU emerged out of a daylong boycott staged by students in January 1964 as part of a COFO protest for voting rights. In April, 200 students gathered at Tougaloo College to formally create the

Figure 1.2. A group sings freedom songs at the Freedom Schools Convention during Freedom Summer, 1964, Meridian, Mississippi. Source: Staughton and Alice Lynd Papers, 1938–2000, WHS-93237, Wisconsin Historical Society, Madison.

group.[94] The group had no real centralized leadership, and its branches acted largely independently according to the wills of the students who made up the chapters.[95] The MSU would carry on the mission of the freedom schools even after the summer ended, when students went back to their freedom schools and, from there, back to their segregated schools. Despite its decentralized nature, the MSU continued to serve as a network for high school student activists and a means through which students could express their own grievances. The MSU would play an important role in the Sharkey-Issaquena button case as members encouraged black students to wear their SNCC buttons to school.

On January 29, 1965, roughly two dozen students at Henry Weathers High School in Sharkey County wore SNCC buttons to school.[96] The protest began, according to one COFO worker, when members of the MSU in Issaquena County met with students to drum up interest in the organization and handed out SNCC buttons. Later, when asked about the students' plan, student Bernice Diggs said that there was not one. "We just wanted to wear the buttons, that's all," Diggs said.[97] Another student emphasized that the buttons displayed support for the work of civil rights organizations in the state. "[The principal] asked me about the organizations like SNCC and COFO, and the MSU," Eugene White stated in an affidavit. White reportedly responded, "I told him that this pin was representing these organizations, which go around telling people about things like voting."[98] Roosevelt White, a tenth grader, reported that he had earlier been asked by a teacher to remove a "Johnson for President" pin after the elections had been held the previous November, although he also said he had worn a SNCC pin on several occasions without incident.[99] As in Philadelphia, students who became part of the lawsuit stated that they acted without adult influence and showed an interest in and understanding of the civil rights protest activity that had been taking place across the state.

The button-wearing students at Henry Weathers were able to attend their first few classes without issue. But at one point, two younger students squabbled over one of the buttons and were sent to the principal's office to sort out the conflict. The principal, Orsmond E. Jordan, was a graduate of Tougaloo College and an Army veteran. He was not pleased by the sight of the buttons.[100] Jordan told the students that he did not approve of their actions, but he also did not ask them to remove the buttons or threaten the students with specific disciplinary action.[101] If Principal Jordan hoped that the issue would be forgotten and abandoned over the weekend, he was mistaken. On Monday morning, roughly 150 students showed up at school wearing SNCC buttons. This time, they were summoned to the office again, although there were too many students for them all to fit. One by one, in an orderly line, the students gave their names to the secretary. They were told to remove the buttons and go back to class. Many of the students refused to comply, and when teachers refused to let them enter their classrooms, the button-wearing students were sent to the cafeteria.[102]

At this point, the student protest became about more than the right to wear a button in school. Everyone at the school soon discovered that an insurrection, however mild, had begun. At a meeting in the gymnasium, the students were allowed to ask the principal questions. They seized the opportunity to pry into Jordan's personal politics and his feelings about the Black Freedom Struggle. Students inquired about the use of corporal punishment at school—how would Jordan "feel about his own daughter having to touch her toes and get whipped on the backside?"—and whether there were any African Americans on the school board. Was he registered to vote? the students inquired. He demurred on this point. He was registered, he said, but in another county, and in any case, he did not want to talk about it with the students.[103] The students were dismissed after one student called Jordan an "Uncle Tom," evidently demonstrating some students' determination about where his loyalties lay.[104] The meeting revealed how many students connected the voting-rights message of the SNCC buttons to their own concerns about racial justice in the schools. Even if they could not register to vote because of their status as minors, the students demonstrated their belief that suffrage was intimately connected to other facets of the state's racial regime.

Jordan's efforts to dismiss the button issue and regain control over the students continually backfired. As he tried to squash the protests, the students only got louder. When he told them they would be punished, even more students showed up to school with SNCC buttons affixed to their shirts and dresses. On Tuesday, roughly 200 students wore buttons to school.[105] By Wednesday, Jordan was forced to either capitulate to the students—and, in doing so, likely enrage the superintendent and school board—or follow through on his threats. And so, on Wednesday, after nearly a week of defiant students wearing buttons, Jordan suspended 300 students. This was roughly a third of the entire school population. Parents who met with Jordan were told that the students would only be allowed to return without their buttons.[106] Some acquiesced and returned to school, but approximately 200 students did not. Students at three schools in the two counties participated, including some at Cary and Mayersville elementary schools.[107] As the boycott continued and news of it spread via newspaper reports, hundreds of black students in Indianola in Sunflower County boycotted their schools in a show of solidarity with students in Sharkey and Issaquena Counties.[108] Parents and students from the area reported that some children who chose to return to school were told they would be paddled before the school would accept them back.[109] Those students who refused were suspended for the remainder of the school year.[110]

Jordan was almost certainly afraid for his job. He had no tenure and could be fired at will by the all-white school board. Jordan was part of a class of black professionals who served as intermediaries between the white ruling class and the state's black population. Jordan had shown himself to be suspicious of and resistant to civil rights activity in schools before he was even hired at Henry Weathers High School. When black parents filed a desegregation lawsuit in Harmony, Mississippi, where he was principal in the early 1960s, Jordan successfully convinced many of them to withdraw their support.[111] He attempted to do the same with the students who wore freedom buttons to Henry Weathers High School. Jordan and a white school board member quietly contacted students' parents and asked them to remove their names from a petition to the school board.[112] When Jordan was asked to choose between ignoring or standing behind the students and attempting to crush the rebellion, he chose the latter. How would it look to the lily-white school board if he allowed the students to promote the voter registration drives at school? Surely this would bring more trouble than the buttons were worth.

But Jordan failed to foresee that, when it came to conflict with students, they held the ultimate trump card in the form of the *Brown v. Board of Education* decision, which had been thus far effectively unenforced in Mississippi. While filing the free speech lawsuit, local activists also asked the NAACP to initiate school desegregation proceedings.[113] Invoking *Brown* in the Issaquena County case meant challenging the very existence of Henry Weathers High School, a place where black teachers and principals worked closely with black students. A successful school desegregation lawsuit would allow students to transfer out of Henry Weathers and into the white school. Furthermore, Sharkey and Issaquena Counties did not have many school-aged children. If desegregation occurred, the segregated black schools might shut down entirely, and Principal Jordan along with teachers, secretaries, school bus drivers, and other staff—all of them African American—could potentially lose their jobs.

Unita Blackwell later mused that, ultimately, it was the decisions made in those moments by Principal Jordan that sparked the free speech and school desegregation suits. The lawsuits came out of a miscalculation on his part. Jordan underestimated the fury students would feel because of his condescension and the determinedness of those parents who were willing to jeopardize the rest of the school year to back up their children's actions. "He alienated the black children," Blackwell later recalled, "And he told them the white folks didn't like it."[114] As a "yes man" who cared only about keeping his job and pleasing his white superiors, Jordan's decision to try to stamp out the protest only caused the fire to intensify and spread.[115] At one point, a student recalled that Jordan lectured to him, "Negroes are the cause of their own problems, and that goes for the negroes both today and yesterday."[116] A button was no longer just a button. It was a symbol of everything that was wrong with Mississippi's schools and an indictment of the role that they played in attempting to promote the ignorance of the state's children.

As was the case in Philadelphia, a number of the children involved in the Issaquena-Sharkey school protests were related to local civil rights workers, including Unita Blackwell and Henry Sias, who was a crucial figure in the Black Freedom Struggle in Issaquena County. One of the few self-employed black men in the area who owned his own land and therefore could not be swayed by threats of unemployment or eviction by whites, Sias served in the dangerous and prominent position of a local civil rights leader. In the years before Freedom Summer, Sias hosted Freedom Riders at his home, and he also served as the head of the local NAACP chapter.[117] Two Sias children served as leaders of the student rebellion.[118] Unita Blackwell's son Jeremiah, Jr., was the first name alphabetically on the lawsuit, making the Blackwells the symbolic representatives of the lawsuit that bore the family name: *Blackwell v. Is-*

saquena County. This was fitting, given Unita Blackwell's organizing acumen and her key role during Freedom Summer.

After the suspensions, roughly one thousand students from the Sharkey and Issaquena County schools began a boycott that lasted for the remainder of the school year. Parents and supporters rushed to reestablish freedom schools for the children to attend during the duration of the boycott.[119] Principal Jordan warned the parents that any work done at a non-accredited school (in other words, the freedom schools) would "not be recognized as an official school." Students would not get credit for attending freedom schools, although, in acknowledgment of Mississippi's lack of a compulsory education law, Jordan concluded his letter with the observation that "what you do with your child is your business."[120] Jordan was able to use the state's lack of a compulsory education law alongside his power to discipline students and quash protest activity at school. In doing so, he demanded that the young people who attended his school adhere to the premise that the buttons were disruptive and outside the realm of "respectable" behavior for black youth.

In both Philadelphia and Issaquena County, the button protests were linked not only to voter registration efforts but also to school desegregation. In both hearings, the inferior nature of segregated schools rose to the surface. Unlike the freedom schools, whose ramshackle nature owed to circumstance, the state's segregated public schools were inferior by design. In the 1960s, Mississippi's schools were some of the worst in the nation. A universal system of public education for Mississippi's children did not exist until the first decades of the twentieth century, and as late as World War I, the state had no four-year public high schools for black students.[121] After all, Mississippi's whites had long expected that black children would work in the fields with their parents. Education for black children was less pressing than the value of their labor to the state's agricultural industry. The school year for many black children in the state was truncated to accommodate the cotton growing and harvesting season well into the twentieth century.[122]

So, for many black children and teenagers, the state's schools offered a mockery of the idea of "separate but equal." Mississippi made efforts to equalize school conditions in the early 1950s in response to the success of the NAACP's campaigns to equalize teacher pay and desegregate higher education.[123] But in practice, Mississippi continued to spend far less per pupil for the education of black students than it did for white students, especially in the Delta. Statewide, a quarter of what was spent on white education was spent on the education of black children. In certain areas, the disparities were astonishing. Holly Bluff schools spent $191.17 per white pupil and only $1.26 per black pupil.[124] Elsewhere, the difference in spending was less stark, although still a fraction of the amount spent on white schools went to black schools. In Sharkey and Issaquena Counties, spending on black students in public schools was a little more than half that for white students.[125] And in many places in the state, black children attended school for only a few months out of the year so they could return to work in the fields chopping and picking cotton with their families.

At the same time, education for black students was valuable even though it was unequal to that offered to white students. For these high school students, the disciplinary policies employed in Issaquena and Sharkey County schools jeopardized the opportunity young people had to earn a high school diploma. This created a thorny problem for students' parents, advocates, and activists: Was segregated education better than no education at all? What would happen to those students who would inevitably be pushed out of the schools? Unlike most other states, Mississippi had no compulsory education law. It had been abolished in 1956 in the wake of *Brown v. Board of Education*.[126] Education was a privilege and emphatically not a right in Mississippi. It could easily be used as another way to punish those engaged in movement activity. As Judge Sidney Mize declared in the *Burnside* case, "High school education is a privilege provided for the young people of this community by adults who recognize the importance of education. It is not a right to be exercised without regard for the welfare of others."[127] Mize's words emphasized the precarious status of public school students. If they did not behave in ways in which administrators or school boards approved, they would lose the "privilege" of being educated entirely.

The initial outcome of the *Burnside* case suggested that the *Blackwell* case would not be an easy victory. By denying the injunction allowing students to wear buttons to school, the court seemed to lend legitimacy to school administrators who punished students for civil rights activity at school. With the principal refusing the students' entrance back into school and the school board ignoring their requests to be heard, a group of parents and guardians consulted with Marian Wright (later, after she married, Marian Wright Edelman), a leading civil rights lawyer in the state.[128] The LDF eventually took up the case, with assistance from staff attorneys Henry Aronson and Melvyn Zarr on the ground in Mississippi and LDF head Jack Greenberg and Derrick Bell in New York. On April 1, 1965, LDF lawyers filed a civil suit against the Sharkey and Issaquena County Consolidated School Board representing 197 of the local black schoolchildren who had been suspended for wearing SNCC buttons. The students ranged in age from six to eighteen, but the majority were junior high or high school aged.

The case did not stand a chance before the local district judge, Harold Cox, who was widely known to be an open and unrepentant racist. Legal Defense Fund head Jack Greenberg referred to Cox, who had been appointed to the court by President Kennedy in 1961, as "possibly the most racist judge ever to sit on the federal bench."[129] Cox's appointment had been part of a deal involving Southern senators in which Thurgood Marshall, the previous head of the LDF, became a federal judge. Like *Burnside*, the case was nonetheless a good one. While the organization faced an uphill battle whenever they sued in state court, the case invoked the First and Fourteenth amendments and was therefore litigated in federal rather than state court. The issue of free speech potentially posed an excellent constitutional issue, as long as the court recognized that the First Amendment protected students in public schools.

Unlike the *Burnside* case out of Philadelphia, *Blackwell v. Issaquena County* came paired with a desegregation suit against the school district. The black plaintiffs from the Delta were not alone in this endeavor. Across the state in places like Shaw, McComb, Moss Point, and Greenwood, students and parents launched boycotts of the public schools to protest unequal education. In Meridian, Canton, and Summit, black parents attempted to register their children at all-white schools in the fall of 1964. As the historian Charles Bolton has noted, "The mobilization of black students during Freedom Summer opened the floodgates of protest against segregated education."[130] Previous efforts to implement *Brown v. Board of Education* failed owing to intimidation, violence, or legislative innovation. Petitions to desegregate Mississippi schools in the wake of *Brown* resulted in the publication of signers' names in local white-owned newspapers. The harassment that resulted pressured many black Mississippians into withdrawing from the suits, leaving school segregation untouched.[131]

By the mid-1960s, Mississippi school boards had another workaround to prevent meaningful desegregation while appearing to comply with the law: If parents filed desegregation suits or attempted to enroll their children in segregated schools, the boards would adopt a "freedom of choice" plan. Such plans declared that black students need only register at white schools if they wished to attend classes there. In theory, any child could apply to attend any school, which meant that the schools were not technically segregated by law.[132] The process of applying to all-white schools for black children and their families meant that there were plenty of ways to make the administrative tasks onerous and time-consuming; this also allotted time for retaliation once the information became public. Freedom of choice meant, for George Metcalfe, who led the local NAACP chapter in demanding desegregation in Natchez, suffering brutal injuries in a car bombing.[133] For others, it meant intimidation. For her civil rights work, Unita Blackwell had shots fired at her house, Molotov cocktails thrown in her yard, and crosses burned out front. The local sheriff, when he received the complaint, blamed Blackwell for staging and lighting the fiery cross herself and threatened to throw her in jail.[134]

So, even a decade after *Brown*, the desegregation case would not be clear-cut. Judge Cox, presiding over another desegregation case from Wilkinson County, declared in 1968 that "everybody knows that the *Brown* case didn't have anything to with anybody down here, and everybody that don't know should know that nobody would be bound by an injunction suit in another State and another Court." Getting directly to the point, he stated, "I think everybody was hoping [*Brown*] would go away if they didn't pay too much attention to it."[135] Cox's claim that the case only involved those school districts that were party to the lawsuit was outrageous. He had, after all, been appointed as the district judge seven years after the *Brown* decision and by a civil rights–supporting president. Nevertheless, Cox claimed that there was no sweeping demand for desegregation of the South or any right of a student in other districts to the equal protection of the law.

In May 1965, Judge Cox denied the request for a temporary injunction in the *Blackwell* case, writing, "We are not dealing with any problem of free speech, due process, fair trial . . . but we are dealing with a disciplinary problem within the framework of a public school system wherein the children seek to defy the school authorities and ignore their instructions." Cox concluded, "That is not and never has been the law and will ever be even good common sense so long as public schools continue to merit their cost of operation."[136] In May, the month after the students' parents and guardians filed suit, Judge Cox ruled in favor of the school officials on the issue of the freedom buttons. "These plaintiffs are school children attending public school at taxpayer's expense for the purpose of preparing themselves to be good citizens and obey constituted authority," the order declared. Cox was especially appalled at a student who displayed "a shocking degree of defiance" in court. "These children must learn respect for the law and constituted authority and should not be encouraged or assisted by any good adult citizen in any course of conduct so detrimental to their welfare at this important stage of life," Cox wrote, castigating both the children and their parents.[137] This outcome was entirely in keeping with Cox's widely known views, but the denial of the injunction was also an invitation for the LDF lawyers to take both button cases to the Fifth Circuit Court of Appeals.

Free Speech and the Fifth Circuit

The button cases gained traction in court owing to Freedom Summer and the resources it brought to Mississippi. Freedom Summer stirred and revitalized organizing efforts, sparked bolder protests, and led to the construction of a framework for legal challenges to white supremacy. The LDF had an office on Farish Street, the thriving black hub of Jackson, which was the central node of civil rights lawyering in the state. The office was composed of a group of older local lawyers, recent law-school graduates from outside Mississippi, and "carpetbagging" lawyers who flew in occasionally from New York and the District of Columbia to work on briefs or argue cases. Melvyn Zarr was fresh out of law school, having arrived in Mississippi in the spring of 1964 at the request of Michael Schwerner.[138] Marian Wright was among the young new recruits who came to assist with the legal challenges created by protests. Wright would eventually become the first black woman to achieve the formidable goal of becoming admitted to the Mississippi bar. Wright graduated from Yale Law School in 1963 "with a mission and Mississippi" on her mind.[139] Graduates of the Ole Miss law school—all of them, at the time, white—were automatically admitted to the state's bar and able to practice law. "Outsiders" like Wright, however, had to live in the state for fifteen months to establish residency before they were even allowed to take the exam, for which there was no course of study and during which the examiner could ask for a verbatim recitation of any part of the Mississippi state code.[140] Wright passed the bar exam, she later recalled, thanks to a sympathetic white law clerk who slipped his notes on the exam's most commonly asked questions to her.

Civil rights lawyers who took on cases in Mississippi were faced with a number of monumental tasks. First, they had to figure out how to avoid the state court system. Arrested civil rights workers were likely to have their cases end up in unfriendly local courts with judges who were dedicated to upholding the state's racial regime, but if their lawyers could get the lawsuits bumped to the federal courts, they could have better luck in getting their clients out of jail.[141] For this reason, the students' free speech lawsuit was somewhat promising, even as it tread upon new legal ground in terms of the reach of the First Amendment. With a clear basis for a constitutional claim, the LDF lawyers could go straight to federal district court. The state was part of the Fifth Circuit, which had shown itself to be relatively liberal on issues of race. As LDF lawyer Melvyn Zarr put it, the Fifth Circuit Court of Appeals in New Orleans was the "ultimate backstop" for civil rights lawyers.[142] While state courts and even the federal district courts in Mississippi might be hostile to civil rights workers, the Fifth Circuit often served as a corrective, instructing the lower courts to adhere to federal civil rights laws.

The two button cases, *Burnside v. Byars* and *Blackwell v. Issaquena County*, landed before the Fifth Circuit in 1966. By this point, it had been a year and a half since the students were suspended for wearing the buttons. School officials forced students in Sharkey and Issaquena Counties who participated in the school boycott for the remainder of the 1964–1965 school year to repeat grades. Many students were transferred to other schools when the district redrew attendance boundaries. Their parents had been thrown off plantations where they worked and lived and threatened with termination of their welfare payments.[143] The gears of the legal process turned slowly, but nevertheless many parents and children in the Delta stuck to their guns.

The LDF strategy in presenting the cases before the Fifth Circuit contrasted the two sets of facts. Henry Aronson took the *Burnside* case, presenting the students as peaceful protesters who only wanted to express their support for voter registration, which was a political issue of utmost importance in the state of Mississippi during the autumn of 1964. This strategy emphasized the quiet nature of the protest and the purity of the students' expression. They had not shut down school or affected teachers' lessons in a measurable way. In the end, Principal Montgomery Moore could not testify to having witnessed a disruption to the regular school day since he was not even on the school grounds that day. Because the principal had been at home on the morning the students wore their buttons, no one provided evidence at the hearing that there was any disruption to classroom activities, even though the principal expressed his concern that there could have been. Furthermore, the rule that students wear only things that could be classified as "educational" withered before testimony that students often wore buttons to school with the initials of the person with whom they were "going steady" or with pictures of the Beatles. "What's a Beatle?" asked Aronson during the trial, perplexed. "Boys who sing . . . sort of like a movie star," his witness, a student, informed him.[144] The Philadelphia case showed that it was indeed possible for students to engage in political expression at school without disrupting the normal school day. But the *Blackwell* case, involving the schools in Issaquena and Sharkey Counties, was imperfect in this respect. The principal first became aware of the buttons when young students were sent to him for squabbling over a button. This argument among children would become the basis for the Fifth Circuit's decision, even as it was presented during the hearing as a minor conflict.

In deciding the cases, the Fifth Circuit played *Burnside* and *Blackwell* off one another to emphasize the importance of disruption and its relationship to free expression in the classroom. In determining whether the students' actions were protected free speech, the court treated the First Amendment as limited by speech that disrupted the regular functioning of schools. It acknowledged that "the right to communicate a matter of vital public concern is embraced in the First Amendment right to freedom of speech and therefore is clearly protected against infringement by state officials." The Fifth Circuit court then added an important caveat: "But the liberty of expression guaranteed by the First Amendment can be abridged by state officials if their protection of legitimate state interests necessitates an invasion of free speech."[145] In sum, the right to free expression was an important one that even young people could claim. But it was not without its limits, and the courts could balance a student's right to free speech with other state interests.

So what constituted a "legitimate state interest" that could allow principals and other school officials to limit the free speech of students? *Burnside v. Byars* established that teachers who punished students for talking during class or otherwise disrupting classroom activities were protected in doing so. But a blanket prohibition that resulted in students being expelled or suspended for wearing political buttons, especially ones that contributed to an important public discussion like voting rights did in Mississippi in 1964? That was not protected, so long as the student protest did not otherwise cause disruption. This ruling was a marginal victory. It was technically a loss for the Issaquena and Sharkey County students, although they later won the school desegregation case. But Canzetta Burnside and her fellow students in Philadelphia were vindicated. If a rule such as a wholesale prohibition on the wearing of buttons infringed upon students' free speech but was otherwise essential to preserving order, then the rule was constitutional. In demarcating this line, the Fifth Circuit declared that "a reasonable regulation is one which measurably contributes to the maintenance of order and decorum within the educational system."[146] The Sharkey-Issaquena school district claimed that the button-wearing students at Henry Weathers created "a state of complete confusion and disturbance" in the school's corridors.[147] And so, because Principal Jordan and others testified that the buttons disrupted the Sharkey-Issaquena schools, the court acknowledged that he was within his power to suspend the students. But in Philadelphia there had been no such disruption shown in court, and therefore the button ban was unreasonable.

The Fifth Circuit's ruling was a small victory for children who participated in civil rights protests. Any indication of dissent or an expression of political consciousness threatened the employment of a black principal under the influence of an all-white school board. It was in part the actions of students that determined whether or not speech was disruptive, but it was also reliant on the response of administrators who feared for their own livelihoods. The line of protected speech was unstable, and the same actions by students—as shown so clearly in the *Burnside* and *Blackwell* cases—could not necessarily be predicted to be covered by the right to free expression. As the situation at Henry Weathers High School escalated into a power struggle between students engaged in a civil rights protest and a black principal trying to keep control and his job, the students moved beyond constitutional protection for their protest.

The Fifth Circuit's decision reflected the politics of representation that were so crucial to the Black Freedom Struggle. What protest was acceptable—or not—and what actions would be legitimated by the courts depended on the adherence of students and parents to specific, contingent ideals of decorum. The efforts by the judge in the *Burnside* case to pin student protest to outside agitators was part of a larger effort to shape the behavior of black Mississippians in public by marking even polite protest as beyond the limits of acceptable behavior. When both principals insisted that the mere presence of the pins could disrupt the school day and, furthermore, that the Black Freedom Struggle had no rational relationship to the education of black children, they carved out a tiny sphere of acceptable activity, even as civil rights protest ratcheted up outside the schools. The politics of respectability have a long lineage in the history of African American organizing and resistance. Rooted in late nineteenth-century conceptions of racial uplift, issues of representation were crucial to the advancement of black civil rights well into the twentieth century even as ideas of proper behavior limited the scope of protest that could be seen as legitimate.[148]

In Issaquena and Sharkey Counties, and elsewhere in the state, local whites punished the parents and students who took civil rights to school, as did the legislature. The state accommodated white parents who refused to send their children to school with black children in 1964 by providing tuition grants for students who attended non-sectarian private schools.[149] The state legislature later passed a law requiring tuition payments for children who were cared for by guardians who were not their parents. Therefore any student in the Mississippi schools whose parent resided outside the state or who did not have a living parent or court-appointed guardian would have to pay up to $375 for the privilege of attending a public school. On its surface, the law targeted parents who had abandoned their children. But Mississippi's agricultural economy depended on the labor of migrants, many who left their children to follow the work as crops ripened or needed tending in other states. The average wage of a fieldworker in the Delta was three dollars a day, and that was only during the growing season and the harvest.[150] It also targeted men and women who migrated north or west in search of better work opportunities, leaving their children with grandparents or extended family.[151] Without directly targeting poor black agricultural workers, the law accomplished that feat nonetheless. Legal Defense Fund head Jack Greenberg labeled the effort as "Mississippi's war on orphans."[152] The move was an extension of previous efforts in Mississippi and in other states to create classifications that targeted African Americans in order to sidestep the reach of equal protection. These classifications stood in for race even as they were ostensibly race neutral, thereby escaping the attention and, ideally, the reach of the Fourteenth Amendment and its condemnation of racial classifications.[153] By targeting orphans and not specifically African Americans, the law could punish black people and poor whites who could not afford to pay the tuition. According to the LDF, the law had the effect of pushing thousands of poor black children out of the state's public schools.[154]

In the *Blackwell* desegregation suit, the students' lawyers attempted to use legal tools to cut out discrimination within the schools, but the court's decrees only glanced the surface. At every turn, the students who opted to attend previously all-white schools found themselves faced with resistance and discrimination. Black students complained that they were made to sit by themselves or in separate rows from white students in classrooms and at lunch; teachers refused to call on black students in class; white students pelted their black peers with wadded-up balls of paper while white teachers did nothing in response.[155] School buses were kept meticulously segregated. Black parents tried to flag the buses down to no avail, watching helplessly as buses full of white children rolled right past their homes on the way to school. Their children had to take an early bus to a segregated black elementary school before waiting for another segregated bus to pick them up and drop them off at their new schools, often late. Furthermore, most of the black students who transferred to formerly white schools were labeled "retarded" and put in remedial classes, separate from their white peers.[156]

Elsewhere in the state, freedom of choice plans put black students in similarly difficult situations. In Philadelphia, Ajatha Morris was one of the first students to desegregate the previously all-white Philadelphia High School in 1966, where she, too, faced difficulties. At the behest of her parents, Ajatha, along with two other black students, enrolled in the high school. Her mother, Ola Morris, encouraged her to enroll even though she worried about the possibility that Ajatha would receive failing grades as punishment for challenging the color line. Ajatha carried her belongings with her to class, concerned that students would rifle through her locker or steal her books. Black students were also instructed not to join any extracurricular clubs or try out for sports teams. But even though white students treated their new black peers harshly, Ajatha later noted that many teachers were kind to her, and she did well academically.[157]

In the Neshoba County schools, just outside Philadelphia, discussions about potential desegregation emerged out of what were termed "impossible conditions" by a COFO fieldworker commenting on the poor state of the county's segregated black schools.[158] After court-ordered desegregation began, white students perpetually harassed the forty-two black students who chose to attend the previously segregated Neshoba Central School during the 1966–1967 school year.[159] The harassment became so severe—reports surfaced of fighting and physical abuse—that the number of black students attending Central dropped to eleven the following year. Within three years, only one black student remained at the school. An attempt to get an injunction to stop the harassment was met with rejection and derision by Judge Cox. All of the other students dropped out of school entirely or transferred back to the segregated black school.[160]

The *Blackwell* desegregation case eventually became part of the landmark 1969 Supreme Court per curiam decision, *Alexander v. Holmes County*. In the case, thirty-three Mississippi school districts were ordered to stop dragging their feet on desegregation. But the case was complicated; it signaled a more aggressive stance on the implementation of *Brown* from the Supreme Court at a moment when Lyndon Johnson's relatively racially liberal Department of Justice had come under the authority of newly elected president Richard Nixon. In *Alexander*, the Court pushed back against the executive's decision to delay the implementation of desegregation plans that had been recently drawn up by the Department of Health, Education and Welfare. These new delays on the implementation of desegregation were wiped away by the court's order, infuriating white supremacist leaders and pro-segregationist Mississippians.[161] Mississippi's schools were ordered to implement the new plans, and school desegregation proceeded in the next several years.

In response, many white Mississippians pulled their children out of the public schools and enrolled them in newly established, lily-white private day schools. One such "segregation academy" opened in 1969 in Rolling Fork, just down the road from the high school that Unita Blackwell and others risked their lives to desegregate.[162] One Freedom Summer volunteer, who remained in Mississippi throughout the year and closely followed the events in Sharkey and Issaquena Counties, recalled the disappointing close to the school boycott and the case. She remarked,

> After all the kids learned about themselves, and about each other, and about their parents and their teachers, and about what teaching is and what learning is, have the schools changed? The kids went back in September without the right to wear their pins. They are still beaten if they ask a question.[163]

* * *

A year after black students in Philadelphia, Mississippi, wore their freedom buttons to school, white schoolchildren in Des Moines, Iowa, tied on black armbands to protest the escalation of the Vietnam War. The children wore the armbands, they said, in support of a proposed Christmas truce in December 1965.[164] As in Mississippi, the Des Moines students' actions infuriated the principal. And they, too, were promptly suspended when they refused to take the armbands off. On its face, the case bore striking similarities to the Mississippi button cases. The students wore symbols that declared their stance on a controversial but prominent public issue. Their case, *Tinker v. Des Moines*, reached the Supreme Court in 1969 and remains the most famous of the student free speech cases. *Tinker* is widely considered the high tide mark for public school students' speech rights.[165] The *Tinker* decision opened the door for American public school students to claim rights at school in an era of dramatic political change and upheaval, and the Court's decision relied heavily on the Fifth Circuit's rulings in the button cases. The majority opinion emphasized that students Christopher Eckhard, John Tinker, and Mary Beth Tinker had participated in a "quiet and passive" protest like the one in Philadelphia, Mississippi, contrasting their situation with the *Blackwell* case, where the court was persuaded that disruption to the school day had occurred. The line between the protection of free speech and its reasonable regulation remained squarely centered on the disruption principle.[166] Those who got to determine what conduct was disruptive—principals, teachers, and the courts—were ultimately the ones who determined the shape of students' free speech rights. Context was everything. The content of the speech was only protected when it was explicitly political and did not disturb the regular functioning of the schools.

Thus, with its limited reach and adherence to the judgment of school administrators, the Fifth Circuit created a complicated legacy for student activists, especially African American students and others whose protest activity might chafe against the strictures imposed by school administrators and teachers. From this perspective, *Tinker* failed to mark out a clear path when it came to the broad interpretation of students' right to free expression. In *Blackwell* and *Burnside*, the deciding factor in whether students' political expressions were protected was the reliability of the testimony of the principal. The disruption principle was therefore problematic at the ground level even as it seemed to establish a clear test on its surface. When the *Tinker* case came before the U.S. Supreme Court, lost was the fact that Des Moines was no Mississippi and that the politics within schools differed tremendously between the two cases. And yet, as the Supreme Court cited *Burnside* and *Blackwell* in *Tinker*, it implied that the cases were substantially similar. But the facts on the ground proved that they were tremendously different. The politics of race played a crucial role in the button cases, even as it was absent from the discussion of their meaning and legacy.

Justice Hugo Black's dissent in *Tinker* is revealing of this unresolved conflict over the proper relationship of students-as-children to the law. Black dismissed the idea that, as minors, students had anything resembling coterminous rights with adults. Indeed, states and local school boards would be justified in making whatever school rules they felt were necessary to preserve a proper educational environment, one in which teachers did the instructing and students did the listening. Black argued in favor of the "original idea of the schools, which I do not believe is yet abandoned as worthless or out of date, [which] was that children had not yet reached the point of experience and wisdom which enabled them to teach all of their elders." It was, therefore, preposterous to assume that students needed free speech protections or that it was conducive to a democratic society to extend constitutional protections past the schoolhouse gate. Echoing the sentiment of Judge Cox, Black concluded, "One may, I hope, be permitted to harbor the thought that taxpayers send children to school on the premise that, at their age, they need to learn, not teach."[167]

Black's dissent presented an argument for the dismissal of any individual rights claims by students in public schools. But the majority opinion, in its sweeping language about the implicit connections between education and democracy, made it possible to imagine that federal courts might be used to make more substantive civil rights reforms in the wake of *Tinker*. "Mississippi is a prison, a prison whose inmates have not been told what crime they have committed," declared a COFO newsletter in mid-1965. It continued,

> The prison has schools for the children of the prisoners, schools taught by prisoners chosen by the warden. Their task under the rules of the prison is to teach the children that they are prisoners by birthright. . . . The purpose of the school is to kill dissent, to give the impression that the prison system is too big to change.[168]

If Mississippi was going to change, its schools had to change, too. The schools were one place where black children were taught Jim Crow.[169] In the process of learning the state's racial hierarchy, schooling had an important place. In the state's separate and unequal schools, black children were reminded that whites held the ultimate authority and that they, as people, held relatively lesser value than white children. Or, at least, this was what the racial curriculum of the schools was supposed to teach. Instead, in the months after Freedom Summer formally ended, black teenagers and their parents brought forceful challenges to the treatment of black students and, ultimately, the very structure of segregated schooling in Mississippi. Despite their modest victories in the button cases, the lawsuits nonetheless showed that litigation under the guise of constitutional rights could be one way to challenge unequal schooling and protect students who were punished for their protest.

Mississippi was no Des Moines, even though the Supreme Court's ruling in *Tinker* implied that "disruption" was a term with universal meaning. In *Blackwell* and *Burnside*, the court effectively brought the politics of respectability into the classroom, making it crucial that students engaging in symbolic protest at school be quietly deferential to school officials on terms that those authorities specified. The only protest that would be tolerated was polite protest that otherwise conformed to standards of obedience and compliance with all school rules and regulations. In *Tinker*, then, the Supreme Court made the disruption test applicable across the country even though such an idea might have wildly different meanings depending on the context. If such mild protest activity by students wearing political buttons in what, in retrospect, is frequently painted as the moment in the Black Freedom Struggle when activists had the most moral authority, what would this mean for students associated with defiant movements like those involving Black and Brown Power?

In the end, the button cases laid the groundwork for future cases involving public school students and the Constitution even as they created a precedent that would limit the scope of students' free speech rights. Although the Fifth Circuit's ruling limited students' rights at school, it also affirmed that students had rights, however circumscribed they might be. In this way, it smoothed the path to *Tinker*. But the contrast between the stories told about *Tinker* and *Blackwell* illuminate how these rulings set up future battles over protest, race, and education. The perceptions of student protest at school and their relationship to challenges to the fundamental mission of education itself would become battlegrounds in future lawsuits, including those related to the Chicano Student Movement in Denver, Colorado, and Black Freedom Struggle in Columbus, Ohio, the subjects of the next two chapters.

2

The Right to Equal Protection

Segregation and Inequality in the Denver Public Schools

In 1969, Reba Yépes was a teenager disillusioned with her school, her teachers, and her position. Yépes grew up in a poor, unincorporated part of Denver, Colorado, where her neighbors lived without running water or indoor plumbing. "The country cousins," her extended family labeled her and her siblings. "I didn't realize I was different than anybody else," she reflected on her younger years. It was at school that she first understood the sting of discrimination and the taint of poverty. The school she attended was mostly white, with affluent children from middle-class families. "By the time we got to school, we were angry and frustrated," Yépes observed. But she came from a family in which organizing was a tradition. Her mother worked for the Southwest Action Center, a War on Poverty program, and she came from a family of farmworkers. As a young girl, she worked in the potato fields and stood in the picket lines with her mother. In 1968, she traveled with the Western Caravan to Washington, DC, to participate in Resurrection City, a massive demonstration that sought to make poverty of all colors and kinds visible to the federal government as part of Martin Luther King, Jr.'s Poor People's Campaign.[1] By the late 1960s, Yépes was no longer a disenchanted public school student. Now she was part of a larger effort to reform the city and its schools.

The frustration she felt at school, along with her family's ties to economic and labor activism, brought Yépes into Denver's emergent Chicano Movement.[2] Across the southwestern United States, the Chicano Movement took root and flourished during the late 1960s, often through the organizing work of high school students.[3] At the same time, black students and parents launched their own challenge to separate and unequal education in Denver. These challenges to the city's system of public education sometimes dovetailed but often conflicted over what shape racial reform should take. Nonetheless, both Chicano and black activists in Denver charged that the city's public schools replicated inequality instead of providing equal opportunities to all students. This chapter examines the early years of *Keyes v. School District No. 1*, the Denver school desegregation lawsuit that eventually reached the Supreme Court, and the cauldron of ideas about racial equality in education from which it emerged. At the time, the reach of the Fourteenth Amendment's equal protection clause in public schools was not yet fixed by the courts, and so the Denver case provides a window into these competing arguments and differing visions for how a truly equal system of education might take shape.

The Shape of Separate and Unequal in Denver

The city in which Reba Yépes grew up was a swiftly expanding and modern segregated city. A prime beneficiary of the federal government's investment in defense spending during and after World War II, Denver grew steadily during the middle of the century.[4] Between 1950 and 1960, the metropolitan population increased by 50 percent.[5] Like many of its Western counterparts, Denver's population was majority white, although a growing percentage was made up of members of racial minority groups. African Americans, who historically made up a very small percentage of the city's inhabitants, moved to Denver in larger numbers as part of the Great Migration during the 1950s and 1960s and settled in the city's northern neighborhoods. To the west and south lived many of the city's Mexican American residents, who historically made up an older and larger population than African Americans did.[6] The Mexican American population in Denver was largely made up of second-generation immigrants, with a much smaller population of foreign-born Mexican nationals.[7] Unlike the South, where the divide between concepts of "whiteness" and "blackness" determined the structure of racial segregation, the presence of a large population of Mexican Americans influenced the shape of the color line.[8]

Denver's schools became battlegrounds in the struggle to secure equal rights for people of color in part because the schooling provided by the district was both separate and unequal. The schools that had large populations of black or Mexican American students were far more likely to be made up of low-income students and have lower test scores than wealthier, whiter schools.[9] Although the most vocal supporters of the school desegregation lawsuit were African American, outcomes for Mexican American children in Denver schools were worse than those for all other racial or ethnic groups. Three-quarters of Mexican American students dropped out of school before graduation.[10] A study of census data put together by the Crusade for Justice, a Chicano civil rights organization, found that the average number of years of schooling among Chicanos in central Colorado was not quite nine. In other words, many Mexican American students left school as soon as they were legally able to do so. The white population had, on average, at least twelve full years of schooling. Even more troubling, 20 percent of adults of Mexican descent in Denver County had fewer than four years of formal education.[11] While high school completion was considered the norm for whites, the same was not true for students of Mexican descent.

As elsewhere throughout the country, a blend of state and private action created residential segregation in Denver, which created segregation within neighborhood schools. Until 1948, the use of courts to enforce racially restrictive covenants—agreements signed by community members that barred homeowners from selling to "undesirable" classes of people—contributed to a logic that put monetary value upon a neighborhood's whiteness and associated financial risk with the presence of people of color.[12] As late as the 1950s, real estate companies in Denver still advertised homes bound by racially restrictive covenants.[13] Through these advertisements, real estate agents sold an idea of protection—a home insulated from neighborhood racial change (and, conversely, an assumed drop in prices if a black family moved in next door)—as well as the desirability of living in a racially homogenous, whitewashed world. Furthermore, federal policy encouraged the practice of racial discrimination in housing across the nation. The Federal Housing Administration's policy of "redlining" residential areas with non-white residents, a practice in which such areas were identified as being investment risks and therefore ineligible for federally backed loans, made it difficult for people of color to secure mortgages and supported the construction of all-white neighborhoods.[14] Blockbusting, also called "panic selling," was a practice employed by unscrupulous real estate agents who used the fear of black families moving to white neighborhoods to encourage white homeowners to sell their homes below market value. They then turned around and sold those homes at a premium to middle-class black buyers looking to live in more desirable neighborhoods, contributing to rapid white flight and racial change in neighborhoods along the color line.[15] Although the Colorado Legislature passed a law prohibiting discrimination in housing in 1959 and the federal Fair Housing Act of 1968 forbade public and private discrimination in the real estate and rental markets, the passage of such laws did not magically undo decades of policies and practices that promoted residential segregation.[16]

As Denver's black population grew in the 1950s and 1960s, historically black neighborhoods became overcrowded, and black residents began to buy homes adjacent to white enclaves.[17] As they moved, so did the color line. This was most noticeable in the northeast neighborhoods of the city, which became the central focus of the Denver desegregation case. Park Hill, located due east of the historically black neighborhoods of North Denver and Five Points, was separated from those neighborhoods by Colorado Boulevard, a major thoroughfare that also served to divide school attendance zones. The class status of the neighborhoods reflected this racial and economic segregation, as Park Hill residents were solidly middle-class, whereas those in Five Points reported far lower average incomes, levels of educational attainment, and rates of homeownership.[18] Historically, Five Points had been a poor neighborhood crowded with black residents. Park Hill residents sought to maintain its place as a model middle-class, integrated neighborhood. This was one goal of the interracial Park Hill Action Committee, which aimed to keep the neighborhood stable and outside the clutches of real estate agents looking to profit through panic selling.[19]

Other factors also increased segregation of the city's schools and set the stage for conflict. Prime among them was the baby boom, in which American women bore higher numbers of children on average in the two decades following World War II.[20] This reversed the late 1940s trend of declining enrollments in the city's schools, which were likely the result of declining fertility rates during the Depression.[21] The 1950s and the 1960s were therefore moments of extraordinary school building and student shifting to accommodate demand. During these years, the superintendent and Denver School Board held more power than ever before to shape the student populations of the city's schools. Critics charged that the board of education did so with an eye to maintaining or increasing the segregation of black and Mexican American children in certain schools.

A 1969 study showed how quickly racial segregation in the city's schools had accelerated in the previous decade. Black and Mexican American students were likely to attend a school where they made up a majority of students, even as together they made up a minority of the district's student population. In 1969, white students constituted 60 percent of all students in the district. Despite making up only 15 percent of the school population, black students made up more than 90 percent of the population of three elementary schools.[22] Mexican American students, who constituted nearly a quarter of the city's public school students, faced segregation that was not quite as extreme. Only one elementary school was more than 90 percent Mexican American, while eleven others had student populations that were more than half Mexican American.[23] Nine of the city's public elementary schools were more than 90 percent white. Most dramatically, of the nearly 33,000 white students in the city's elementary schools, only 5,035 attended schools that were less than 70 percent white.[24]

As these children left their elementary schools, they attended junior high schools and high schools that were no less segregated. A number of schools opened up during the decade before the lawsuit was filed, including four brand-new high schools. Abraham Lincoln accepted its first students in 1959, while two other high schools, George Washington and Thomas Jefferson, opened the following year. John F. Kennedy High School opened its doors to students in 1966. All of these schools had high enrollment capacities and overwhelmingly white student bodies. Kennedy, a gleaming, new, combined junior high and high school on the city's southwest side, had the most students of any school. More than 2,700 young people filled its halls and classrooms, but only 79 of those students were black, Mexican American, or Japanese American.[25] White students who attended high schools in these parts of the city had access to college preparatory classes that launched them into selective colleges. North, West, South, East, and Manual High Schools were all older and—with the exception of South High School—had larger minority student populations.[26]

Located in Five Points, Manual High School stood for a quite different approach to education. Manual, which had been called Manual

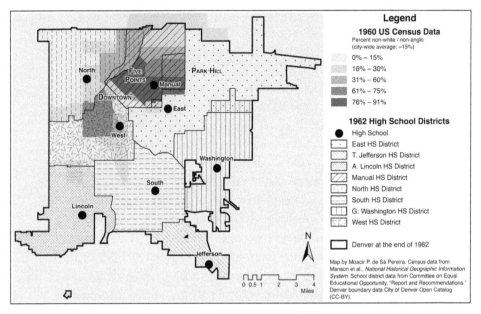

Figure 2.1. Map of Denver public high schools and attendance boundaries in 1962. Shading indicates percentage of non-white/non-Anglo students in 1960. School districts as of 1962 are outlined. HS = high school. Source: School data are drawn from *A Special Study Committee on Equal Educational Opportunity in the Denver Public Schools, Report and Recommendations to the Board of Education, School District Number One, Denver, Colorado,* March 1, 1964, Papers of the Mexican American Legal Defense Fund, box 708, folder 9, RG 5, Special Collections and University Archives, Stanford University, Palo Alto, CA. Geographic racial distribution data are drawn from Steven Manson, Jonathan Schroeder, David Van Riper, and Steven Ruggles, *IPUMS National Historical Geographic Information System: Version 12.0* (database, Minneapolis: University of Minnesota, 2017), doi: 10.18128. Historical geographic data on Denver city limits are drawn from the City of Denver Open Data Catalog, http://data.denvergov.org.

Training Academy until the early 1950s, earned its name from its original emphasis on vocational education. After the building burned in a fire, Manual High School reopened in the early 1950s with new attendance boundaries. It quickly became clear that the boundaries would send more black and Mexican American students to Manual while decreasing the numbers who attended East High School.[27] Black parents immediately criticized the decision. Many felt especially betrayed by the redrawn boundary lines. The "new" Manual High School was meant to be the pride of the neighborhood, but it appeared to black parents that it was yet another way for the city to cordon off their children in separate and unequal schools.[28] By the 1960s, Manual was majority-minority and emblematic of the inequities of the city's public school system.[29] Whereas five of the city's nine high schools (and all of those named after American presidents) were at least 85 percent white, Manual High School's population was, by this time, only 8 percent white. Sixty percent of the school's students were black, and the rest were Mexican American and Japanese American. Japanese-American students were overrepresented at Manual, constituting 4 percent of the student body even as they made up a much smaller percentage of the total student population in Denver public schools.

During the 1950s, after the district redrew attendance boundaries to channel most of the city's black students to Manual, parents pointed out that the school offered more remedial classes and fewer college preparatory courses than the nearby, mostly white East High did.[30] The school's vaunted pre-medical and pre-law programs merely allowed students to see what doctors and lawyers did "on the job" rather than providing a challenging program of study that would prepare them to follow such a path through graduate and professional school.[31] It appeared as if the district created two standards of high school education for the city's children: rigorous college-preparatory classes for white students and vocational training for students of color.

In addition to building new schools, the school board found ways to accommodate more students in older schools when it chose to do so. In 1962, the district brought in mobile units in order to handle overcrowding in the schools of northeast Denver without disturbing attendance zones.[32] The district administration also proposed a new elementary school in North Denver. The school, Barrett Elementary, infuriated black parents when they realized that it would be "built small." The building would be constructed to take in a relatively small number of students, which would mean that students from nearby white schools would not be transferred to relieve overcrowding at their schools. Soon after, a new junior high school was also announced; it, too, would be built squarely within a segregated black neighborhood and appeared to reinforce the color line at Colorado Boulevard. The school would feed its students into Manual High School and steer them away from East High School. After witnessing the segregation that resulted from the construction of

Barrett, outraged parents managed to halt the school board's plans for a new junior high school.[33]

The issue of where to build the new, sorely needed junior high school became a central issue for parents who were outraged by the racial segregation overtaking city schools. Parents in the Park Hill area wanted the school built in an area that would create a stable, desegregated student population. The school board resisted these suggestions. Meanwhile, Cole Junior High School in Five Points remained overcrowded and segregated even as open seats existed at other predominantly white junior high schools.[34] At odds with neighborhood residents, the board did not move forward on plans to build the new school for years. As children crowded into classrooms in schools in Five Points, Park Hill, and the surrounding neighborhoods, the board brought in mobile classrooms rather than change attendance boundaries. The inability of the board to deal with such a straightforward problem—it simply needed to choose a site on which to build a school—became a clear sign to area parents that their frustrations were being ignored and fed the perception that the school board deliberately built schools in order to perpetuate residential segregation.[35]

Even as the schools became increasingly segregated in the late 1950s and early 1960s, the school board's internal assessments downplayed the importance of race in relation to the quality of education Denver's children received. A survey conducted by the Denver School Board in 1963 found that most parents with children in the city's schools highly regarded the quality of education that the schools provided. Of the 23 percent of parents surveyed who said that "some schools [were] not as good," black parents pointed to Manual and East High. Mexican American parents listed North, Manual, and West High Schools. Black and Mexican American parents were also more likely to express concern that their children's schools were overcrowded. The survey found the most dissatisfaction with the schools among black parents. Half of the black parents surveyed wanted the system to abandon the neighborhood school zoning system for high schools and expand the district's open enrollment policies in order to allow students to choose which high school to attend. This desire was especially strong among parents whose children attended high school at West and Manual. In opposition, virtually all of the parents whose children attended South High School or Jefferson High School—nearly all of whom were white—opposed open enrollment and favored the neighborhood school scheme. The report, in the end, declared that the survey demonstrated that "there is no substantive accusation that the city's schools have failed to provide 'an equal educational opportunity for all.'"[36]

The report downplayed the importance of concerns about unequal educational opportunities by relying on stereotypes of Mexican American parents as more interested in employment than in higher education for their children. The committee interpreted the self-reported detachment of Mexican American parents from their children's education as proof that they cared less about school than black and white parents did, concluding that Spanish-surnamed parents were "seemingly . . . somewhat less concerned about the vitality of the educational system or process."[37] What might have been a glaring signal of the marginalization of the city's largest minority student population became, instead, an excuse for their needs to remain a low priority for the school board. Board members expressed relatively little interest in addressing the high percentage of Mexican American children who dropped out even as parents presented evidence at meetings that poor students were being pushed out of school because their parents could not afford to pay school fees.[38]

In May 1964, in response to pressure from parents and students and after years of complaints from parents in northeast neighborhoods, the Denver School Board adopted a policy on equal educational opportunity: "This Board of Education recognizes that all children within the District, regardless of racial or ethnic backgrounds, are equally entitled to the benefits of a good education," the statement declared. But it stopped short of taking any responsibility for inequities within the system, and the definition of equality of educational opportunity was ambiguous in its meaning and scope. It did define what equality of educational opportunity was emphatically not:

> Because individuals vary greatly in their backgrounds, their capacities, and their motivations, equality of educational opportunity must not be conceived as the same opportunity for each person; that is, for example, as schools with the same curriculum, guidance, and instruction.[39]

The reforms proposed were relatively minor, and they did little to stem the tide of increasing segregation within the schools. The district's student population grew steadily during these years, and so did the patterns of racial isolation. After the 1964 study, the school board allowed some schools that had open seats to accept student transfers, but this did virtually nothing to challenge segregation beyond a token basis. Fewer than 200 black students transferred to other schools, and not a single white student transferred to a majority-minority school.[40]

The autumn after the board announced its statement on equality of educational opportunity, members of the local National Association for the Advancement of Colored People (NAACP) chapter appeared before the board of education and warned that the growing, young population of Park Hill meant that segregation would increase in the neighborhood's schools. Irving Andrews, an at-large board member for the national NAACP and local lawyer, presented the board with an article from the May 1965 issue of the *Case Western Law Review*, a special edition that examined the issue of de facto school segregation. Andrews informed the board members that the arguments for the unconstitutionality of de facto segregation might "enlighten" them, suggesting that should the board continue to ignore the existence of separate and unequal education, they effectively invited a lawsuit.[41] A month later, the local chapter of the NAACP and the Park Hill Action Committee presented a plan to relieve overcrowding at Stedman Elementary, which had 200 more students than it was built to accommodate, by allowing those students to transfer to three nearby elementary schools that had majority-white student populations.[42] At a special board meeting intended to discuss the issues facing schools in northeast Denver, residents spoke before the board to register their concerns about racial segregation in the schools and the unequal nature of education.[43] Time and again in the early 1960s, the local NAACP and black parents in Park Hill pointed out segregative actions. And time and again, the board ignored them. Two weeks after the meeting to discuss racial isolation in northeast Denver, a member of the city's newly founded Citizens' Council, an extension of the organization that terrorized black people in the South after the *Brown v. Board of Education* ruling, expressed opposition to any actions that would dismantle segregation, requesting that the board consider "the rights of white children also."[44]

Rachel Noel, the board of education's sole black member, eventually tired of the board's recalcitrance on segregation and inequality in the city's schools. A resident of Park Hill, Noel saw for herself the variation in quality between schools with mostly white and black student populations.[45] After years of forming advisory committees, receiving their reports, and listening to residents complain about the unequal education and increasing segregation in the city's schools, by the spring of 1967 Noel voiced her frustrations with the inaction before the board, reading aloud a section of a report from the U.S. Commission on Civil Rights that stressed the urgency of dealing with racial segregation in education.[46] Noel also worked behind the scenes with school board members, conducting what she described as "sensitivity training" to teach them about the effect racism had on the lives of black Americans, a tactic that persuaded at least one other board member, John Amesse, to change his mind and support her position. Noel also had the support of another board member, Edgar Benton, who worked closely with her on developing proposals to combat school segregation.[47] In June, Noel introduced a measure that would forbid the board from building a new junior high school in northeast Denver, where it would certainly become quickly segregated, arguing that the board should begin a program of busing to relieve crowding in the area's schools. Amesse agreed with Noel, stating that the time to act was now. He added that, as a member of the Colorado National Guard, he had been warned that officials were worried that if action was not taken on civil rights issues Denver could become "another Watts," invoking the six days of rioting that took place in Los Angeles in 1965.[48]

While people like Rachel Noel worked for administrative solutions to inequity in the schools and the plaintiffs in *Keyes v. School District No. 1* turned to the courts when that strategy stalled, new and more radical movements brewed in the city's streets and in its schools. A 1967 report from Denver's Commission on Community Relations warned about the tinder box of disillusionment and frustration that many Denver teenagers felt, stating that the city faced "a real threat of riots this summer." The preliminary report on the neighborhood of Northeast Park Hill, written in early July, clearly had an eye toward the long, hot summer that had just begun and would culminate weeks later with riots in Detroit. In assessing the likelihood of such an event in Denver, the report warned about hostility toward police, "covert bias" in hiring that limited opportunities for young people of color, increasing residential segregation as a result of the actions of "panicky whites," and a "white middle class educational system which is unable to communicate with many Negro children."[49]

There were no riots in Denver during the summer of 1967, as there were in many other places. But there were near misses. During the last weekend in July, the tension nearly boiled over between black residents and police. When a police officer ticketed a black teenager for jaywalking after a dance at the downtown YMCA, young people congregated in Northeast Park Hill's shopping center the following day. Shop owners reported that some windows were broken and merchandise was stolen. Two days later, police officers pushed into a crowd of young people at the same center in order to disperse them. Again, the situation did not escalate. Neighborhood residents aggressively worked to head off any potential conflict, hosting dances several nights in a row to give local teenagers a place to go and enjoy themselves, steering them away from the shopping center.[50]

In late March 1968, the board of education voted to study the Kerner Commission's recently released report on the riots that had spread like wildfire through American cities the previous summer.[51] Concerned parents also spoke before the board of education and echoed Amesse's warning that its inaction on segregated and unequal education in the city could lead to riots in Denver.[52] Just a few weeks later, Martin Luther King, Jr., was assassinated in Memphis, and civil disorders once again convulsed the nation. Rachel Noel arrived at the next school board meeting with a plan. Capitalizing on anxieties about the possibility of unrest in Denver, Noel presented her own solution for reducing the isolation of children of color in separate and unequal schools. Resolution 1490, later referred to as the "Noel Resolution," called for a multipronged dismantling of racial segregation and required that the superintendent submit a plan for effective desegregation by the end of the year.[53] The school board voted to table the resolution.

In response, a vocal and persistent group of Denverites moved quickly to pressure the board into passing the Noel Resolution. Supporters picketed the homes of resistant board members. Black teachers in the system formed their own organization and planned a boycott in support of the measure. More than half of the district's black students stayed home on May 16, the day the board was to vote on the resolution.[54] And perhaps

Figure 2.2. Black men and women demonstrate in favor of passage of the Noel
Resolution in Denver, Colorado, May 16, 1968. Source: Western History and Genealogy
Collection, X-28759, Denver Public Library.

no less compellingly, the specter of another long, hot summer did its own work to persuade reluctant members of the public and the school board that taking steps to alleviate racial tension and the frustration of young black men—many of whom were also students in the city's schools—might be a worthwhile investment in the city's future. As Rachel Noel explained, some school board members "were afraid of what might happen if the black kids started roaming the streets."[55] The *Denver Post* ran an editorial supporting the resolution, and the *Rocky Mountain News* likewise printed favorable coverage.[56] By May 1968, enough moderate board members agreed that it was time to do something that the measure passed, five votes to two. Desegregation was on its way to Denver, one way or another.

Student Protest and Equal Protection

The passage of the Noel Resolution marked the high tide of educational reform efforts that focused on administrative paths toward change in Denver. Rachel Noel later noted that King's death particularly impressed upon her the responsibility her position on the school board gave her. "I thought any black person in a position of policymaking should see to it that there is equal opportunity," she later observed.[57] But the 1968–1969 school year also marked the virtual end of such efforts. With the filing of the *Keyes* case in the summer of 1969 and the rise of the Chicano Movement, the courts, schools, and streets became the theaters in which the struggle to create and define equal education would play out in the city. Fatigue with the slow and unsteady pace of institutional reform took its toll. And increasingly, young people saw themselves as the agents of change.

In the months following the passage of the Noel Resolution, the board discussed and voted on three measures that called for the desegregation of a small section of the city's schools. The superintendent produced a plan in response to the resolution that called for some improvements to city schools but limited desegregation to the expansion of voluntary open enrollment. Led by Rachel Noel and Edgar Benton, the school board amended the plan to make it more ambitious in regard to reducing segregation. In order to stave off the falling numbers of white students at East High, which appeared to be on its way to becoming a segregated school, Resolution 1520 changed attendance boundaries to include white neighborhoods to the south. Resolutions 1524 and 1531 tackled segregation at Smiley Junior High and the elementary schools in Park Hill, respectively.[58]

At the same time that the board considered measures to reduce segregation, black and Chicano activists sought their own reforms. In some Five Points schools, black activists sought to implement community control measures, inspired in part by the Ocean Hill–Brownsville school experiment in New York.[59] The local branch of the Black Panther Party, led by Lauren Watson, was primarily focused on employment discrimination and police abuse and brutality during its short, active life. The chapter, arguably synonymous with its leader, effectively shut down after Denver police raided its headquarters and arrested Watson.[60] But before Watson's arrest, Black Panther Party members picketed the entrance to Cole Junior High, where they managed to convince 200 students to boycott the school for two weeks in the fall of 1968 in support of a transition to community control. Later, after administrators at Cole responded to an altercation between students and a teacher in the parking lot by hiring a police officer to patrol the hallways, the Black Panthers again picketed the school with hundreds of boycotting students.[61] They later claimed victory when the principal was replaced with a respected black teacher who then hired an assistant principal who hailed from Five Points. The new administration removed police officers from the school and arranged for the school to offer courses in black history.[62]

The city's burgeoning Chicano Movement spurred its own conversations about justice and equity, especially in education. Corky Gonzales, the leader of the Crusade for Justice, encouraged student participation in the movement. The Crusade for Justice was born in 1966, initially describing itself as "a national civil rights organization that has been created for and by the people" that "was born out of frustration and determination to secure equality with dignity for the Mexican American and Spanish-surnamed people."[63] The decision to target the schools was inspired by the mass protests in East Los Angeles that occurred the previous March, where more than 10,000 students staged walkouts, gave and heard speeches, picketed, and generally created headaches for school officials.[64] The East Los Angeles "blowouts," as they quickly became known, represented a collective rejection of the inferior education that Los Angeles schools offered Mexican American students.[65] They also provided a template for young Mexican Americans across the nation who chafed against the strictures of school systems that expected very little from them and provided very little in return.

By late 1968, the Chicano Movement gained steam in Western cities, including Denver. In early November 1968, an energized Gonzales appeared at a school board meeting, flanked by Black Berets, a group made up of Chicano student activists that served as a security force. The meeting had been called to discuss a desegregation plan in response to the Noel Resolution, and Gonzales was direct in voicing his disapproval. "From Head Start through college, our students and our people have suffered psychological ethnic destruction by the overwhelming brainwashing machine called education," Gonzales roared at the meeting. "We can no longer remain silent in the face of this devastating monster that perpetuates the myth that European whites or Anglos are the only symbols of success and power in this society." He then finished (with a bullhorn, as someone disconnected the public microphone in the middle of his speech) by listing a set of demands that included bilingual instruction, the teaching of Hispanic heritage and culture, free education from preschool through college, and community control over the schools. Three infuriated school board members left the stage in protest.[66] But Gonzales had made his case for a competing idea of equal education for Mexican American children that did not include desegregation. From this vision would emerge Chicano challenges to inequality in education that largely remained outside the courts until the mid-1970s.

In March 1969, Mexican American students took matters into their own hands. Harry Shafer, a social studies teacher at West High School, was known to students for making demeaning comments about Mexican Americans during class. While more than half of the students and most of the teachers at West were white, nearly 40 percent of the student population was Mexican American.[67] A month earlier, after a student filed a complaint about Shafer's remarks with the school's administration, the school held an informal hearing during which Shafer did not deny making the remarks but instead claimed he made them in a context that was intended to "stimulate debate over current social problems."[68] This message was apparently not clear to the Mexican American students in his classes, who felt humiliated and angered by his remarks.

Figure 2.3. Members of the Black Berets stand guard in front of Corky Gonzales as he delivers a speech during a demonstration at the Colorado State Capitol Building, Denver, on November 3, 1968. Source: Western History and Genealogy Collection, X-21596, Denver Public Library.

On the morning of March 19, 150 students decided that they had had enough. They walked out of school in protest, demanding that Shafer be fired.[69] What began as a peaceful demonstration quickly spiraled out of control. The students were met across the street by police officers in riot gear. Some students threw rocks and bottles at officers who teargassed and beat the students with nightsticks. It was a scene of total chaos that terrified many of the teenaged protesters. In the end, Gonzales and twenty-four other people were arrested, including twelve teenagers.[70]

The Denver police department had a fraught relationship with young Mexican Americans. In the previous few years, the shootings of Mexican American young men by police officers had outraged many people and had become a central issue for the Crusade for Justice, as it was in other cities with large populations of persons of Mexican descent.[71] The presence of police in the midst of a protest driven by young people ratcheted up the stakes. With riot-gear-clad police the first thing students saw, many young people who already felt that Denver police officers targeted Mexican Americans became infuriated. As the protesting students moved into the gardens in the park across the street from the school, police officers formed a line and aggressively pushed the students back. This was the moment when the protest shifted from a peaceful scene to a chaotic one. Witnesses later testified that the protest became a riot only when the police began to treat students roughly.[72]

The blowout was followed by days of protest, sometimes turning violent, in which students from other schools joined in solidarity. African American students joined the movement to protest discrimination in their own schools. On Friday, March 21, approximately 100 students, including members of their schools' Black Student Alliances, walked out of East High and marched to Manual High School, where the group more than doubled in size.[73] The students, now more than 200 strong, marched on to West High, where they joined hundreds of students who protested across from the school.[74] Mexican American students distributed handbills that listed their demands, which echoed those made before by Gonzales, including demands for bilingual education, separate school boards for individual schools, and the teaching of Mexican-American history and culture.[75] After the protest at West High, the groups dispersed throughout the city. A large number marched to a nearby park, where they listened to a speech by Gonzales. Another group that included many of the African American students from East High marched to the district administration building downtown, where they demanded to meet with board member Rachel Noel. When told she was not in the office, they met instead with the superintendent and asked him to hire more black teachers in the system who could teach black history.[76]

A week after the initial walkout, District Superintendent Harry Gilberts declared that he had found no wrongdoing on the part of Shafer. "It is our judgment that these charges have not been substantiated and do not seem to reflect either Mr. Shafer's philosophy or conduct," Gilberts declared.[77] Shafer was later transferred to another school at his request.[78] Field agents for the FBI reported to the national office on the parades and protests staged by the Crusade for Justice, and informants were present at the West High blowouts, for which the FBI reports blamed the Crusade and the Black Panther Party.[79] Denver Police Chief George Seaton blamed adult "anarchists" who used students as a "cute trick" to avoid police aggression.[80] Despite the FBI's insistence that the students had been manipulated into carrying out a "harassment campaign," the participation of so many young people on such a large scale indicates that more was at stake.[81] By joining Chicano protesters at West High, black students at East High and Manual were able to voice their own concerns as part of a larger demand for reform in the schools.

Meanwhile, the city geared up for another school board election in May. The school board members who voted with Noel to take affirmative steps toward desegregation had been inundated with hate mail. One board member described the messages he received as "vituperative, vitriolic, and sometimes outrageous."[82] Anti-desegregation and anti-busing fervor in Denver was as strong and furious as anywhere else in the United States. That year's school board elections, which took place in the spring of 1969, were defined by race and busing, and they occurred in the midst of student walkouts and boycotts and increasing defiance on the part of student protesters. Opponents of the Noel resolution were elected to the board, and, now outnumbering those who favored the plan, they quickly dispensed with the policy. On June 9, 1969, the newly seated board of education voted to rescind the three resolutions that would have reduced segregation in the city's northern neighborhoods. Infuriated by the board's action, parents of children in the city's schools—including African Americans, Mexican Americans, and whites—enlisted the assistance of local lawyers and sued the school district, asking for an injunction against the resolution's retraction. Rachel Noel, Wilfred Keyes, and Fred Thomas, all of whom lived in Park Hill and who had children in segregated schools, convinced white lawyer Gordon Grenier to take the case by relaying their stories about the experiences of their children. The first hearings in *Keyes v. School District No. 1* took place in a Denver federal courtroom in July 1969 before Judge William Doyle, where the plaintiffs asked the court to temporarily hold off on the school board's actions by granting a temporary injunction against the rescission of the Noel Resolution.[83]

In crafting the initial complaint, the lawyers for the plaintiffs claimed that there were "alleged injuries resulting from the plaintiffs having been subjected to unequal treatment with respect to their right to an education."[84] Intentional racial segregation within city schools, they argued, deprived students of their right to educational equality as guaranteed by the U.S. Constitution. On July 23, 1969, Judge Doyle gave an oral order to temporarily reinstate the Noel Resolution and to move forward with the district's plans to desegregate until a full hearing could occur. Doyle stated that, by repealing the Noel Resolution and the attendant plans to desegregate, the board had taken actions that would undoubtedly perpetuate the segregation of the schools. In his written order, issued a week later, Judge Doyle declared that the "denial of an equal right to education is a deprivation which infringes this constitutional guarantee" under the Fourteenth Amendment.[85] Furthermore, Doyle's order declared that the "right to equality in education has, since *Brown*, become recognized as a sensitive constitutional right."[86] But what did "equality in education" look like in Denver? What did the Constitution demand? These questions became central to the *Keyes* litigation.

After Doyle's order was issued, lawyers for the school district quickly appealed the decision to the Tenth Circuit of Appeals, which reversed Doyle's ruling on August 27, one week before classes were scheduled to resume in Denver public schools. The district court acted too quickly, the judges said, and a more prudent course would be to delay implementation in order to nurture public support for desegregation. Rebuffed, the plaintiffs' lawyers scrambled to take action, racing to the U.S. Supreme Court and asking for a review of the Tenth Circuit's decision.[87] On August 29, Justice William Brennan sided with the plaintiffs' lawyers and chastised the appeals court for overstepping its bounds in issuing the injunction. According to Justice Brennan, "Where a preliminary injunction has issued to vindicate constitutional rights, the presumption in favor of the District Court's action applies with particular force."[88] The argument in favor of waiting until public support amassed was not, Brennan wrote, sufficient to continue to deprive students of their rights when the district court had found evidence of de jure segregation. Doyle's order reinstating the Noel Resolution and the district's desegregation plans was once again in force. Just after Labor Day in 1969, despite the protestations of many white parents, several hundred black and white children were bused to new schools in order to begin desegregation on a limited scale.[89]

Student protests continued during the 1969–1970 school year. Another Chicano boycott took place on Mexican Independence Day in September, with thousands of students walking out of school and joining a peaceful parade that ended with a speech by Corky Gonzales at the state capitol building.[90] When a Chicano student activist, Manuel

"Rocky" Hernandez, was suspended from North High School in February, students supported him with a protest outside the school that drew nearly 200 people. The school administration claimed that Hernandez had been suspended for "truancy and failing grades," but students suspected that his suspension was part of a larger effort to remove student activists from the school and quash their activities. Among the administration's claims were that Hernandez "distributed literature" in school without permission and made "demands and threats" toward teachers and the school's principal.[91] Hernandez had been one of the most visible and vocal leaders of the Chicano student movement at North High and one of the original Black Berets.[92] During the Mexican Independence Day celebrations in September, Hernandez organized a protest by Mexican American students at nearby schools.[93] Their list of demands echoed the ones articulated previously, demanding that the schools recognize Chicano and black history and hire more Chicano and African American teachers and administrators. They also asked for the dismissal of "racist" school board members, the removal of police officers from the schools, and an end to corporal punishment.[94]

As conflict within the schools ratcheted up after 1968, so too did antibusing fervor. Late on the night of February 5, 1970, someone snuck over a fence, planted bombs, and destroyed forty-one school buses. This was a third of the school district's fleet. Police blamed Baltazar Martinez, a member of the Crusade for Justice. Mexican Americans immediately decried the accusation, arguing that Martinez was a scapegoat intended to make the Crusade's tactics look like violent extremism and, therefore, make them illegitimate in the eyes of Denver's public. Martinez was arrested when a paramedic, who had treated someone with wounds on his hands soon after the bombing, picked him out of a lineup. Martinez's lawyer was quick to point out that his client's hands were uninjured, and therefore there was no physical evidence that he had been involved. He was eventually cleared of the charges, and the case was never solved.[95]

Equal Protection and the Law

In February 1970, District Judge William Doyle once again heard the *Keyes* case, this time on the merits. While the initial hearing had been focused on the passage of the Noel Resolution and the school board's decision to retract it, this trial approached the broader question about racial segregation and inequality in the Denver schools. It therefore brought forth arguments from both sides about the meaning and scope of the Fourteenth Amendment's equal protection clause. Much as black and Chicano students articulated their own meaning of the idea on the streets and in classrooms, the courtroom was likewise a venue for experimentation. Several questions framed this conversation. First, did the right to equality of educational opportunity exist for students who were subject to de facto segregation, or was it limited to cases of de jure segregation? In either case, the second question was paramount to any litigation over school segregation: What was the difference between de facto and de jure segregation? And how should the courts treat Mexican American children? All of the school desegregation cases previously heard by the U.S. Supreme Court had dealt only with black students.[96] In crafting their arguments, the plaintiffs' lawyers reached beyond *Brown v. Board of Education* to older cases that dealt with the substantive meaning of educational equality, including *Plessy v. Ferguson*, the decision that protected the legality of state-imposed racial segregation in the United States.

Concerns about educational equality had roots even deeper than *Brown v. Board of Education*, a fact that the lawyers hoped would provide them with guidance while litigating a case that did not fit the Southern model. Two key cases were the landmark 1950 decisions *Sweatt v. Painter* and *McLaurin v. Oklahoma*, which rested upon the concrete ways in which segregated graduate schools and law schools could never provide equal education or career opportunities for their African American students.[97] Just a few years later, in *Brown*, the Supreme Court applied these principles to elementary and secondary education. The Court argued that "to separate [black children] from others of similar age and qualifications solely because of their race generates a feeling of inferiority . . . that may affect their hearts and minds in a way unlikely ever to be undone."[98] The unanimous decision emphasized how the nation's changing economy gave new importance to education. It implied that perceptions of inferiority would follow children throughout their lives, hindering their ability to succeed in adulthood. Quality education made good employees and, most important, good citizens.

But how would the Court know when a violation of the right to equality of educational opportunity existed? Certainly, according to *Brown*, a deprivation of the right existed where schools were segregated by state action, but the boundary between de jure and de facto segregation had never been perfectly clear. Even in Mississippi, a bulwark of Jim Crow well into the 1960s, state officials sought creative ways to avoid the reach of the Fourteenth Amendment, claiming that "freedom of choice" plans protected the racial segregation in the state's schools from the taint of state action. White schools were open to black children, officials argued. The problem was that black children simply chose not to attend such schools. In 1968, the Supreme Court struck down such plans as old forms of illegal segregation masquerading under a new guise.[99]

Cases outside the South would prove more difficult to litigate, although anyone who paid attention to federal district and appellate cases in the early 1960s knew it was possible to win such a case. In 1961, federal courts in New York found that the school board of New Rochelle intentionally created illegal segregation in one of the city's elementary schools, and as the remedy, the courts ordered desegregation.[100] But cases from Gary, Indiana, and Kansas City, Missouri, were unsuccessful. In each case, the courts determined that, while students were segregated in schools by race because of residential segregation, the district courts had not proven that the action was intentional on the part of the school board.[101]

A two year-old case from Washington, DC, provided similar facts and arguments for the *Keyes* lawyers and, perhaps, the best template for their own arguments.[102] In his 1967 decision in *Hobson v. Hansen*, federal judge J. Skelly Wright ruled that schools in the District of Columbia were both unconstitutionally segregated and unequal. As in Denver, the plaintiffs' lawyers in *Hobson* argued that optional attendance zones had been used to segregate students, that teachers had been placed in schools according to their race, and that schools with predominantly black student populations offered lower-quality education. Crucially, Wright's decision included language that indicated that students had the right to equality of educational opportunity regardless of whether the schools were de jure segregated. In the opinion, Judge Wright wrote, "The court assesses the *de facto* segregation question and holds that the District's neighborhood school policy, as presently administered at least, results in harm to Negro children and to society which cannot constitutionally be fully justified."[103] The harm here, defined as providing unequal education within a district, was a separate issue from whether the racial segregation that existed was de jure. The decision therefore opened up an alternative path toward defining the right to equality of educational opportunity.

Writing in the *Journal of Negro Education*, NAACP Legal Defense Fund lawyer Robert L. Carter argued in the wake of *Hobson* that the de facto approach was not inconsistent with judicial precedent and represented a fuller understanding of the *Brown* decision than focusing on the South alone could do. "As historic an advance as *Brown* is presently believed to be, it is safe to assert that the 14th Amendment neither ceases to operate nor loses its potency once the situation moves beyond the facts of that case," Carter wrote.[104] He concluded, "*Sweatt* and *McLaurin* make clear that the total educational experience must be evaluated in determining whether equal educational opportunity has been accorded."[105]

The *Keyes* lawyers decided to press both arguments presented in *Hobson*, making the case that the district's predominantly black and Mexican American schools offered unequal educational opportunities to their students and that the school board intentionally funneled students of color into those schools. Making both arguments presented a workaround for the court, which theoretically could order relief even if it rejected the argument that schools were segregated by intentional state action. In their opening statement, the plaintiffs' lawyers therefore employed arguments from both *Brown v. Board of Education* (that schools were illegally segregated) and *Plessy v. Ferguson* (that even if legally segregated, they were unconstitutionally unequal).[106] As attorney Gordon Grenier introduced the *Plessy* argument in court, which he argued was "premised primarily upon general Fourteenth Amendment principles," he called it a "simple theory. It poses that . . . there is no adequate justification existing for the continuation of that unequal educational opportunity." Owing to this deprivation, which existed independently of the question of whether segregation was de jure, plaintiffs deserved the "equal protection of the laws."[107]

The plaintiffs' lawyers crafted the equal protection argument by introducing a number of witnesses who testified, as Gordon put it, that "the minority schools are failing miserably in their task of educating minority children."[108] The data targeted drop-out rates, which were higher at black and Mexican American schools, and test scores, which were lower—a fact that the school board had refused to acknowledge until 1966.[109] Teachers at these schools had less experience, too. Lawyers for the school board fired back that, if inequalities existed, it was because students of color had not taken advantage of educational opportunities at the lower-performing schools. This argument mirrored the "freedom of choice" principle employed by Southern district officials who claimed that they had opened enrollment in white schools to black children who simply did not take up the opportunity.[110] The argument, therefore, placed blame on students rather than the schools. Students, and not institutions, were at fault for their own poor academic performance and the schools' lackluster reputation.

The plaintiffs' lawyers further argued that not only did Denver school policy channel children of color into segregated schools but the district's administrators also assigned teachers to schools on the basis of race. Most teachers of color—most of whom were black—taught in predominantly black and Mexican American schools. The district claimed that it had abandoned its practice of requiring headshots with applications (which could easily be used to identify a teacher's race without an application ever explicitly asking for the information), although the segregation of teachers continued. The district practiced a kind of "colorblind" employment; officials argued that the best practices were ones that ostensibly did not take race into consideration in the hiring of teachers or their placement. And yet almost all of the teachers of color in the system ended up at predominantly minority schools. The key to this pattern may have been the fact that every teacher was interviewed at the administrative level before hiring and placement. Therefore, whoever interviewed the candidate knew the race of a prospective teacher or staff person even if the district claimed not to solicit such information.[111] Ethel Rollins, a black woman who worked as a school counselor, testified in *Keyes* that administrators covertly marked the files of African American job applicants with a "C," perhaps to indicate that the person was "colored."[112] Rollins also testified at trial that she had been transferred out of a school where she was the only black staff member. She did not want to leave the school, but she was sent to another predominantly minority school regardless of her wishes. She testified that, in her case, the school's principal did not realize her race until she showed up for work and then quickly attempted to get her placed elsewhere. Rollins testified that the school's faculty and staff held a vote to decide whether they thought the school was "ready" for a black staff person. They decided that it was not.[113]

Furthermore, the teachers at segregated schools tended to have fewer years of teaching experience than those at the district's white schools, potentially creating a lower standard of education. Some black teachers told the lawyers in *Keyes* that administrators seemed reluctant to offer them long-term contracts on par with those that white teachers received.[114] By 1969, the district's 191 black elementary school teachers were clustered at schools with substantial black student populations, such as Fairview, Mitchell, Park Hill, Smith, Stedman, Whittier, and Wyatt. There were far fewer Mexican American teachers in the system; only forty taught at the elementary level, and nearly all of them at schools with large percentages of minority children. The district's twenty-three Asian American elementary school teachers, however, were distributed more evenly throughout the system. More than half of the district's forty-eight black high school teachers taught at Manual; another ten taught at East High. Six of the twenty-five Mexican-American high school teachers worked at Manual and ten at West High.[115]

Judge Doyle initially rejected the argument that racial segregation was de jure in Denver, but he agreed with the plaintiffs' lawyers that, even if the segregation was legal, the district provided unequal educational opportunities to students of color. Doyle's decision pointed out that the school board acknowledged its role in transferring neighborhood segregation patterns to schools by creating attendance zones that matched racially identifiable residential areas. Furthermore, after passing its resolution on equality of educational opportunity in 1964, the district did virtually nothing to address the problem. Especially damning was the decision to build Barrett Elementary and draw its attendance zones in a way that created a student population that was nearly entirely black. The building of Barrett in a neighborhood that was racially identifiable, and with boundaries that so clearly matched the color line, meant that the school board knew it would become a segregated school when it opened.[116] A nearby school was overcrowded and remained so after Barrett opened; therefore it only made sense that the size and zoning of Barrett were kept small in order to ensure that nearby Stedman Elementary, on the other side of Colorado Boulevard, would continue to have a majority-white student population.

The remedial hearing, held in May 1970, examined the question of what the proper solution was to the unequal educational opportunities provided by Denver public schools. While the arguments made for finding that students' rights to equal educational opportunity pushed beyond questions of state-sponsored racial segregation, the proposed remedies pointed to desegregation as the cure. Experts who testified focused on the importance and efficacy of school desegregation as the primary means by which inequality could be addressed in the city's schools. James Coleman, lead author of the influential 1966 "Equality of Educational Opportunity" report, which chronicled the persistence and effects of school segregation in the United States,[117] testified that desegregation could have meaningful, positive effects on the academic achievement of black children.[118] Other experts likewise testified about the importance of desegregation in providing "compensatory education" for students who had been subjected to racially segregated schooling.[119]

Doyle therefore ordered desegregation of the Park Hill schools as well as of the seventeen other inner-city schools, including Manual, that he identified as providing an inferior education. The ruling largely left those schools outside the city's core untouched by the plan.[120] The remedial order sliced up the school district into those schools that were in compliance with the Fourteenth Amendment and those that were not. It therefore included just those schools in north Denver that were clearly segregated by race along with the predominantly white schools nearby without consideration of the effect segregation had on the system as a whole. Few on either side of the issue were pleased with this result, and both sides appealed the decision to the Tenth Circuit of Appeals. The school board protested any finding of unequal education, whereas the plaintiffs were frustrated with the limits that the Doyle plan put on desegregating the entire city.

Students weighed in, too, though indirectly. In September 1970, George Washington High School—one of the newer, wealthier, and whiter schools—faced its own turmoil. Busing in students of color without much preparation on the part of administrators and teachers led to conflict. Hundreds of black students who arrived at Washington under the district's newly enacted plan that fall found themselves in an uneasy position reflective of the challenges faced by students who desegregated white schools all over the nation. Just as black students in rural Mississippi found themselves forced to swallow the bitter pill of discrimination as they interacted with their white teachers and peers, the new students at Washington felt frustrated by the manner in which white students, teachers, and administrators treated them. Mutual suspicion between old and new students and the stereotyping of black students by their white peers created tension in the hallways and the classrooms. The school board failed to provide for adequate buses to transport the students, leaving them waiting in study hall or relying on parents to get them home when school ended.[121] On September 24, a fight between white and black students broke out that quickly escalated as more students joined. By the time teachers and administrators finally regained control of the situation, dozens of students had been injured in the fighting.[122]

In a meeting held at Macedonia Baptist Church on September 28, black students expressed their grievances, which documented the difficulties presented by being in the vanguard of those who desegregated American schools. Many of the students had been upset to learn that they would be excluded from the school's clubs, which had formed memberships over the summer before many black students enrolled under the new policy. The students complained of insensitive white teachers and counselors who were overwhelmed by students and therefore unable to help them. Students also felt that the continuing presence of police at school after the protests only made things worse for them; they wanted police removed and, in their place, a committee made up of students, parents, and teachers who would tackle the school's ongoing racial issues. They also wanted more black teachers and a black staff person who could serve as an advocate for their needs.[123]

The controversy at George Washington continued in the following weeks, with more fights breaking out in October. Police officers and dogs patrolled the school, as they continued to do at West High more than a year after the blowouts. Tension was high between student cliques, students and teachers, and students and the administration. The school board was split over how to manage the situation, with board members Rachel Noel and John Amesse agreeing with students who argued that the situation would improve only if the board removed police from the schools. Edgar Benton, a former board member who lost his reelection bid the previous year because of his strong support for the Noel Resolution, also lobbied for the de-escalation of the situation.[124] At a school board meeting, Benton quoted a federal government study that found that violence increased in schools where police were brought in to maintain order, only making things worse. Board members James Voorhees, Noel, and Amesse voted to remove police officers, splitting the vote evenly with those who wanted police to remain. The measure failed, and the police officers continued to patrol the schools.[125]

The students' concerns brought to the fore the limitations of desegregation as a path to providing equal educational opportunities on its own. The students wanted an end to their marginalization within the district, but especially within their schools. Rather than being treated as minorities, the students wanted their teachers and administrators to be receptive to the particular issues that students of color faced in the district. It was not enough to be bused to the white schools in the wealthy parts of the district; the students wanted to feel a sense of ownership and belonging. The meaning of educational equality, in this moment of change, was imbued with deeper concerns about representation and fairness at school for black and Mexican American students alike. The task of providing equal educational opportunity was not finished when they got off their buses at their new schools.

As the school board hedged on addressing the crisis at George Washington High School, Chicano leaders decided to address issues of equity head-on by forming their own school. The move was in part an effort to address the number of Chicano student activists who had been suspended or expelled from school for their activities.[126] In the autumn of 1970, after two tumultuous years of protest in the Denver schools, the Crusade for Justice opened La Escuela Tlatelolco, an elementary (and later, secondary) school that embraced the ethos of the Chicano Movement.[127] In the previous two summers, the Crusade organized summer freedom schools, just as black and white activists had done in Mississippi during the summer of 1964. The freedom schools, with their emphasis on team teaching and student-centered learning, built upon the traditions of the Mississippi freedom schools and their predecessors, the citizenship school curriculum developed by Septima Clark and the Highlander Folk School in Tennessee where labor and civil rights activists trained.[128] The Chicano freedom school drew upon the same ideals of community involvement and collaborative learning and teaching, and educators sought to nurture a sense of self and awareness of the world among their students. Dual missions existed in the freedom schools, just as they had in the South: They focused on critical thinking and developing a political consciousness in the young. One hundred and fifty children participated in the first Chicano freedom school in 1969. The following summer, that number doubled.[129]

In the freedom schools, children learned Mexican history and folk dancing, geography, and art. They also learned Spanish. For many Mexican American children in Denver and elsewhere, their parents emphasized the speaking of English at home and assimilation into Anglo culture. Thinking this would help their children get ahead and have more opportunities for education and work, these children were not necessarily taught Spanish even when it was their parents' first language. According to one former student and teacher at Tlatelolco, Mexican American parents worried that teaching their children Spanish as a first language would hurt their chances for success in Anglo schools.[130] At Tlatelolco, teachers inverted the idea—children would be better prepared for the world if they spoke their parents' and ancestors' tongue, and doing so would be a good thing. The school's curriculum emphasized pride in Chicano culture, in the Spanish language, and in the history of Mexico.[131] Named for the Mexico City square where the Mexican government massacred hundreds of students and other civilians in 1968, Tlatelolco became the most successful and enduring example of the promise of Chicano educational reform at the elementary and secondary level.[132] According to the school's yearbook, students who attended the summer freedom schools felt stifled by the rigid curriculum, traditional teaching, and harsh discipline of the Denver public schools.

The original prospectus for Tlatelolco emphasized the shortcomings of public schooling, which had "only one pragmatic goal . . . produce 'ALL AMERICAN' products."[133] Classes were initially held in the offices of the Crusade for Justice, and Corky Gonzales served as the school's head. Reba Yépes, who returned to teach at the Escuela after graduating and earning her college degree, recalled her parents' initial reluctance to send her to the school. It was not accredited, and her parents feared that by rejecting the public system, their daughter could suffer from a lack of options for postsecondary education. But Yépes insisted, and eventually her parents relented. Yépes recalled how they, too, soon became involved with the school. Her father worked as a custodian, and her mother cooked traditional Mexican fare for the students and staff.[134] Her father was sometimes tasked with taking difficult young male students under his wing. The enterprise was a community affair from top to bottom—in order for the school to survive without much funding and for it to provide a quality education to students, people donated their time and services to making the school run. If the system of public education would not provide quality schooling to Mexican American students, Chicano leaders would do so on their own.

Desegregation, Equal Protection, and the Supreme Court

The Tenth Circuit Court of Appeals handed down a decision in March 1971 that challenged Judge Doyle's original ruling. First, the court ruled that Judge Doyle erred in limiting desegregation to only one section of the city. The district must be treated as a whole, the Tenth Circuit judges ruled, and if school board policies violated the Fourteenth Amendment in one portion of the district, then it followed that the entire system was infected with unconstitutional state action. But the court agreed with Judge Doyle on the charge that the schools had been segregated by state action in the first place, arguing that the plaintiffs had made a persuasive case for finding a Fourteenth Amendment violation in regard to the construction of Barrett Elementary and the use of mobile classrooms in Park Hill.[135]

The Tenth Circuit also grappled with the link between segregated education and unequal education. The decision directly dealt with the charge that the educational opportunities being offered in many Denver schools attended by black and Mexican American children were not equal to those offered to white students regardless of whether segregation was intentional. If education was found to be unequal within the school system, that, too, was a violation of equal protection. The Tenth Circuit agreed with this argument on its surface, stating that it could see "no valid reason why the constitutional rights of school children would not be violated by an education which is substandard when compared to other schools within that same district" without the district offering legitimate reasons to justify offering such variations in educational quality between schools. In the end, however, the Tenth Circuit rejected the application of this principle to schools in Denver, choosing instead to accept arguments that poverty and cultural difference accounted for lower achievement and higher dropout rates among black and Mexican American students. The court accepted the argument that any inequality existing in Denver schools was the result of a curriculum that was "not tailored to their educational and social needs."[136] Once again, the plaintiffs appealed the ruling.

But while the litigation involving the Denver schools worked to define equality of educational opportunity beyond its linkage to segregation, other factors worked to reinforce the idea that it only applied to segregation. By the autumn of 1971, the issue of busing—or, "forced busing," as it was often called to sidestep the issue that many American children were already bused to and from school each day—had emerged as a national issue that appeared increasingly likely to affect cities outside the South.[137] In December, the Department of Health, Education, and Welfare put school officials in Boston on notice that the city's schools were illegally segregated, thereby putting the district at risk of losing federal funds and being subject to a desegregation suit.[138] In early January 1972, a federal judge in Virginia ordered the merging of Richmond's school district with two of its suburbs to facilitate desegregation in the face of white flight.[139] And the following week, the U.S. Supreme Court agreed to hear the appeal of the Tenth Circuit's ruling in *Keyes*.[140]

As the lawyers involved in *Keyes* prepared to present their arguments before the Supreme Court, other branches of the federal government joined in on the conversation over equal educational opportunity and busing. Congressmen scrambled to position themselves as anti-busing, proposing new federal laws and constitutional amendments that would prohibit the practice. President Richard Nixon met with members of Congress the month after the court announced it would hear the *Keyes* case, assuring anti-busing congressmen that he would not "leave things as they stood."[141]

In March, Nixon introduced a law that would attempt to curb the use of busing for desegregation purposes. Titled the Equal Educational Opportunities Act, Nixon proposed a federal law that inscribed the idea of equal educational opportunity into law while condemning busing and

promoting the merits of neighborhood schools. Nixon described busing to achieve desegregation as "a classic case of the remedy for one evil
creating another evil." The courts, he declared, had "gone too far." Nixon
would propose extra funding to help upgrade poorer schools, conflating
problems of racial discrimination in education with the effects of poverty. His acting attorney general announced plans to encourage lower
district courts—including those in Denver—to comply with a moratorium on new busing plans that would give Congress time to act in order
to "clear up confusion" about the meaning of the Fourteenth Amendment's promise of equal educational opportunity.[142] In short, Nixon's
plan was for Congress to pass legislation that would guide the courts as
they interpreted the meaning of illegal segregation, effectively defining
it along the Southern model. This would preempt court decisions that
might expand illegal segregation to include de facto segregation.[143]

When the Supreme Court heard oral arguments in *Keyes* in October 1972, lawyers James Nabrit III and Gordon Grenier made the case
that Denver schools were both illegally segregated and unconstitutionally unequal. "We think that either ground, segregation or inequality, is sufficient to justify an order to desegregate the schools," Nabrit
declared. "Both grounds together"—as they argued was the case in
Denver—"justify such a complete remedy."[144] Grenier made the case
that "Denver's provision of the inferior schools and schooling for minority children who are black and Hispano and the provision of superior
schools and schooling for Anglo children" constituted "a denial of equal
protection under the Fourteenth Amendment."[145] "Tangible inputs and
outputs" and perceptions of those inside and outside the schools all
demonstrated the inequalities that were built into the system along with
racial segregation. "The minority student in Denver" would find him
or herself "assigned to a school with twice as many brand-new teachers, twice as many probationary teachers and only half as many teachers
with 10 or more years [of] experience" as a white student. Furthermore,
the high teacher turnover rates at majority-minority schools contributed to an "aura of inferiority." As Greiner described it, a "minority
student found that his teachers did not expect very much of him, that
he was neither challenged nor motivated to do better." And in the end,
"Although he didn't do very well, he always seemed to be passed from
grade to grade."[146] Greiner drew a line directly from *Sweatt v. Painter* to

Keyes. In essence, he asked the justices to look beyond the fact of state-sponsored segregation and consider, too, that the Fourteenth Amendment should protect the rights of children to receive substantially equal schooling within a district.

In response to this argument, the school district's lawyer, William Ris, made the case that the low achievement of black and Mexican American students was a product of "cultural deprivation" rather than intention by the school board, echoing Nixon's arguments that it was poverty—not racial discrimination—that caused inequities. There was, perhaps, a certain "aura" over Manual, he conceded, that made it seem like a lesser school. But the curriculum was built for the "special needs" of its pupils, and the district should determine what was best for those students. School officials did "what seemed the best thing for the kids in that community." When Justice Potter Stewart pressed Ris about whether there were college preparatory schools in the district, he admitted that there were and that they were in higher income areas where there were "more children who go to college."[147] He then argued that the only way to prove that the quality of education was lesser was through discrepancies in financial resources, which were not contested in Denver. An intangible like lower achievement scores could not necessarily be proven to be linked to the school board's actions. The connection between the quality of education that black and Mexican American children received had no direct relationship to the decisions made by the school board. The problem, Ris emphasized, was due to "cultural deprivation" experienced by students from "lower socioeconomic family groups and neighborhoods."[148]

Justices Lewis Powell and William Brennan were the most vocal about being willing to abandon the de jure/de facto distinction of racial segregation altogether.[149] Powell had the most experience in school policy, as he had served on the school board in Richmond, Virginia, while it was subjected to a desegregation suit. His experience and his status as a Southerner certainly influenced his ideas about whether it was fair that Southern states were solely accused of racial segregation and therefore the targets of desegregation lawsuits and busing mandates issued from judges. This was a sensitive point; after all, there had been school segregation in Northern cities that preceded the Civil War.[150] Powell's clerk, Larry Hammond, argued that the *Plessy* claims had some merit.

"But, the state may not maintain segregated schools, no matter how they became segregated, unless the education offered is equal," Hammond wrote in a memo. "To this extent I believe *Plessy v. Ferguson* is still good law."[151]

On June 21, 1973, the Supreme Court handed down its opinion in *Keyes v. School Dist. No. 1*. The case generated several separate opinions, including a concurrence by Justice William O. Douglas, a lengthy opinion that concurred and dissented in part by Justice Powell, and William Rehnquist's dissent. Both Powell and Douglas argued that the de jure/de facto distinction should go. In William Brennan's majority opinion, the Supreme Court reaffirmed the Tenth Circuit's narrow vision of the equal protection. Importantly, the decision classified Mexican American students as being similarly situated to black students for the purposes of school desegregation litigation. Like black students, the court would treat Mexican Americans as a racial minority group. The majority opinion also ruled that a close look at the school board's actions might show that state action had been involved in the segregation of children in Denver schools on the basis of race. When there was evidence of intentional state-created racial segregation in even a small part of a school district, it meant that a *prima facie* case existed for illegal segregation in the whole system. In such a case, the burden of proof would shift to the school board, which would have to prove that it had not intentionally segregated schools in the system—making it much more likely that state-sponsored racial segregation would be found. The Supreme Court therefore did not rule directly on whether Denver's schools were unconstitutionally segregated; instead it provided these points as guidance for the lower courts to determine whether the school board's actions violated the Fourteenth Amendment.[152]

Under this standard, Judge Doyle found the Denver school board responsible for de jure segregation under the Supreme Court's guidelines from *Keyes* once the case came back to the district court in December 1973. This time, however, lawyers representing Mexican American students joined the suit. The Mexican American Legal Defense Fund (MALDEF) began discussions with the plaintiffs' lawyers in *Keyes* shortly after the Supreme Court issued its ruling, and MALDEF lawyers officially joined the case in early 1974 on behalf of children of Mexican descent in the Denver schools. They argued that the plaintiffs' current lawyers could not effectively represent the needs of the city's large Mexican American population and that, in particular, the schools needed to hire more Mexican American teachers. Of particular concern for MALDEF lawyers was the inevitable conflict between desegregation as a remedy and the nascent bilingual-bicultural education programs that existed in some Denver public schools.[153] The Finger Plan, which was the desegregation plan presented by the school district's expert witness, recommended closing several schools that had student bodies that were primarily Mexican American. John Finger asserted that such schools were too "dreary" to be acceptable to white children; MALDEF lawyers disagreed.[154] Even as Chicano activists in Denver expressed concerns that echoed those of black residents about the quality of education their children received, the vision of reform put forth by Chicano activists took a substantially different shape than the litany of school desegregation cases litigated by the NAACP's Legal Defense Fund. Even if the problems were similar, the proposed remedies were different.

One of the most troubling developments to MALDEF lawyers was the initial plan to desegregate Del Pueblo Elementary School, which hosted an experimental bilingual-bicultural program aimed at incorporating Mexican-American culture and Spanish language instruction into the school day.[155] The desegregation program put forth by the district's expert would effectively dismantle the program, which was funded by federal grant money. Colorado passed its own bilingual education act in 1975, which called for an elected advisory committee of community members to oversee implementation of the programs. Some school board members excoriated the program, claiming it was a disaster.[156] But others, including the district superintendent, argued that the program was working well for its students.[157]

In fashioning their own arguments for the proper remedy for the wrongs done by the Denver school board, MALDEF lawyers recruited José Cárdenas, the executive director of Texans for Educational Excellence. Once MALDEF decided to enter the lawsuit, they contacted Cárdenas and asked him to put together a plan that would identify the ways in which Denver schools disadvantaged Mexican American students and seek to remedy them.[158] Cárdenas presented a plan that promised to overhaul education in Denver and provide equitable education for Mexican American children. This was a goal, MALDEF argued, that could not be accomplished through a plan that provided only for school desegregation. The Cárdenas Plan called for the Denver school board to "look to the Chicano and Black communities" to refashion public education around the core principle that "all children have worth," privileging "the concept of self-acceptance as a person of worth [to] be fostered and developed in minority children."[159] These children began falling behind as soon as they began to attend school in Denver—an effect that, Cárdenas argued, snowballed over the course of a student's education, creating increasingly unequal opportunities and poorer outcomes for minority children. This was an effect that desegregation alone could not solve. "Regardless of ethnic mix schools continue to be racist institutions with instructional programs developed for white, Anglo Saxon, English-speaking, middle class children," the plan declared.[160] Instead, Cárdenas outlined a different approach. In other words, teachers would work individually with children to find successful learning strategies, while school environments would embrace a multicultural approach and encourage all students to feel a sense of belonging.

The plan outlined changes in school administration, teaching, and curriculum. Specifically, it called for the hiring of more Mexican American teachers, the teaching of Mexican American history and culture, and specialized training for teachers. Minority-group students should be integrated into school activities; poor children would benefit for the elimination of activity and library fees and costs associated with field trips and student clubs.[161] The plan would eliminate the need for schools to hold Black History Week or Chicano Month programs as such subjects would become part of the everyday classroom experience for children in the city's schools. Minority children would not be treated as if their family histories and cultural backgrounds made them different or deficient; rather, the schools would acknowledge and celebrate them. It also called for the creation of a community council made up of white, black, and Mexican American parents who would oversee the plan's implementation. The plan also paid close attention to the issue of poverty, calling for school breakfast and lunch programs and the provision of basic clothing items to the poorest students so that they would be less likely to skip school because they were hungry or had no clean clothes to wear. The plan also paid particular attention to reducing suspensions and expulsions.[162] These suggestions, of course, echoed the school reforms already in place at La Escuela Tlatelolco, the private school founded by Chicano activists who were disillusioned with the city's public school system, and the pilot program at Del Pueblo Elementary. The Cárdenas Plan suggested that such a program did not require beginning from scratch but that the existing system could be reformed from within the classroom walls. It was, to say the least, ambitious.

What the Cárdenas Plan presented offered was a vision of "bilingual-bicultural" education. The theory and methods behind bilingual-bicultural education differed in fundamental ways from traditional bilingual education programs, which focused on teaching English and assimilating children into the traditional school structure. Such programs received a boost in federal support owing to the end of the Vietnam War. Congress passed the Indochinese Refugee Transition Act in 1975 to create assistance for the men, women, and children who fled Southeast Asia in the wake of American withdrawal from the region.[163] As a city that was home to a major Air Force base, Denver received so many refugees that, by the early 1980s, the top five languages other than English spoken by students in Denver schools were Spanish, Vietnamese, Hmong, Laotian, and Cambodian.[164] There were more than 2,400 students with limited English-speaking ability in the schools who either spoke no English or very little.[165] But ten years prior, when the *Keyes* case was at the peak of its litigation, the city's Mexican American community was predominantly made up of second-generation English-speaking students whose parents spoke Spanish. This was the crucial difference between the expansion of bilingual education in the late 1960s through the 1970s and what Cárdenas and other advocates demanded: The former was a minimal response to a child's inability to understand English, the latter a holistic response to an education system that did not serve the interests of children who were not middle-class whites.

But the aims of MALDEF to fundamentally restructure American public education, especially the ambitious Cárdenas Plan, faced hostility from the courts. The Tenth Circuit Court of Appeals eventually ruled that the Cárdenas Plan went too far. The district court had outpaced its obligations by ordering bilingual-bicultural education, especially considering that many Mexican American students in Denver did not require English language-learning services.[166] They were of the second generation, mostly born and reared in the United States. *Keyes* thus became another case about who went to school where and erased the alternative meanings of equality of educational opportunity, particularly as they embodied schemes of profound racial reform. As Charles Zelden has written on the desegregation law in the South, "Rights without effective remedies are meaningless rights."[167] In *Keyes*, the Supreme Court reaffirmed that a right to equal educational opportunity existed for students, but it also reinscribed that idea around racial segregation and a limited conception of the state's obligation to immigrants and their children. Segregation became the key to identifying deprivations of equal educational opportunity, neatly making desegregation plans—often through busing—the only possible remedy. Other valences of meaning were collapsed into a simple determination by the courts: Did the school board purposefully racially segregate children? If the answer was yes, a desegregation order would follow. If not, those students effectively had no right to equality of educational opportunity. By conflating a busing scheme and a bilingual program with equity, the struggles and stories of parents, students, and others to create meaningful educational equality within the district were ignored by the courts. Lost were the vibrant and difficult conversations Denver residents held about their schools and their children. Lost, too, was the role of students in demanding their own measure of justice. The meanings of the right to equality of educational opportunity to those in the schools, on the streets, and in the courts diverged.

* * *

"There should be no single doctrinaire remedy for inequality," lawyer James Nabrit III told the justices of the U.S. Supreme Court when he argued the *Keyes* case in October 1972.[168] This was a statement with which many of the people involved with school reform in Denver during this period likely would have agreed. As the first school segregation case to reach the Supreme Court that did not fit the Southern model, the *Keyes* case was heard in a moment in which the right to equal educational opportunity was tested and defined. For a moment it seemed possible that the courts might extend the reach of the Fourteenth Amendment beyond public schools that had been segregated by law and confer the right to equality of educational opportunity to every student in the country.

But when the Supreme Court issued its ruling in *Keyes*, it did so in a narrow way that constrained conceptions of educational equity. The plaintiffs won this particular battle, but advocates for educational equity were in the midst of losing the war. The right to equality of educational opportunity could only be employed to remedy racial discrimination in places where the state created segregation or, in the case of immigrant children, when they had the most severe limitations on their ability to speak and understand English. Other forms of discrimination—the provision of a superior education in schools in wealthier and whiter parts of the city, for example, or evidence that the quality of instruction was poorer at majority-minority schools—did not qualify as deprivations. And holistic visions of how to make equality of educational opportunity a reality for minority children through bilingual-bicultural education or other means did not register as important enough to qualify as protected by the law. States and local governments could choose to make education more equal, but the courts would not demand it.

By the early 1980s, the student population in Denver schools was roughly 60 percent minority and 40 percent white; those numbers had been reversed when the *Keyes* lawsuit was first filed. In 1977, the school board caved to pressure from parents to respond to the district's "discipline problem." Administrators used suspensions too readily, especially when it came to disciplining black and Mexican American students. In the late 1970s, the Denver public schools suspended more "Spanish-surnamed" students than any other district in the United States.[169] In accounting for the expected rates, given the total number of students suspended annually, the district ranked sixth in excess suspensions.[170] The district responded by encouraging schools to establish "in school" suspension programs in the place of out-of-school suspensions.[171] But the Community Education Council, which advised the school board as part of the 1974 desegregation order, released a report in 1981 that noted that suspension rates of minority students continued to be disproportionately high. In the spring of 1980, 80 percent of suspended students were students of color. The figures for other recent semesters consistently hovered above 75 percent. Community Education Council member Rachel Noel lamented the "awful" rates of suspension for minority students, noting that "these disparities have become almost etched in concrete."[172] Such measures of educational inequality profoundly shaped the experiences of students of color in American public high schools, but they remained off the table in discussions of the extent of equal protection. But there were other ways to challenge the discriminatory use of discipline in schools. The equal protection clause of the Fourteenth Amendment would only take protesting students and their allies so far. And yet there were other tools within reach, including principles of due process, as the next chapter explores.

3

The Right to Due Process

Student Discipline and Civil Rights in Columbus, Ohio

It was March 1971, and Tyrone Washington was fed up with the way administrators ran his school. A senior at Marion-Franklin High School in Columbus, Ohio, Washington and a group of several dozen black students occupied the auditorium and refused to leave until the principal acknowledged their grievances over the treatment of all black students in the schools. When confronted by the principal, Washington informed him that they would no longer passively obey—it was the administration's turn to listen to the students. Washington was not alone in his decision to stand up to school authorities, as similar protests by black students roiled schools around the city and sent administrators and the school board into a panic. For weeks the protests went on as students and their supporters staged sit-ins, walked picket lines, planned rebel assemblies, and—on a couple of occasions—got into fistfights with hostile white peers. This was likely not what officials in the Columbus public schools anticipated when they planned to celebrate Black History Week in late February 1971. Instead of a polite observance of black history and culture that would signal the school district's acknowledgment and inclusion of its substantial black population, the week triggered an outpouring of student frustrations over issues of race and discrimination in the schools. Black students seized the opportunity to criticize the marginalization of African Americans in curricula and to accuse administrators of racist policies and teachers of discriminatory attitudes. In junior highs and high schools across the city, black students disrupted classes and caused a ruckus, igniting a series of intense protests that lasted through April.[1]

Tyrone Washington was, of course, suspended. The plainclothes police officers who patrolled the school's halls forcibly removed him and his co-conspirators, and the principal sent his parents a note blaming him for inflaming an already "explosive situation."[2] Dozens of black students received punishments for participating in protests at school that spring. While some, like Tyrone Washington, served as leaders of the student rebellion, others claimed that they were innocent bystanders who had been swept up by administrators' actions and suspended unfairly. Indeed, the authority of school administrators to punish students at will was a perpetual challenge to the protest activity of students at school. Black History Week and the ensuing conflict over school discipline launched a case that reached the Supreme Court in 1975. Parents and guardians sued the school district on behalf of suspended students, claiming a deprivation of the Fourteenth Amendment right to due process of law in relation to the punishments. Their case, *Goss v. Lopez*, with its disruptive student plaintiffs, has been the subject of pointed criticism both in the 1970s and in more recent scholarly works.[3] This chapter puts *Goss v. Lopez* into its historical context, revealing that the case was not merely a product of the late 1960s rebellious youth culture but the apex of a much longer struggle for civil rights protections that had accompanied desegregation since the 1950s. Indeed, through *Goss*, advocates for black children sought to reframe school discipline as a pressing issue of racial justice. The history of the case and its origins in the struggle in Columbus reveal how difficult achieving meaningful racial reform can be and also how crucial such reform is for providing equitable public education for all students.

Protest and Punishment

Tyrone Washington was only one of the many high school students who participated in protests across the nation during the late 1960s and the early 1970s. These students decried everything from strict dress codes and prohibitions on long hair for men to the Vietnam War and racial discrimination.[4] As discussed in the previous chapter, calls for Black and Brown Power increasingly and loudly rose from the streets as students influenced by and involved in these movements pushed for their own reforms in classrooms in cities across the nation.

Student protesters in the nation's secondary schools challenged the meaning of the right to free speech, as examined in the first chapter of this book, and they complicated discussions about school desegregation and efforts to make educational opportunity equal, as the second chapter shows. But in all of these cases, one particular problem vexed nearly all students who defied authority and spoke out in school: the virtually unchecked ability of school administrators to suspend or expel them for their actions. This problem became especially acute as protests became more common in public schools, and it was especially pressing where Black Power ideas influenced students' actions. Marked as rebellious and troublemaking, these student protesters could easily find themselves afoul of student codes of conduct and state laws permitting administrators to suspend or expel students who were considered disorderly, defiant, or disrespectful.

The protests in Columbus capped off a much longer struggle over racial segregation and discrimination in the city's schools. The capital city of Ohio, Columbus grew steadily during the 1960s. It had never been a manufacturing mecca in the way neighboring cities like Toledo, Akron, and Cleveland had been; instead, state government, higher education, and the service industry dominated the city's economy. This largely insulated the city from the economic crises that gripped other Ohio cities as manufacturing plants closed. Columbus surpassed a half-million residents even as many other Rust Belt cities began to lose substantial populations to Sunbelt states and the suburbs.[5]

Despite avoiding the fates of Detroit and Cleveland, Columbus experienced its own growing pains in the postwar years, which spurred organizing by local black activists. In 1970, approximately one-fifth of the city's population was made up of African Americans, a percentage that more than doubled in the previous two decades. During that time span, urban renewal policies and the construction of new Interstate highways demolished homes in neighborhoods near the downtown area, pushing residents out of historically black neighborhoods.[6] Like many other cities in the nation, real estate agents capitalized on the city's growing black population and its demand for housing. Real estate agents employed "panic selling" methods to sell homes in mostly white neighborhoods at a premium to black buyers while encouraging white homeowners to quickly sell their homes inexpensively owing to the looming threat of residential integration.[7] This practice of "blockbusting" meant that city blocks experienced rapid turnover in homeownership, creating newly segregated black city blocks that had previously been lily-white.

Segregation in city schools dated back much further, but the city's growing black population and the flight of white residents into the suburbs meant that old color lines dissolved and reorganized along new axes. School board gerrymandering in 1910 began the practice of segregating black and white children in neighborhood schools.[8] But as the color line moved with population growth in the 1950s and 1960s, city schools experienced waves of desegregation. Black families moved into neighborhood school zones where there had previously been only white families, and their children were then assigned to previously all-white schools. In at least one case, the Columbus school board attempted to bus black children to a segregated black school in order to avoid even token desegregation at a white school, but the students' parents successfully resisted.[9] These shifts in the racial makeup of city high schools created conditions that were ripe for interracial conflict. The Columbus Board of Education had long resisted the demand for a comprehensive desegregation policy, but white flight and neighborhood change ensured that black and white students within the schools were less segregated in the early 1970s than they had been previously.[10]

When demographic changes put black and white students in the same classrooms and hallways, tension and conflict often followed. Reflecting on student unrest in the city's schools, the school district's chief psychologist observed that "you could almost pinpoint the disruptions with where the boundary lines of housing were."[11] As one white student explained, after she began attending a high school that had a substantial black student population, she was seized by her fear of black students. "People think you're going to walk down the hall and you're going to get mugged by a black—right in the middle of the hall," she told researchers from Ohio State who were studying the effects of racial change in the city's schools. She added that she and other white students understood that "you don't go into restrooms with them."[12] The student assured researchers that she eventually overcame these initial prejudices and made friends across the color line, but her words powerfully illustrated how the hallways could became theaters in the drama of segregation. Changing neighborhood demographics—and, therefore, a change in the racial makeup of the schools—could easily spark conflict between white and black students, and especially between white teachers and administrators and black students. The *Goss* case grew out of this struggle over the schools, and it was both a product of desegregation created by racial changes in city neighborhoods and a rebellion by black students against discrimination in the city schools.

The eruption of protest and conflict during Black History Week in 1971 followed years of black discontent with the city's public education system. In the 1960s, African Americans in Columbus repeatedly accused the school board of providing separate and unequal education to the district's black students. In 1964, the district opened a new junior high school in a predominantly African American neighborhood, leading to accusations that the board was intentionally segregating children. In 1966, the local chapter of the National Association for the Advancement of Colored People (NAACP) presented complaints that the district segregated black children and provided them with inferior education, and in 1967, the Urban League joined in support of desegregation in the spirit of equality of educational opportunity. Both organizations produced detailed reports that pointed to a historical pattern of isolating black children in particular schools with zoning that followed the lines of residential segregation. Even more troubling, data on test scores and teacher experience showed that the education provided at schools with predominantly black student populations was of a poorer quality than that provided to the children at predominantly white schools.[13]

In response, black parents took matters into their own hands. Marian Craig became an organizer when she learned that her son, a seventh grader who perpetually earned good grades, was in fact reading at a fourth-grade level.[14] Furious that the school had misled her about the quality of education her son received and disappointed with the school board's weak response to her complaints, Craig organized parents into the Ohio Avenue School Ad Hoc Committee. The committee sent a list of twenty-seven demands to the school board, requiring the board to take action to improve education at the school, including requests that the district provide "intercultural" textbooks for children and training to faculty and staff. When the district failed to respond to the committee's requests, they held a boycott of the city's schools in September 1967. Three hundred students stayed home, and most of those who participated in the boycott attended freedom schools set up at local churches.[15] In the spring of 1968, the committee produced its own report on the education of black children in Columbus schools, calling for community control. While not explicitly rejecting desegregation as a means to improving education for black children, Craig emphasized the desire of black parents to be involved in the schools' governance, curricula, finance, and hiring of teachers and the importance to the community of such control.[16]

In 1969, students began to offer up their own demands.[17] On February 16, 1969, students at Franklin Junior High School boycotted classes after the school removed a counselor. Students protested that the counselor's only mistake was teaching students "Black Power" ideas. The following day, black students at Eastmoor High School, where whites constituted 90 percent of the student body, held a sit-in in the schools' gymnasium to protest racial discrimination by the school's white administrators, teachers, and students. Students at West High School, which had a racial makeup similar to Eastmoor, held their own sit-in the following week after the principal refused to meet with them to discuss their grievances. The principal called the police, who arrested eighty black students for trespassing.[18]

Two years later, black student protests once again disrupted the schools. These protests produced the mass suspensions that would lead to the filing of *Goss v. Lopez*.[19] During the weeks of protest and disruption, students used Black History Week as a way to talk about and challenge what they saw as persistent racial discrimination at school. Carter Woodson first proposed Negro History Week in 1926 with the hope that black history and culture would soon find their way into the mainstream of American education.[20] To hold a weeklong celebration of the achievements of black Americans was radical in the 1920s, but by the 1970s it seemed to mark the defeat of efforts to make substantial racial reforms in American schools. While racial moderates in Columbus touted the week's existence as a signifier of progress, young black men and women chafed at the idea that the entirety of the black experience could fit into a single week's time and that it needed to be set apart from the regular curriculum. At the same time, schools that ignored the week and refused to offer programming faced condemnation from many students who saw avoiding celebrations as worse than a token acknowledgment of black history. As black students aired their grievances at one school and then another, frustration swelled and spilled over into conflict at schools across the city. By now, the "Black Power" slogan was five years old, and impatience peaked among black students who were tired of waiting for change to come from the top down.

When students and staff at Central High School met on Thursday, February 18, for a "patriotic" assembly with no mention of African American achievements or history, a group of black students walked out in protest. Angry that the school failed to recognize Black History Week, seventy-five students staged a sit-in in the school's auditorium the following day, while four black student leaders met with administrators.[21] They then embarked on an eight-day boycott of the school.[22] At Linden-McKinley High School on the north side of town, white students dropped what was later referred to as "anti-black literature" from the balcony onto the main floor of the school's auditorium during that school's Black History Week assembly. Scuffles broke out after the disruption, and school officials called in the police. Black students later asked administrators to play the black national anthem, "Lift Every Voice and Sing," each Monday morning through the building's public address system, but their request was denied.[23] African American students at West High School held their own assemblies on Friday, and during one meeting, an argument between white and black students came to blows.[24] At another predominantly black high school, someone set fire to gym mats and a stage curtain, causing students and faculty to evacuate and black, acrid smoke to roll down the halls. The administrators suspected arson but were unable to identify any culprits.[25] One student described the atmosphere at West High School as "damn tense" to the *Columbus Evening Dispatch*.[26]

Many protesters wanted Black History Week abolished. They argued that it was yet another reminder that black history remained separate from the schools' regular curriculum. What the district needed, instead, was an overhaul of how and what students were taught. The director of the Columbus community relations center, Clifford Tyree, said his organization refused to appear at Black History Week assemblies, arguing that it was an example of "tokenism." Tyree had long worked to combat racial discrimination in Columbus as an employee of the city's Juvenile Court and, later, in the cabinet of the mayor, and he used his position of prominence to reject such halfhearted measures by the schools.[27] Instead, Tyree argued, black history "should be a total and integral part of our curriculum."[28] At a school board meeting held a few days after the end of Black History Week, a member presented the recommendations culled from a parents' meeting at Hilltonia Junior High School. Several parent groups recommended abolishing Black History Week and integrating all curricular materials. Several groups also requested that the district make a more concerted effort to hire black teachers and staff members.[29] Tyree further accused white teachers and administrators of "insensitivity" about matters of race. This attitude frustrated and infuriated the African American students in the schools, making a tense situation worse.[30]

The protests and disruptions continued well into the spring. In early March, a radio broadcast that city leaders denounced as "inflammatory" encouraged black residents to turn out and protest at the central school administration building. But after the demonstration ended, dozens of young people "rampaged" through downtown, breaking shop windows and—in an incident that received wide attention in the local news— stealing merchandise from a convenience store operated by the State Services for the Blind.[31] In late April, the principal at Mohawk Junior High sent all students home after protests turned to disorder in the school's cafeteria and hallways. Students at the school, where African Americans made up two-thirds of the population, demanded the firing of twelve teachers that they claimed were racist. They also asked for the replacement of the principal. No students were suspended or expelled, but police arrested three young people—two for throwing rocks at a police car and the other for using "improper language" with an officer.[32]

In order to regain control over the schools, administrators suspended students, sometimes dozens at a time. The day after a white seventeen-year old shot two black Central High students as they walked down the street, black students at the school rebelled and, at one point, ran through the halls and disrupted classes. In response, an administrator suspended between fifty and seventy-five students at once after a disturbance in the school's lunchroom.[33] This mass suspension included Dwight Lopez, who would become one of the nine plaintiffs in the *Goss* case.[34] Lopez testified during the trial that he and several other students were studying in the cafeteria during a free period when a group of black students stormed into the room and began overturning tables. Lopez claimed that he and his friends, worried about being caught up in the melee, left the cafeteria without participating. Panicked school officials cancelled classes for the rest of the day and sent all of the students at Central High School home. It was not until later that the school's principal called to inform him that he had been suspended and should not return to school until further notice. A letter sent to his parents accused him of being "in the group" that caused the trouble at Central High and notified them that Lopez would not be readmitted to school until he met with administrators in a conference. But Lopez and his parents were unable to attend the conference. On the morning on which it was scheduled, hundreds of black parents and students picketed the board of education's policies and, in doing so, blocked the school's entrance. Lopez and his parents never did get a conference with the principal, and he never returned to Central High School. He was later informed that he had been transferred to the Columbus Adult Day School, supposedly because of his age.[35]

The other plaintiffs in the case, who were all African American, provided similar accounts of the events that led to their suspensions. Some were leaders in the protests at their schools, but others claimed that they were not involved but were swept up in the mass suspensions. Several received suspension notices that did not explain why they were being punished. Betty Crome, a student at McGuffey Junior High, claimed that first-period classes had just been dismissed when disruption occurred in the school, but that she was not involved. Students broke light bulbs and glasses in the cafeteria, and when Crome had difficulty navigating the hallways, she left the building with other students and went to the school's playground. After being told to go home, Crome and other students stopped at Linden-McKinley High School, where another student protest was taking place. Crome was arrested along with other students and taken to the Juvenile Bureau of the Columbus Police Department. No charges were filed, but Crome's parents were informed by administrators that she was suspended from school, although they failed to provide a reason.[36]

Other students who became plaintiffs did not disavow their role in the disruptions or claim they were not involved. Indeed, many of the students were leaders of the student rebellions. Tyrone Washington, the student suspended during the occupation of the Marion-Franklin High School auditorium, was one. Two other African American students at Marion-Franklin who were suspended the same day as Washington were also active participants in the auditorium protest. One, Rudolph Sutton, was arrested alongside his father at school for assault and battery on a police officer and resisting arrest.[37] Bruce Harris, another black student leader at Marion-Franklin and a plaintiff in the case, was suspended with several other students when they stood and turned their backs during a lecture from the principal to the senior class, raising their fists in a Black Power salute.[38]

The facts of other students' suspensions were presented in a conflicted and contradictory manner in the lawsuit. One such instance was that of Susan Cooper, a junior at Marion-Franklin High School. Cooper and the school's assistant principal disagreed about what, exactly, led to her suspension and whether she was a troublemaker or an innocent bystander. On March 15, Cooper sensed that the tension at school might boil over into conflict and possibly into violence—something she said her mother had instructed her to avoid. And so, in order to obey her mother, Cooper said that she went to the attendance office to ask to be excused from school for the day. An assistant principal insisted that she return to class, and when she replied that it was her mother's wish for her to go home, he suspended her. The assistant principal later wrote to Cooper's mother, asserting that Cooper had been one of the instigators of the racial conflict at the school and that she had been "disrespectful" toward him. The principal claimed that Cooper showed "insolence" toward school authorities and persuaded other students to skip class. According to the principal, her insubordination earned her a suspension.[39]

Like Lopez, several other students were transferred from their schools as a result of their suspensions. School administrators involuntarily transferred students as punishment for being disruptive at their schools, figuring that the way to put down "militant" activities was to separate the students from their friends.[40] Plaintiff Deborah Fox, who had been pegged as a "militant" by her school's administrators, was transferred from Marion-Franklin High School after two suspensions in which she was accused of "extremely defiant and disrespectful" behavior. Administrators also transferred Rudolph Sutton from Marion-Franklin to South High School. Others were sent to alternative schools, where they finished their coursework. Two other plaintiffs, Bruce Harris and Carl Harris, were also transferred in March 1971 from their high schools to the Columbus Evening School, where they graduated the following spring.[41]

In addition to the spike in suspensions, off-duty police officers brought in by the school board to patrol the schools sometimes arrested students for offenses inside the schools. Sometimes these arrests involved issues of safety or were made in response to fighting at school, but they were just as often made for minor infractions. Two black students received sentences of ten days in a juvenile detention center for assault-and-battery charges stemming from a fight between black and white students at Hilltonia Junior High School.[42] In other incidents, an officer arrested a fifteen-year-old student at McGuffey Junior High School for using "improper language," the same charge used to arrest a student at North High School.[43] Another teenaged girl was arrested for trespassing when she was found "dancing on chairs" in a classroom at her school while she was supposed to be serving a suspension for another infraction.[44]

Many disagreed with the decision to send police officers into the already-tense situations in the schools. As the wife of one Columbus schoolteacher put it in her letter to the *Columbus Dispatch*, "The prolonged presence of the police force will only antagonize the students."[45] On Wednesday, March 17, school officials at North High School called in police officers, ostensibly to "keep the peace" when a dozen black students held a demonstration in the school's halls, even though it was police involvement in school affairs that prompted the protests in the first place. Citing information gathered from unidentified "outside sources," the school's administrators had previously sent letters to the parents of certain black students asking for information about "drug pushers and users." The protesting students assumed that the letters were meant to implicate them in drug use.[46]

In addition to increased police presence in the schools, the city council made it easier for officers to arrest students outside school grounds. In March, the Columbus City Council passed an ordinance that criminalized cutting class. The new ordinance made it a misdemeanor for any student under the age of eighteen to be out of school during regular class hours without permission. The law therefore criminalized protest activities such as picketing and boycotting that students might undertake without the written consent of their parents. The penalty—a $300 fine, 90 days in jail, or both—was notably harsher than that allowed by the state code governing punishment of juveniles (and therefore was probably unenforceable, as many critics of the law argued). Ohio state law permitted police to pick up students who were "habitually truant" as "unruly" children, but the Columbus ordinance criminalized even one day of skipping class. Even the city attorney told the *Columbus Dispatch* that he thought the law was "unconstitutional, unreasonable, vague and arbitrary."[47] Further undermining the appearance of legality, the measure appeared to target black students. A student at Whetstone High School explained that he supported the ordinance so long as it was not applied to "ordinary students cutting class."

Students protested the new law, diligently attending city council meetings to voice their demands. One week after the passage of the ordinance, students presented the city council with a petition signed by more than a thousand students and community residents asking that the council rescind the ordinance, which students claimed duplicated already-existing laws while infringing on students' civil rights owing to its vague language.[48] As Toni Shorter, a student at Eastmoor High School pointed out, the law imposed penalties that were harsher than those that punished sex work. "In such an All-America city as Columbus, surely prostitution is more abhorrent than cutting class," Shorter told the city council, eliciting calls of "Right on!" from fellow students in the audience.[49]

Columbus's civil rights organizations backed the students and their protests. The local NAACP blamed the unrest on the failure of school and district administrators "to protect students" and do anything in response to the "violation of Black civil rights." The Hilltop Civic Council likewise pointed to school officials for fomenting unrest in the schools by refusing to implement Black studies programs in all city schools, including those that were majority white.[50] When the superintendent announced that the district would respond by creating a ten-person task force to "investigate" the situation, the Columbus NAACP retorted that the findings would only be acceptable if they reiterated the complaints students, parents, and civil rights organizations had already been making for years.[51] Local religious leaders joined the NAACP in criticism of the task force, suggesting that its true purpose was to find a "scapegoat."[52]

The state legislature, meanwhile, fretted over how to handle the unrest that boiled up in public secondary schools. Columbus was not the only Ohio city where students were in revolt; there had also been recent disturbances in the schools in Lima, Sandusky, Lorain, Dayton, Cincinnati, and Middletown. Some legislators sponsored bills that would increase the power of administrators to expel students, whereas Mack Pemberton, a representative from Columbus, recommended a new law that would allow for the one-year expulsion of teenaged students who lacked "the proper attitudes and motivation to profit from further instruction."[53] The city's mayor, Jack Sensenbrenner, used the school disorders as a handy way to kick off his reelection campaign, telling a crowd, "This is a new age. It's time we stop this crap in the schools. Any of these dumb kids who slap a teacher deserve to be expelled."[54]

School Discipline in the Desegregation Era

What the students in Columbus experienced during February and March 1971 was not uncommon in schools around the nation. As the number of protests at American high schools rose sharply in the late 1960s, so did the use of suspensions and expulsions to control and punish students for their actions. The disciplinary crackdown on students engaged in protest attracted attention from lawyers, legal experts, and organizations concerned with students' rights. And when civil rights and child advocacy organizations examined school suspensions, they discovered that, across the nation, black students were suspended far more frequently than students of other races. While students of all racial and ethnic groups were disciplined for their participation in protest activity, advocacy organizations began to frame fairness in school disciplinary practices as a pressing civil rights issue that threatened the ability of black students to get a quality education.

Earlier civil rights cases established some protections for college students as the dismantling of *in loco parentis*, the end of formal segregation, and a rise in enrollment on university campuses increased the presence of students of color. Secondary school students faced the opposite problem: They were required to go to school by state law, but they legally had no right to education and therefore could find themselves pushed out of public schools with no recourse.[55]

Surveys of public school principals demonstrate that many American high schools were troubled by protest and disorder during these years. In a 1969 study, the National Association of Secondary School Principals declared that 60 percent of principals surveyed reported active protest at their schools. Others reported anxiety at the possibility of unrest.[56] Robert H. Finch, the Secretary of Health, Education and Welfare under President Richard Nixon, predicted that the problem of student disruptions at junior high and high schools could become so widespread in the near future that it would eclipse the number of protests on college campuses.[57] These concerns were not limited to school administrators. According to a 1971 Gallup poll, half of all those polled were very concerned about discipline in American public schools. Forty-eight percent of respondents told pollsters that discipline in schools was not strict enough, while only 3 percent believed it was too strict. Amid the upheavals that accompanied student protests and school desegregation, the poll indicated that many Americans feared that teachers and school administrators were concerned about the inability to control young people.[58]

It is impossible to know precisely how many protests took place at American junior high and high schools, although those who turned their attention to the issue found plenty of evidence of its commonality. In gathering statistics to determine how common protests were, academics grouped small-scale protests involving a few students with large-scale protests and disorders, such as those that took place in the Columbus public schools during Black History Week. Alan Westin soon became a leading expert on this kind of study owing to his personal involvement with student protests. Westin was an expert on privacy law teaching at Columbia University Law School when he found himself in the midst of a student rebellion on the university's campus. The protests, which began in April 1968, were in part sparked by the university's decision to build a new gymnasium in New York City's Morningside Park, but they also drew together members of two disparate organizations, the Students' Afro-American Society and Students for a Democratic Society, in a joint critique of domestic racism and the United States's involvement in the Vietnam War.[59] Westin became a kind of faculty mediator and peacekeeper.[60] The university called on the New York City police, who sent 1,000 officers. They arrested 700 students.[61]

With these experiences in mind, Westin expanded his research interests to include secondary schools. As the director of the Center for Research and Education in American Liberties, Westin, along with his research assistants, monitored 1,800 newspapers over the autumn of 1968 and the following winter. His findings captured national headlines, as he described a widespread situation created by student grievances that ranged from the local to international in nature.[62] Students protested in places as diverse as Billings, Montana, and Edcouch, Texas—a town of 2,800 people just outside Brownsville, where a high school senior who had spent the summer as an auto worker in Detroit returned that fall to lead a Chicano student walkout.[63] The students in Edcouch faced a similar situation to the students involved in the Columbus protests. In response to the low expectations that white teachers had for Mexican American students and the humiliating treatment they received at school, where rules forbade students from speaking Spanish, the students walked out of class in November 1968. Police arrested some students, and administrators suspended many more. As in Columbus, the students sought legal help, and a local judge eventually sided with them.[64] This was one of the first lawsuits initiated by the newly founded Mexican American Legal Defense Fund, and it served as the organization's first success in the field of education.[65] In places as diverse as Columbus and Edcouch, American students of all stripes embraced the walk-outs, sit-ins, picket lines, and petition drives of other protest movements of the era, employing them whenever they felt local injustices merited it.

Predictably, some critics of student protest placed blame on organizations such as Students for a Democratic Society or other "outside agitators."[66] Other experts cited a "cultural phenomenon" that embraced youth dissent.[67] Westin argued that the protests were indicative of "a growing tension between basic democratic ideals and two operating realities of American education: an authority-centered system of teaching and school governance and an unreal and distorted content-presentation of American social and political realities."[68] In other words, the purpose of education—to socialize children and bring them into the polity—was at odds with the methods of teaching in the modern era, which emphasized authoritarian methods of school governance in growing contrast to the democratization of American society and culture. Conflict in the schools was the result of that tension between schooling and society and between what students witnessed in the news and on the streets and how they were treated in the classroom.

According to Westin's research, racial conflict drove more protests than any other single issue. He counted 132 race-related protests and disorders reported in American schools by local newspapers over the course of just three months.[69] The following year, a federally commissioned report examined a large sample of junior high and high schools in urban and suburban districts. Stephen K. Bailey, a political scientist at Syracuse University and a member of the New York State Board of Regents, directed the study, which found that 85 percent of the 700 high schools and junior high schools studied experienced "some type of disruption" between 1967 and 1970.[70] The report stated that desegregated schools were more likely to experience disruptions than segregated schools. Furthermore, desegregated schools with large percentages of black students were far less likely to experience disruptions if they had high percentages of black staff members; in schools with higher percentages of black students than black teachers, disruptions were much more likely to take on "a racial tone."[71]

The report's findings suggest that the unrest in many American high schools in the late 1960s and early 1970s could be traced to the friction created by local conflicts. In some places, such as Mississippi, desegregation plans put white and black students and teachers together for the first time. Elsewhere, as was the case in Denver and Columbus, other factors led to racial changes in school populations, stoking the dissatisfaction many students of color felt with white school authorities. The fact that disruptions were more likely in schools with fewer black teachers indicates that at least some of the unrest in this era can be traced to serious problems in the relationships between white teachers and principals and their black students and the lack of African American authority figures who could champion the students' interests. These concerns echoed the complaints provided by the students who protested during Black History Week. They also aligned with the concerns of students in the Chicano Movement who wanted an education that included and celebrated their history and cultural past as part of the regular curriculum and who demanded the hiring of teachers and administrators of Mexican descent.

As the situation in Columbus illustrated, Bailey's report concluded that disciplinary measures taken in schools experiencing disruptions only made the situation worse. In sum, traditional means of dealing with student disruptions such as suspension, expulsion, and police intervention were likely to create "perverse and contra-productive results."[72] It appeared that attempts by school administrators to shut down student protest benefited no one. If student unrest was a result of frustration with school authority, administrators who relied on authoritarian means only fed student discontent within the schools and increased resentment toward school officials. In his examination of the evidence, Westin agreed that harsh crackdowns by administrators were unlikely to yield good results from students, whose frustrations were often reactions to the perception that school administrators were unyielding in their views, unwilling to listen to students, and unreceptive to suggestions for reform. Westin also pointed to school censorship of student newspapers, violations of privacy through locker and desk searches, and the lack of students' rights to self-expression and due process when disciplined as adding fuel to the fire of student dissent. Westin concluded that, "when students hear democratic messages in their classes but experience autocratic treatment in the decisions that shape their lives, the clear message of our era is that such treatment will not go unchallenged for long."[73]

This was especially true in matters of race—an issue that was more pertinent than ever as schools moved toward desegregation through the adoption of integration plans, court orders, or white flight and neighborhood racial change. In the early 1970s, an expanding literature on the problems attendant to school desegregation appeared in response to complaints from parents and students. Evidence gathered by civil rights organizations indicated that increased conflict in desegregated schools was a result of African American students having white teachers who were either unprepared to handle the transition or resistant to the idea of teaching black students. They, too, found an increase in the number of conflicts between black and white students during the late 1960s and early 1970s.

Education experts also weighed in on the linkages between school discipline policies and the persistence of racial discrimination in education. New pedagogical theories and practices claimed to target persistent and structural forms of racial discrimination while a new curriculum that was no longer centered upon a white, Eurocentric view of American history and culture became ever more accessible through the publications of academics and journalists. The racial reform of education, some academics argued, needed to begin with a reassessment of the practice of teaching itself. Rather than emphasizing the cultural deficiencies of black families, radical pedagogues of the 1960s argued that the schools were operating in ways that fit a white, middle-class ideal that encouraged conformity and obedience. According to the education scholar Philip Jackson, students who did not adhere to the mores of such an environment were at a higher risk for discipline, suspension, and expulsion. Calling this agenda the "hidden curriculum," these radical pedagogical theories suggested a need to reform the practice of teaching itself in order to deliver upon the promise of *Brown v. Board of Education*. Desegregation and the Black Freedom Struggle necessitated new approaches to education and, especially, to school discipline. Higher rates of suspension and expulsion meant that black students around the nation were more likely to be deprived of an education than their peers for what the law professor Mark Yudof termed "trivial violations of the hidden curriculum."[74] In response, scholars and educators sought to pump life back into teaching, reveling in its revolutionary capacity.

Academics began to identify the ways in which a hidden curriculum structured education and stymied the development of children in the 1960s. Phillip Jackson's 1968 work, *Life in Classrooms*, introduced the idea of the hidden curriculum into university courses on education. The curricula offered in schools, including the lessons, homework, and in-class exercises, were only one part of what schooling sought to accomplish. The hidden curriculum, in contrast, was made up of the "crowds, the praise, and the power that combine to give a distinctive flavor to classroom life . . . which each student (and teacher) must master if he is to make his way satisfactorily through the school."[75] The hidden curriculum encompassed structures of power and authority that all children learned implicitly through the rules and discipline given to them by teachers. Schooling was, in its essence, as much about learning obedience to institutional figures as it was to learning reading, writing, and arithmetic. A successful student must master both curricula. Jackson concluded, "It is certainly possible that many of our valedictorians and presidents of our honor societies owe their success as much to institutional conformity as to intellectual prowess."[76] In its essence, Jackson's idea of the hidden curriculum pointed to the power imbalances that were essential to the student-teacher relationship. A student's ability to please his or her teacher was vital to academic achievement.

This turn toward a reassessment of the classroom and the unveiling of its power dynamics led other educational scholars and theorists to put forth radical solutions to the problems inherent in education. Some, such as Ivan Illich in *Deschooling Society*, took an avant-garde approach and called for the abandonment of institutionalized education altogether.[77] Others, such as Neil Postman and Charles Weingartner, argued instead that remaking teaching within the existing institutions of education was a better solution. Postman and Weingartner's bestselling polemic on American education, *Teaching as a Subversive Activity*, served as a scathing indictment of the methods in fashion with education schools. These pedagogies discouraged independent thought and challenges to authority by emphasizing obedience to the status quo. Postman and Weingartner argued that, rather than learn to become cogs in the "democratic" machine, children should become "experts at 'crap detecting.'"[78] Students' crap detectors would equip them with an anthropological perspective: the ability to "be part of his own culture and, at the same time, to be out of it."[79] Blind obedience to authority, learning just to learn was the poison in the well of American education. To teach independent thought and a hunger for questioning everything was the way to cultivate young minds. And this reform must come from the inside, through remaking how teachers and students saw themselves while transforming the purpose of education.

The "crap detector" approach would potentially undermine American prejudices, including those related to race. Postman and Weingartner argued that, by changing the frame through which young people saw the world, they might acquire the tools to see social and cultural constructions all around them and, importantly, question them in the process. "A person who is prejudiced against Negroes, for example, cannot 'see' a Negro; he can only see 'niggers' and decide that they are whatever his closed system predetermines them to be," they wrote. "We act on the basis of what we 'see.' If we 'see things' one way, we act accordingly. If we see them in another, we act differently."[80] By questioning the racial essentialism that was elemental to race prejudice, Postman and Weingartner argued that teachers and schools might be able to remake society to be more democratic and pluralistic. What they proposed was potentially a solution more satisfying than the general assumption that desegregation would create true equity and an opening of the American educational system.

The book swiftly became a bestseller as the public took notice. In a review for the *New York Times*, Peter Schrag identified the explosive potential of the recommendations of Postman and Weingartner. "They propose just what the title suggests: a form of subversion—teaching kids to ask real (and therefore often unwelcome and threatening) questions," he observed. But this was unlikely to be well received in an environment experiencing the convulsions of busing and its fiery resistance and the anti-war movement: "What will the local patriots say in Southern California, or the Citizens Councils of Alabama or the various ethnic pressure groups in New York or Chicago?" While neither *Teaching as a Subversive Activity* nor Schrag's review was explicitly about race and American education, concerns about the tensions created by civil rights activism and school desegregation undergirded their arguments. The book's eighth chapter, titled "New Teachers," began with a *New York Times* article discussing how black and Puerto Rican students argued before the board of education that a lack of communication with teachers and administrators—exacerbated by the school's nearly all-white teaching staff—pushed them out of New York City schools. The chapter focused on how teachers communicate, but the introduction makes it clear that racial issues were uniquely problematic in the classroom and its hidden curriculum. But Schrag's concerns about the book also presaged—if wrongly—the *Tinker v. Des Moines* decision that the Supreme Court would issue the following year. He concluded, "The fact is that students have never had rights and that the society shows no intention of recognizing them now."[81]

Brazilian educator Paulo Freire's classic 1968 work on anti-colonialism and education, *Pedagogy of the Oppressed*, was first translated into English from its original Portuguese in 1970. The book entered into conversations about education in America at a moment when radical pedagogy dominated discourses. Freire's work turned pedagogy upside down: It fused together the decolonizationist works of philosopher Frantz Fanon with the humanistic inquiry methods of psychoanalyst Erich Fromm. According to Freire, the oppressed must find their own humanity independently, discovering the extent of their oppression along the way. The role of the teacher should not be authoritarian but instead collaborative. Rather than assuming that teachers "deposit" knowledge in their students, Freire's pedagogy called for dialogues between students and teachers in partnership.[82] He rejected strict obedience to any ideology—capitalistic, communistic, or anywhere in between—instead championing the essential value of free inquiry. Freire argued, "This, then, is the great humanistic and historical task of the oppressed: to liberate themselves and their oppressors as well."[83] Freire's idea targeted the power imbalance assumed to underlie all student-teacher relations.

In 1973, the Southern Regional Council (SRC) and the Robert F. Kennedy Memorial Fund published a joint report on a new problem they called the "student pushout." As opposed to students who dropped out of school voluntarily, "pushouts" were young people unjustly expelled or suspended from school by teachers and administrators. The report, titled *The Student Pushout: Victim of Continued Resistance to Desegregation*, was compiled in response to complaints from students and parents about disproportionately harsh disciplinary actions taken toward black students in desegregated schools. The report argued that African American students were "victimized by racial discrimination and arbitrary acts of school authorities."[84]

The Student Pushout articulated the problem as especially acute and pressing in the wake of desegregation of Southern schools. The SRC argued that administrators at previously all-white schools suspended and expelled black students at higher rates than white students as a method of resegregating public schools. As black students were "pushed out" of school systems, administrators could indirectly subvert desegregation policies. Setting aside arguments about the wisdom or efficacy of desegregation policies, these concerns took a pragmatic look at the challenges that accompanied desegregation. They also pinpointed a great weakness in arguments for desegregation: Busing children and creating racial "balance" in schools would not necessarily mean that African American students did not face racial discrimination once they got to their newly desegregated schools. And as the SRC claimed, these worries were indicative of a systemic problem in the way students were treated by teachers and administrators. If there was no oversight for the way administrators dispensed punishments, students would remain vulnerable to the discriminatory actions of those in charge of schools.

The Student Pushout focused on student suspensions and expulsions in the South, and the report identified higher rates of suspension and expulsion for young African Americans than their white peers. The report used data from four Southern states: Georgia, South Carolina, Louisiana, and Arkansas. The most extreme case was Little Rock, Arkansas. In the 1971–1972 school year, the first year of implementation of wide-scale desegregation plans, although only 33 percent of the high school population and 42 percent of the junior high school population were black, nearly 80 percent of all suspensions were of black students.[85] Although black students constituted a higher percentage of student suspensions before desegregation, the percentage of those students suspended who were black jumped by 10 percent during the first year of desegregation.[86]

According to the SRC report, the student pushout was another tactic in a prolonged effort to deny black children equal educational opportunities. It could be used, the report warned, as a tool to punish those who protested against racial discrimination and was an extension of the Massive Resistance campaign that doomed the implementation of the *Brown v. Board of Education* decision in the mid-1950s. The invisibility of these pushouts worried the SRC, as they constituted a population deprived of their civil rights without recourse within rehabilitated "desegregated" school districts. Although school policies had changed to eliminate the dual systems of de jure Jim Crow, the people in power had not necessarily changed with the times. Part of the problem was a lack of protections for students who had been subject to unfair disciplinary practices and possible legal recourses for the students and their guardians.

After the publication of *The Student Pushout*, some school districts took notice. In Dallas, a student's lawsuit against the district forced officials to consider what might underlie the tremendous disparity between suspension rates in the city. In the 1972–1973 school year, black students in Dallas accounted for only 38 percent of the population but 60 percent of all student suspensions. The lawsuit accused the school of using suspensions in a racially discriminatory manner, and a local judge ordered the district to revise its policies to address the problem. Nolan Estes, the superintendent of Dallas schools and a former associate commissioner of education under Lyndon Johnson, acknowledged the disparity as stemming in part from "institutional racism." Estes described the district's efforts to expose and remedy forms of institutional racism as in the national fiscal interest. "It seems to me that it's cheaper for our society to educate these children than it is to put them out on the street where they become tax eaters rather than tax payers or send them to a juvenile detention home where the cost is $5–10,000 a year for care," Estes declared during an interview with National Public Radio.[87] In Estes's view, reforming the way teachers and administrators treated black students would be a boon to both the individual student's prospects and those of society.

Student Discipline and the Courts

In response to the mass suspensions of students in the Columbus Public School System, the local branch of the NAACP declared on March 5, 1971, that it would file suit in the local U.S. District Court on behalf of all African American children suspended during February and March in the Columbus public schools. The student unrest in Columbus schools was in response to racism, the NAACP asserted, and the students were being disciplined unfairly. The chairman of the local NAACP education committee, Marian Craig, condemned "the increasing number of school officials who, using various disciplinary actions as the rationale, are expelling or suspending black students for minor violations." The NAACP sought an injunction on the student suspensions and "immediate amnesty to all black students suspended or expelled."[88] On March 31, their lawyers filed a class-action lawsuit on behalf of all similarly situated public school students, claiming that the state law permitting suspensions of fewer than ten days' length without hearings violated the students' First and Fourteenth Amendment rights. The complaint charged that the state law and district policies governing disciplinary procedures were unconstitutional owing to "vagueness and overbreadth."[89] The situation of the student protesters was exemplary of the "widespread, invidious practice among defendants to arbitrarily suspend and transfer students without hearings and to keep students suspended without hearings for substantial periods of time at their pleasure."[90] The decision to use language in the lawsuit that indicated that school discipline in Columbus was "invidious" and "arbitrary" was part of an effort to signal to the court that the case was not about protecting unruly students but instead an effort to restrain state actors who overstepped and abused their authority, using it in an unjust and discriminatory manner.

The students' lawyers explained that all students' constitutional rights were at stake in the case. "Suspension, involuntary transfer, and the threat of expulsion are common administrative tools to prevent students from exercising such Constitutionally protected rights as free speech and peaceful assembly," the complaint noted. The Supreme Court asserted that students had free speech protections in *Tinker v. Des Moines*, but the decision meant little for students in public schools so long as the disciplinary authority of school administrators remained unchecked. To underscore this point, the NAACP noted a lawsuit filed the year after the Supreme Court handed down its decision in *Tinker*, in which a high school in Florida suspended students who participated in a Black History Week protest under a policy that automatically punished any student who protested school rules or discipline.[91] Due process protections in the form of hearings were necessary to protect other fundamental rights. In sum, as the students' lawyers explained, "The failure to provide fair hearings goes hand in hand with the vice of granting unfettered discretion to local school administrators."[92]

Because it challenged the constitutionality of the Ohio law governing student suspensions, the case was heard by a three-judge court in Ohio's Southern District.[93] The students' lawyers argued that, by suspending the students without hearings, the Columbus public schools had violated the students' right to due process of law under the Fourteenth Amendment. The Ohio statute that allowed administrators to suspend students for up to ten days without hearings was overly broad, and it deprived students of their right to property in education, which they termed "an important public right."[94] During the hearing, lawyers for the Columbus public schools sought to shroud the extent of student suspensions in the schools and downplay the use of punitive measures as a means of controlling student protest. The school district did not submit any evidence at all regarding the number of suspensions in order to substantiate its claim that suspensions were not widespread or used in a racially discriminatory manner.[95] In fact, of all the school districts asked to provide racial data on the use of suspensions by the Department of Health, Education, and Welfare, the Columbus district was the only Ohio district that did not respond.[96]

In *Goss*, the students and their parents and lawyers challenged the foundations of *in loco parentis*, which, in 1975, still largely dictated the

contours of school law. The common-law doctrine temporarily transferred part of the parent's natural right over his child to the teacher.[97]
In addition to authority over what a child was taught, this power also
gave the instructor the right to discipline the student as he saw fit.[98]
The doctrine of *in loco parentis* did not, however, give school administrators and teachers absolute authority. And the development of public
education after the Civil War and the passage of compulsory education
laws complicated the theory. Before laws made education compulsory,
parents were given discretion to determine how and if their children
would be educated. But when states began requiring children to attend
school, legislatures seized that power from parents. Compulsory attendance laws gained popularity during the Progressive Era, and their ef-
fectiveness was strengthened by the initiatives of reformers who sought
to end the practice of child labor.[99] These laws sought to ensure that
children would be neither in the factory nor on the street but in the
classroom—where reformers believed they belonged. Child labor laws
were not always popular, as many parents and employers disagreed with
the exclusion of children from the workplace.[100] Nonetheless, the push
to get children into schools was quite successful. By 1918, every state
in the Union had a compulsory education law on the books.[101] By the
late 1930s, enforcement of compulsory education laws therefore made
education into a function of the state.[102] They could no longer choose to
send a child to the field or the factory instead of the classroom. Children
were educated in part for the public good, and the state was therefore
responsible with ensuring the provision of education for all. Although
the central premise of *in loco parentis*—that a parent voluntarily relin-
quished some rights over the child, from which the instructor drew his
authority to educate and discipline—was compromised by compulsory
education, the courts continued to rely on the doctrine in school cases.

There was precedent for students challenging their suspensions and
expulsions in federal court. College students were the first to gain constitutional protections. Token desegregation of college campuses spurred
initial challenges, as white administrators punished student civil rights
activists with suspensions and expulsions. Autherine Lucy, one of the
first black students admitted to the University of Alabama, experienced
this firsthand. When white students rioted after she enrolled, the university expelled her. Her initial admission to the school was made possible

by a 1955 Supreme Court case, *Lucy v. Adams*, but the courts claimed that they could not protect her once she was finally enrolled at the University of Alabama. Her lawyers returned to court to protest her expulsion, only to have it upheld.[103]

The following year, in 1957, Warren A. Seavey, a professor of law at Harvard University, wrote a brief piece in the *Harvard Law Review* making a passionate case that the University of Alabama's treatment of Lucy deprived her of basic constitutional rights. He argued,

> Our sense of justice should be outraged by denial to students of the normal safeguards [of constitutional law]. It is shocking that the officials of a state educational institution, which can function properly only if our freedoms are preserved, should not understand the elementary principles of fair play. It is equally shocking to find that a court supports them in denying to a student the protection given a pickpocket.[104]

Seavey's keen observation that American students were denied the same constitutional protections of "pickpockets" emphasized the way that schools were special spaces in the public sphere and young people a special class of citizens within their walls. Desegregation was only the first step toward providing equitable education to black students; if they were not protected once they got to school, desegregation could never fulfill the basic promise of *Brown v. Board of Education*: the idea that it could facilitate equality of educational opportunity.

The sit-in movement and the Freedom Rides spurred new litigation challenging the authority of college and university administrators to retaliate against students who participated. *Dixon v. Alabama State Board of Education* was a lawsuit brought by six African American students who had been expelled from Alabama State College, a historically black teachers' college in Montgomery. The students were punished for participating in a sit-in on February 25, 1960, just weeks after four students in Greensboro, North Carolina, began a national sit-in movement with their protest at a Woolworth's lunch counter.[105] In Montgomery, the students' target was the lunchroom in the basement of the Montgomery County Courthouse—a place the students claimed they should be served, as it was a publicly owned and operated restaurant. They were denied service, and the lunchroom closed early. Informed of the students' actions, Alabama governor John M. Patterson, who acted as the chair of the State Board of Education, called the president of Alabama State College and advised him to consider expelling the students. The lunchroom sit-in was part of a series of mass demonstrations by black students from Alabama State College; in the following days, students engaged in a number of protests, in which they marched by the thousands. The governor identified the students who participated in the sit-in as "ring leaders" of the student protest movement, and with this information, the State Board of Education then decided to expel nine of the students and put twenty others on academic probation.[106]

Governor Patterson testified in the students' trial that he recommended expulsion because the student protests threatened to cause disruption. He told the district court, "I felt that the action should be prompt and immediate, because if something had not been done, in my opinion, it would have resulted in violence and disorder."[107] The students sued, declaring that they had been expelled without fair hearings—a denial of their Fourteenth Amendment right to due process of law. Although the district court sided with the college and declared that the State Board of Education had the right to expel the students without a hearing, the U.S. Court of Appeals for the Fifth Circuit found in favor of the students. The district court relied on the assertion that because the students did not have a constitutional right to attend Alabama State College, they could not claim due process protections after being expelled. But the Fifth Circuit judges declared that this was not the case—education was protected under the due process clause. In a decision written by Judge Richard Rives that echoed the language in *Brown v. Board of Education*, the court declared,

> It requires no argument to demonstrate that education is vital and, indeed, basic to civilized society. Without sufficient education, the plaintiffs would not be able to earn an adequate livelihood, to enjoy life to the fullest, or to fulfill as completely as possible the duties and responsibilities of good citizens.[108]

Furthermore, the court determined that the State Board of Education's powers were "not unlimited and cannot be arbitrarily exercised." Giving the students a hearing at which they could give their side of the story would at least satisfy the "fundamental principles of fairness," regardless of whether the students were then expelled or not.[109]

In his dissent, Circuit Court Judge Benjamin Franklin Cameron wrote that, by giving courts authority over the day-to-day decisions made by administrators, *Dixon* would only "add to the now crushing responsibilities of federal functionaries, the necessity of qualifying as a Gargantuan aggregation of wet nurses or baby sitters."[110] Were the judges in *Dixon* only reiterating the due process rights students already held, as the Fifth Circuit majority claimed? Or were they tasking the federal government with the responsibilities of "wet nurses or baby sitters," as Cameron's dissent dourly complained? These rhetorical questions presented by the Fifth Circuit judges revealed competing ideas of what role public schools should play in shaping a democratic society and challenged the basic premise of *in loco parentis*. If an education was a student's right, then common-law ideas about the power of administrators to punish children however they saw fit no longer made sense. The majority opinion reflected the idea that schools should be training grounds for participation in the citizenry, where students had certain rights and responsibilities, with limited power given to administrators in order to protect each student's interest in obtaining an education. The dissent argued, however, that administrators rightly held absolute authority over students who should abide by the rules or risk losing the privilege of being at school. College administrators took advantage of that power, as the facts of *Dixon* so powerfully demonstrated, and it was not the only place where black student protesters faced harsh punishments for civil rights activity. In the midst of the wave of sit-ins, the Tennessee Board of Education approved a rule ordering colleges and universities to expel students who had been arrested or convicted of "personal misconduct." The president of Tennessee A & I State University invoked the rule a year later to punish students who participated in the Freedom Rides.[111]

But *Dixon* was a case that dealt with college students. Courts sometimes borrowed from cases involving higher education when ruling on cases involving elementary and secondary education, but it could not be assumed that *Dixon* would straightforwardly apply to the circumstances involved in *Goss*. Another case from Alabama indicated that courts would review disciplinary actions under certain circumstances. Two years after the sit-in movement spurred the Fifth Circuit's decision in *Dixon*, civil rights organizations were still on the ground in Alabama, battling racial segregation. As part of the Birmingham Campaign in the spring of 1963, the Southern Christian Leadership Conference launched the Children's Crusade, which recruited young people to participate in direct action. Beginning on May 2 and lasting for a week, young people—including children as young as six years old—gathered at the Sixteenth Street Baptist Church, where they set out to march to City Hall. Along the way, Bull Connor and his police officers waited for them, wielding German shepherds and water cannons. In a scene that horrified many who saw the images, including President John F. Kennedy, police brutalized many young people, and they arrested many more.[112]

Among those arrested for "parading without a permit" was ten-year-old Linda Cal Woods, the daughter of Reverend Calvin Woods, who showed up to the demonstrations with two siblings and three cousins and without the knowledge or permission of their parents. Two weeks later, the school board notified Linda and a thousand other school-aged children in Birmingham arrested for their participation in the Children's Crusade that they would be suspended for the remainder of the school year. Students would not be eligible for promotion to the next grade unless their parents paid for summer classes to make up the missed time. And more important, suspended high school seniors would not be allowed to graduate.[113] Constance Baker Motley, a lawyer for the NAACP Legal Defense Fund, took up the students' case, arguing that the school board's actions were arbitrary and that they deprived students of their rights to due process and equal protection. The Fifth Circuit eventually sided with the students in a decision that sidestepped the questions of whether there had been constitutional violations of due process or equal protection.[114] Nonetheless, the decision denounced the use of discipline to punish protest activity that took place off campus, with the majority stating, "To be sure, discipline for truancy or for any other wrongdoing cannot be made an instrument of racial discrimination or imposed for asserting a constitutional right or privilege."[115]

The issue was bound to make its way before the Supreme Court as black student protests continued in the years following the court's ruling in *Tinker v. Des Moines*. The lower courts were divided on these questions. Whereas the three-judge panel that initially heard *Goss* was troubled by a lack of procedural protections for students, other district and circuit courts disagreed that the issue presented a constitutional problem. One such case came from a formerly all-white high school in Tyler, Texas, where a desegregation order was newly in place.[116] Racial conflict over the composition of the school's cheerleading team led hundreds of black students to gather around the school's flagpole in the early morning before classes began; most of these students then refused to attend classes. Students who participated in the boycott were required by the school to meet with administrators before they returned, creating de facto suspensions for protesting students. They were also put on academic probation, with the school requiring they sign a form that acknowledged that they would be expelled if they violated any school rules for the remainder of the year. Nearly 200 of the boycotting students refused to attend the interviews and were thus kept out of school. The Fifth Circuit sided with the school, finding no substantial issue with the school's treatment of its protesting black student population.[117]

The Fifth Circuit continued to rule in favor of the disciplinary authority of school officials. Black students suspended en masse in January 1972 during a "disruptive demonstration" in Port Allen, Louisiana, sued the district, claiming that the state law governing student discipline was overly vague, violating students' rights to free speech and due process. The law allowed suspensions for "willful disobedience," "intentional disruption," and "immoral or vicious practices" that disrupted school in addition to prohibiting students from showing "intentional disrespect" to any school official; any teacher could punish students for such activity. The Fifth Circuit denied that the statute gave administrators and teachers too much leeway or deprived students of due process of law through mass suspensions. Citing the Mississippi button case, *Burnside v. Byars*, the decision concluded, "Furthermore, a minority of the students, be they black or white, have no First Amendment right to convene their own assembly during school hours in defiance of the administration and thereby disrupt school order."[118] The previous year, the Fifth Circuit declined to find a Texas state statute that allowed suspensions for students deemed "incorrigible" unconstitutionally vague.[119]

The issue surfaced in Denver, too, where North High School administrators suspended Chicano student activist Manuel "Rocky" Hernandez and eight other students for wearing their black berets at school. After participating in protests, he was also arrested and later convicted for committing "unlawful acts in or about a school."[120] Hernandez sued the school district in October 1969, claiming that the school violated his right to free speech and due process of law. The Tenth Circuit upheld the suspension, finding that the Colorado law that allowed school administrators to suspend students for up to five weeks without a hearing did not violate the Constitution.[121] Hernandez was later expelled, a decision that the city's school board approved without much debate.[122]

Goss Goes to the Supreme Court

The case of the Columbus students attracted the support of numerous national organizations dedicated to preserving the civil liberties of young people at school. New attention to the issue of children's rights spurred organizations to spring to the defense of students. Several organizations prepared amici curiae in support of the students' claims, including the recently founded Children's Defense Fund, the American Friends Service Committee, the American Civil Liberties Union, the National Education Association, the National Committee for Citizens in Education, the NAACP, and the Southern Christian Leadership Conference.[123]

The work of the U.S. Commission on Civil Rights and the Southern Regional Council was key to the students' case. The immense store of data they had compiled and analyzed underscored and supported the students' complaints that suspensions were meaningful deprivations of their right to an education. In a joint amicus brief, the NAACP and the Southern Christian Leadership Conference used *The Student Pushout* to emphasize that student suspensions were a real threat to the civil rights of black students. Disproportionate rates of student suspensions negated other efforts to equalize schooling, undoing efforts to root out racial discrimination in American education through desegregation. The brief argued "that the vague standards and lack of due process implicit in Columbus, Ohio, school disciplinary rules and procedures result in a body of essentially unreviewable decisions that strike most harshly at minority children."[124] The state and local policies at issue clouded the decision-making processes of school authorities and protected them from scrutiny, resulting in harm to black children in the district. The brief cited evidence collected by a California sociologist showing rampant racial prejudice in how teachers perceived black students, making them subject to harsher discipline than white students. The study revealed that white teachers in California schools saw black children as being "more disobedient" than white children, just by virtue of the color of a child's skin.[125] The use of school discipline in racist ways may cause black students to drop out of school—a decision that would disadvantage them for life. According to the brief, "When dropout occurs, the consequences for Blacks in the job market are particularly serious since Blacks are already disadvantaged by higher rates of unemployment, lower incomes, and a greater proportion of low-prestige or part-time jobs."[126] At stake in the issue of racially discriminatory school discipline was its contribution to creating an economic underclass. Suspensions and expulsions could create a chain reaction that left minority youth at the margins of society with few options for elevating their socioeconomic status.

The amicus briefs of the Children's Defense Fund and American Friends Service Committee emphasized the argument that children were "persons" under the Constitution and that an era in which children were grouped with "imbeciles and beasts" over whom "there is no law" was a bygone one.[127] The brief also argued that the suspension process in the Columbus schools was inherently unfair and biased against students. Relying on the testimony of Philip Fulton, the principal at Marion-Franklin High School, the brief emphasized how one-sided considerations about student suspensions were. Even when students were allowed a hearing, Fulton testified that a teacher's word was always taken above a student's, effectively giving students no ability to respond to the allegations that got them suspended in the first place.[128] Furthermore, these suspensions—warranted or not—created real harm for the students involved. Students received no credit for work missed during the suspension period, and many of the plaintiffs were transferred to other schools, which they felt left them behind their peers academically. Evidence of their suspensions as noted in their permanent records was available to the police and to teachers who might write them recommendations for college or jobs.[129]

The brief of the American Civil Liberties Union (ACLU) focused on the *Goss* case as a natural extension of the legal logic in *Tinker v. Des Moines*.[130] *Tinker* laid the foundation for litigation in the *Goss* decision as the Court declared, "In our system, state-operated schools may not be enclaves for totalitarianism. School officials do not possess absolute authority over their students."[131] This language, coming from the highest court in the land, aligned with what many critics of harsh disciplinary practices contended: that the school environment must be reflective of the values of a democratic society. The ACLU brief echoed these concerns about totalitarianism at school, citing a 1970 report from the U.S. Office of Education, *Civic Education in a Crisis Age.*[132] According to the report, students at American secondary schools felt oppressed by teachers and administrators and that the educational process was anything but democratic. According to the report, "A large majority of the students feel they are regularly subjected to undemocratic decisions. These are seen as unilateral actions by teachers and administrators that deny fundamental rights of persons to equality, dissent, or due process." Public education in the United States should be a training ground for democratic participation, or it risked jeopardizing the very foundations of democracy: an informed and loyal citizenry. "At stake," the brief stated, "may be whether students will enter society with respect or contempt for the law."[133] Students who felt alienated by public education might become disillusioned with the entire democratic system—an argument that powerfully invoked the specter of the Cold War and was perhaps especially resonant in an era of unprecedented youth protest on high school and college campuses.

In response, the lawyers for the school district insisted that the case was based on a trivial premise: A student's suspension was not a meaningful deprivation of his education, and it in no way deserved the protections of the Fourteenth Amendment. The lawyers insisted that public education was primarily created in the interest of serving societal needs. Common schools were intended to protect the state against an "uninformed citizenry," which was an extension of the obligation of parents to educate their children. The provision of public education was a melding of the state and the home; schools were spaces intended to facilitate a parental duty that would help to achieve republican ends. In other words, education was not an individual right. Young people mattered only in their potential to become informed citizens once they achieved the age of majority.[134]

Settling the question of whether due process protections extended to secondary school students, the Supreme Court handed down its decision in *Goss v. Lopez* on January 22, 1975. Ruling on the side of the plaintiffs in a five-to-four decision, the court agreed with the lower court ruling that the Ohio statute that permitted suspensions and expulsions without hearings violated the students' Fourteenth Amendment rights. Justice Byron White wrote the majority opinion, in which he was joined by Justices William Douglas, William Brennan, Potter Stewart, and Thurgood Marshall. Students could not be suspended for even one day without hearings or proper procedures.[135]

The Supreme Court's decision held that students held both property and liberty interests in education, which were key to establishing a student's entitlement to public education. In other cases, such as those involving welfare benefits, the Court had previously ruled that if the law provides an entitlement, the government could not then take away that benefit without due process of law.[136] Like welfare benefits, the state's law providing free public education for all children and its laws requiring students to attend school created an entitlement. The state could therefore not deprive students of an education without proper procedures.[137] The Court acknowledged its earlier ruling in *San Antonio v. Rodriguez* that the Constitution did not require states to provide public education. Instead, state legislatures voluntarily created an entitlement protected by the due process clause when they passed laws making education free and compulsory.[138]

In his dissent in the *Goss* case, Justice Lewis Powell argued for pushing back at the sweeping language of *Tinker* and reasserting the absolute authority of teachers and administrators. Powell's dissent argued that, by establishing an entitlement to education that required the protection of the due process clause, the Supreme Court would make the jobs of teachers and administrators more difficult than ever. According to Powell, the Court's ruling in *Tinker* had unleashed a torrent of lawsuits—"literally hundreds," he stated—that inundated the courts, and the *Goss* decision would mean that school administrators would be overburdened by the necessity to provide hearings for all suspended students. Powell used the suspension data from the amicus briefs in order to argue that suspensions were becoming ever more necessary in an era marked by student unrest. The Court should not impede the expediency of school discipline in times of great difficulty for administrators and teachers who relied on it as a powerful method of student control. Powell wrote, "It is common knowledge that maintaining order and reasonable decorum in school buildings and classrooms is a major educational problem, and one which has increased significantly in magnitude in recent years." Beyond concerns of student and teacher safety, Powell wrote that the ruling would interfere with the ability of administrators to attend to other parts of their jobs beyond disciplining students. "If hearings were required for a substantial percentage of short-term suspensions," Powell wrote, "school authorities would have time to do little else."[139]

But it was precisely the minutiae of everyday school affairs that frustrated those who sought to defend the civil rights of students in public schools. The concerns captured by the reports of the Southern Regional Council and others showed the way that discrimination remained embedded in the American educational system, even as school boards trotted out desegregation plans as evidence of progress in civil rights reform. For students in desegregated schools, these were pyrrhic victories if they jeopardized the ability of a young person to receive a public education at all. At the same time, the Court's ruling in *Goss* subsumed concerns specific to the experience of black students to those that addressed a broader problem about students and rights. While the origins of the case were in the civil rights struggle, the decision was not a civil rights case, per se.

But the *Goss* decision was only as important as the number of school administrators who knew that it existed and complied with it. This problem was partially resolved by the decision in a closely related case out of Arkansas, which was argued before the Supreme Court on the same day as the *Goss* case. A month after the *Goss* ruling, the Supreme Court handed down its decision in that case, *Wood v. Strickland*. The plaintiffs in the lawsuit were two high school students, Peggy Strickland and Virginia Crain, who had been expelled from their Arkansas high school. Seized with the idea of playing a prank on students and parents attending an evening meeting at their high school, the two young women drove across the border to Oklahoma, where they could purchase liquor, as their county in Arkansas was dry. Strickland and Crain then used the Right Time malt liquor they bought to "spike" the punch at the meeting, although, as the Court dutifully noted, meeting attendees drank the spiked punch "without apparent effect." When school officials discovered the plot, the girls were expelled for the remainder of the semester.

The students and their parents sued the district to have them reinstated, and they also sued the school board for damages. Citing *Tinker*, the flag salute case *West Virginia State Board of Education v. Barnette* (1943), and *Goss*, the Court once again affirmed that "public high school students do have substantive and procedural rights while at school."[140] The majority decision—like *Goss*, written by Justice White—declared that, in accordance with this, school board members who knowingly violated the constitutional rights of students could be sued for damages.

The ruling in *Wood* was an important corollary to the *Tinker* and *Goss* decisions. *Wood* lifted the veil of immunity that had protected school administrators, applying the legal logic of a clause from the 1871 Enforcement Act (known alternately as the Civil Rights Act of 1871 and the Ku Klux Klan Act). The Enforcement Act, passed in the wake of Southern resistance to Reconstruction, was the Radical Republican solution to state agents in the South who deprived African Americans of their constitutional rights. Under Section 1983 of the act, a person could sue and receive monetary relief if an official, acting under the guise of state authority, deprived him of his constitutionally granted rights.[141] Before the ruling in *Wood*, school board members were, according to the common law, shielded by "qualified immunity," meaning that they could not be held individually liable for the deprivation of student rights. But in *Wood*, the Supreme Court declared that school board members could no longer claim qualified immunity "if they knew or should reasonably have known that the action they took within their sphere of official responsibility would violate the constitutional rights of the student affected."[142] School board members acting "in good faith" would still be cloaked in qualified immunity, but those who willfully deprived students of their constitutional rights were not. This language provided a concrete way for students and parents to pursue redress if school board members ignored the new mandate for public schools to actively work to protect the constitutional rights of students. School boards still acted with relative independence, but now members did so in ways that flaunted the *Tinker* and *Goss* decisions at their own peril.

Writing in the *Phi Delta Kappan*, Ronald J. Anson, the director of the Legal Research Branch of the National Institute of Education, embraced the *Goss* and *Wood* decisions as creating a more ideal balance in schools between the authority of school administrators and students' rights.

Anson declared, "Together, *Goss v. Lopez* and *Wood v. Strickland* stand for the idea of fair and responsible treatment of students in disciplinary actions. While such treatment has always been sound educational practice, it has now become sound practice legally as well."[143] Anson insisted that *Goss* and *Wood* would be beneficial to students and to educators—except those educators and administrators who saw themselves primarily as authoritarians. The Court did not seek to overturn centuries of the tradition of local control over American schools; instead, it sought to balance that tradition with the new constitutional imperative to protect students' rights. If *Goss* brought the Fourteenth Amendment into the classroom, then *Wood* demanded that administrators respect the *Goss* ruling. According to Anson, the final result of this move would not be an unwarranted federal intrusion into public schools. Instead, the two decisions could help standardize administrative practices throughout the nation around a new principle of student rights. The most promising outcome of the decisions would be a fairer shake for students, who would now be protected from the capriciousness of administrators.

* * *

In September 1975, nine months after the Supreme Court handed down its ruling in *Goss*, the Children's Defense Fund (CDF) published a report that focused exclusively on the problem of student suspensions. Marian Wright Edelman, whose work as a lawyer in Mississippi in 1964 and 1965 contributed to the button cases, founded the CDF in the early 1970s after moving to Washington, DC, and deciding that young people deserved an advocacy organization that responded directly to their interests. The CDF emphasized that suspensions solved few real problems and were often used in discriminatory or arbitrary ways. The report used data compiled by the Office of Civil Rights in the federal Department of Health, Education, and Welfare. The report's conclusion, answering the question in the title, *School Suspensions: Are They Helping Children?*, was a resounding "No." Noting that student suspension rates varied wildly at schools across districts, the report concluded that "the incidence of suspension is more a function of school policies and practices than of students' behavior."[144] Moreover, it was difficult to quantify how often student suspensions were being used to remove violent children from schools, as some districts used the catchall term "disruptions" to group together civil rights and anti-war protests along with fistfights and other incidents of violence. According to the CDF report,

> No one knows how much school violence there is. . . . Earlier studies included political protests against the war in Vietnam, against violations of the rights of minorities, and in defense of student liberties as "disruptions" in all cases, even when the protests were legal in every respect.[145]

It was unclear, in the end, why some schools relied so heavily on suspensions. A Chicago school principal told the CDF, "The basic point to remember is that suspension solves very little."[146] Ultimately, as the CDF pointed out, there was little evidence that suspensions were anything more than a short-term solution to deeper problems with how schools operated.

Meanwhile, in Columbus, parents and student advocates tired of the district's inaction on racial reform in the classroom. The school board, faced with growing enrollments and overcrowding in the city's schools, found itself unable to deal with the issue. A three-person minority on the board refused to approve a bond issue that would address overcrowding and underfunding of public schools for the ballot without the inclusion of some concession on desegregation.[147] A majority of board members refused. The NAACP's statement condemning any school bond issue that did not fund equal educational opportunities for black students declared, "Inner city urban and Black children face hostile teachers, suppressive administrators, segregated and inferior classrooms."[148] Years passed as an indecisive board of education refused to take any meaningful action to deal with segregation in the city's schools. In June 1973, students and their parents sued the district for deliberately segregating students by race. The initial hearings were held three years later, and the district court ruled that the district had violated the students' Fourteenth Amendment rights. The Sixth Circuit Court of Appeals agreed, and *Columbus Board of Education v. Penick* was finally heard before the U.S. Supreme Court in 1979. Leaning heavily on the precedent set by *Keyes v. School Dist. No. 1*, the court ruled that the Columbus schools were unconstitutionally segregated.[149]

The *Goss* decision's limitations on the authority of teachers and administrators was its most important legacy, although its legal heritage lies in the realm of administrative reform—not necessarily in extended civil rights protections for African American children. The Children's Defense Fund, the Legal Defense Fund, and the Southern Regional Council all recognized the importance of the relationships among students, teachers, and administrators as key to making constructive civil rights reform in the desegregation era. The *Goss* decision forged a path for further articulations of students' rights and marked a victory for those who worked in child advocacy—particularly for those advocating for the rights of children with disabilities, as the next chapter explores. The case gave all students access to procedural guarantees put in place to prevent arbitrary exclusion from schools. But at the same time, the erasure of the case's civil rights past reveals some of the unfinished business of the Black Freedom Struggle. Making these procedures "fair" did not address the continuing problem of racial inequity in public schools or disparate rates of suspension by race. While Congress argued over busing policies, millions of African American students faced the comparatively invisible challenges of navigating everyday life in schools that had purportedly been "reformed" through desegregation.

As Justice Felix Frankfurter wrote in 1945, "The history of American freedom is, in no small measure, the history of procedure."[150] Procedural fairness is one of the basic tenets of American constitutionalism. The due process clauses of the Fifth and Fourteenth Amendments were intended to balance the power of the law and individual rights in the interest of justice and fairness. Procedural due process was not the concern of high school administrators until *Goss*. While legal scholars have considered the *Goss* case to be an afterthought of the "due process revolution," the history of the case shows different stakes for public school students, especially those protesting racial discrimination at school.[151] Students who perceived discrimination in the actions of those in charge of schools realized the necessity of creating pressure for change. In recognizing a student's right to fair procedures—even if the process resulted in suspension, anyway—*Goss* gave the student a voice and established his right to be heard. The *Goss* decision recognized the student's own interest in education, challenging the foundations of *in loco parentis*, even if it was only a small step toward eradicating the racial discrimination that ignited the suit.

4

A Right to Equal Education

The Fourteenth Amendment and American Schools

Oliver Brown initially filed suit against the Topeka, Kansas, public schools after the district denied his daughter Linda enrollment at Sumner Elementary School, which was closer to their home than the segregated black school she attended. Sixteen years after the Supreme Court ruled in his favor in *Brown v. Board of Education*, black students and their white allies staged walkouts and protests at Topeka High School. They formed a black student union in 1969, and much like the rebellious students in Columbus, Ohio, these teenagers targeted the exclusion of black students from school clubs and the lack of black teachers and administrators, and they demanded the inclusion of black history into curricula.[1] A year later, perhaps following the cue of their black peers, Chicano students in Topeka organized their own walkouts.[2] Even in the symbolic home of the *Brown* decision, student protest roiled the schools and revealed the chasm between the kind of educational opportunity promised by the case and the reality of its implementation. While the *Brown* decision addressed the issue of state-sponsored segregation, the student protests of the late 1960s and early 1970s demonstrated that desegregation alone could not remedy racial discrimination in American public education.[3]

As the previous chapters show, in debates over racial reform at school, students often expressed their own grievances and ideas. The intensified involvement of young people brought the stakes of constitutional change into relief. But when the Supreme Court decides cases, it purposefully narrows the legal questions at stake, meaning that the outcomes of Supreme Court cases are seldom fully satisfying to the social movement actors who set them into motion. Some scholars, most notably Gerald Rosenberg in *The Hollow Hope*, make the case that pursuing social change through the legal system is unwise, especially since court rulings often invite political backlash.[4] Nonetheless, as the Supreme Court began to more aggressively enforce the mandate of *Brown v. Board of Education* in the late 1960s, other groups saw the Fourteenth Amendment's equal protection clause as offering a path toward meaningful change for young people in schools across the nation. Just as the higher education cases that preceded *Brown* employed a broad idea of equal protection, the 1970s saw a range of students' rights cases testing the reach of the clause. Witnessing the strides made on the issue of school segregation, advocates for other minority-group students wielded their own theories about the relationship between public education and the spirit of the equal protection clause. And yet, reading these cases together reveals that the Burger Court dramatically limited the extent to which students could claim equal protection during the 1970s. This chapter explores these efforts to leverage the power and promise of the Fourteenth Amendment in education from the late 1960s until the early 1980s, as the Supreme Court set firm limits on how it could be used to counter discrimination as it defined the amendment's scope.

Desegregation and the Limits of the Fourteenth Amendment

In the 1970s, many would agree that the role of the courts in remedying racial inequality in public education could largely be summed up in one word: busing. Indeed, in the late 1960s and early 1970s, the Supreme Court issued a series of rulings that required school districts to finally implement meaningful desegregation policies, including through the use of busing children to achieve "racial balance" in previously segregated schools. This interpretation of the Fourteenth Amendment's equal protection clause was one that sparked great debate and, in some places, violent resistance.[5] The school desegregation cases that followed in the wake of *Brown* often focused primarily on the question of segregation itself even though the provision of poorer quality education to racial minority students was not solely tied to the physical separation of students by race. Claims that the state violated students' rights to equal protection were common in litigation in the 1960s, although the cases that garnered the most attention involved questions of racial segregation in schools.

For the courts, the central question involved in school desegregation litigation was whether state actors purposefully created racial segregation in public schools. The Fourteenth Amendment to the U.S. Constitution declares in part that a state shall not "deny to any person within its jurisdiction the equal protection of the laws." To violate the Fourteenth Amendment, racial discrimination must be shown to be a result of state action. But what constituted "state action"? In cases where law or school board policy required the separation of white children from black, Mexican-American, or Chinese American students in public schools, for example, the state was clearly responsible. In response to this violation of constitutional rights, the courts could then require that the state take on the responsibility for desegregating schools through a variety of remedies. School segregation that was not created by a formal law or public policy required more evidence to prove state action in order to require a state-sponsored remedy, as was the case in Denver. According to the courts, de facto segregation was the result of private action and, owing to a list of precedents that dated back to the nineteenth century, outside the reach of the Fourteenth Amendment.[6]

When the courts engaged in questions about the reach of state action, new and difficult questions arose. Could the state be implicated in creating and maintaining the residential segregation that often led to school segregation outside the South—thereby obliterating the old bright line between de jure and de facto segregation? What about school board decisions that placed new schools in racially segregated neighborhoods and drew attendance lines that encouraged racial segregation? Did this count as "state action" and make racial segregation de jure? Furthermore, what kinds of remedies could the courts employ in instances of de jure segregation? Such questions animated litigation during these years as the court rigidly adhered to the de jure/de facto divide.

The Supreme Court's more aggressive stance toward the implementation of school desegregation as a remedy was first signaled in *Green v. New Kent County*. The schools of New Kent County, Virginia, were strictly segregated by race until 1965, when the district adopted a "freedom of choice" plan that virtually ensured that only token desegregation would occur by placing the burden on individual black families and students to opt to transfer to white schools. In *Brown v. Board of Education II*, the 1955 decision that dealt with implementation of the Court's original ruling in *Brown v. Board of Education* in 1954, the Supreme Court instructed school districts to desegregate "with all deliberate speed."[7] The

New Kent County school board's response to the mandate of *Brown II* was to take limited steps that would ensure that very little desegregation would take place. As they predicted, no white families chose to enroll their children in the segregated black schools. The Supreme Court's ruling, which confronted the question of whether the "freedom of choice" plan satisfied the demands of equal protection as expressed in *Brown*, revealed impatience with the slow pace of desegregation by a unanimous Supreme Court. In its ruling, penned by Justice William Brennan, the Court declared that "the plan has operated simply to burden children and their parents with a responsibility which *Brown II* placed squarely on the School Board." Instead, the justices asserted that the school board was tasked with an "affirmative duty" to dismantle racial discrimination "root and branch." Furthermore, the Court stated, "The burden on a school board today is to come forward with a plan that promises realistically to work, and promises realistically to work *now*."[8]

Green's powerful language spurred renewed litigation over school desegregation and the efforts of states to evade implementing the *Brown* decision. A lawsuit out of Charlotte, North Carolina, involving the racial segregation of students within the city became an important milestone in demarcating the reach of equal protection. A previous lawsuit found the city's school board responsible for creating and perpetuating racial segregation in public schools, and *Swann v. Charlotte-Mecklenburg* addressed the appropriate remedy. Noting the failures of the local school board to remedy equal protection violations, in 1971 the Supreme Court upheld the constitutionality of a school desegregation plan that would mandate the busing of students from predominantly white schools to predominantly black schools, and vice versa. Noting that nearly 40 percent of all students were already bused to school, the Court emphasized that busing was "a normal and acceptable tool of educational policy."[9] The ruling in *Swann* extended the authority of lower courts to adopt desegregation schemes that directly challenged the existence of residential segregation.

At the same time, the language of the decision made it clear that *Swann* applied exclusively to the circumstances of de jure segregation. As the majority opinion declared, "The elimination of racial discrimination in public schools is a large task and one that should not be retarded by efforts to achieve broader purposes lying beyond the jurisdiction of school authorities. One vehicle can carry only a limited amount of baggage." In other words, desegregation should only be used to target the past harm of state-sponsored segregation. The Court added, "It would not serve the important objective of *Brown I* to seek to use school desegregation cases for purposes beyond their scope."[10] President Richard Nixon later lifted this language from the decision in order to justify his proposed limits on the remedies that courts could impose for illegal school segregation. As Nixon put it, "Schools exist to serve the children, not to bear the burden of social change."[11] Nixon's interpretation of school desegregation litigation erased the years of efforts made by students, parents, lawyers, and other advocates for young people to transform public education into a system that truly provided equal educational opportunities to all.

And yet, how the Court defined the contours of the state action doctrine made it difficult to demonstrate in court that school districts intentionally segregated schools. *Swann* dealt with the actions of a local school board. But what about other state entities? Did their actions amount to a violation of the Fourteenth Amendment rights of children in schools in segregated neighborhoods? Numerous examples, including federally supported and locally implemented urban renewal policies, show how state action contributed to residential segregation.[12] The practice of redlining neighborhoods with racial minority populations and thus marking them as "risky" and ineligible for federally backed mortgages was institutionalized through the Home Owners Loan Corporation.[13] Even the law was not much help. While the Supreme Court struck down racial zoning laws in 1917,[14] in the 1948 *Shelley v. Kraemer* decision, the Court ruled that racially restrictive covenants were constitutionally permissible even though the enforcement of such contracts through the courts was not.[15] Federal support made the expansion of largely white suburbs possible, effectively subsidizing the extension of residential segregation through white flight.

The Detroit school desegregation case, *Milliken v. Bradley*, which the Supreme Court heard in 1973, led the Court to address the question of how it would interpret state action and its limits. *Milliken* diverged substantially from the facts of the case in *Swann*. Although Detroit's schools had been formally segregated by race in the mid-nineteenth century, by 1871 the district ended the practice.[16] A century later, Detroit's schools were once again segregated by race. Decades of state-sponsored and private discrimination in real estate led to residential segregation that isolated white and black students in neighborhood schools, which the school board exacerbated through drawing school attendance zone boundaries that aligned with the residential color line.[17] As whites fled the city for the suburbs in the decades after World War II, the percentage of black students in the district population grew.[18]

Black parents organized in response to the provision of separate and unequal education in the Detroit schools, and black high school students launched protests targeting the inferior quality of education they received in 1966.[19] In 1970, lawyers for the local National Association for the Advancement of Colored People (NAACP) branch filed a desegregation suit against the district, the state board of education, the governor, and the state attorney general. At the trial, they made the case that the school board intentionally segregated students in city schools. At the same time, they also pursued a novel strategy by arguing that the housing discrimination that created residential segregation in the city and in neighborhood schools was also the product of state action.[20] The NAACP lawyers presented evidence of the use of racially restrictive covenants to keep neighborhoods lily-white and pointed to Federal Housing Authority policies that encouraged residential segregation.[21]

The ruling in *Swann* was handed down by the Supreme Court just as the Detroit trial concluded. But in Detroit any school desegregation plan that included only students in the city would have a virtually undetectable effect on racial isolation in city schools because such a high percentage of the district's population was made up of black students. Lawyers presented evidence of state action in creating the affluent white suburbs that surrounded the city and the policies that prevented black families from following whites to suburban communities.

The case inflamed racial tensions and, in particular, white accusations of judicial overreach in school desegregation cases. A national fervor over the issue of busing was only fueled by the court's ruling in *Swann*. Irene McCabe, a white housewife from Pontiac, Michigan, who led the city's anti-desegregation campaign, launched her "Mother's March to Washington" in March 1972 in response to a judicial order to desegregate the Pontiac public schools.[22] The Detroit case laid bare the principles that undergirded ideas about school segregation and the reach of the

Fourteenth Amendment. Judge Stephen Roth eventually sided with the plaintiffs, finding that segregation in Detroit schools was the product of state action. Roth controversially issued a remedial order that called for busing between the city and its suburbs, setting off a firestorm of opposition.[23]

After the Sixth Circuit upheld most of Roth's ruling, the Supreme Court agreed to hear *Milliken v. Bradley*, and it became one of the most closely watched cases of the 1973–1974 term. In the Supreme Court's decision, Chief Justice Warren Burger announced that the majority rejected this busing scheme. The decision, Burger explained, rested upon the fact that "without an interdistrict violation and some interdistrict effect, there is no constitutional wrong and there is no constitutional basis for an interdistrict remedy."[24] The ruling denied that the growth of lily-white suburbs could be enough evidence of state action to warrant a court-ordered interdistrict remedy. The lower court had been willing to consider an even more expansive definition of state action, arguing that

> governmental actions and inaction at all levels, federal, state and local, have combined with those of private organizations, such as loaning institutions and real estate associations and brokerage firms, to establish and to maintain the pattern of residential segregation throughout the Detroit metropolitan area.[25]

The court acknowledged the difficulty of establishing direct causality that would confirm state action, noting, "Perhaps the most that can be said is that all [governmental units], including the school authorities, are, in part, responsible for the segregation that exists." But the Supreme Court disagreed and drastically limited the extent to which state actors could be held responsible for remedying the racial segregation that their policies indirectly created.

In short, the Supreme Court identified the limits of what could be considered a remedy, even as it acknowledged the broader definition of state action. And so, although the Supreme Court ruled that plaintiffs had proven that the Detroit school district had taken actions that perpetuated segregation, they were unable to provide direct evidence that any suburban districts did so. The Court chastised the lower courts, declaring, "With no showing of significant violation by the 53 outlying school districts and no evidence of any inter-district violation or effect, the court went beyond the original theory of the case as framed by the pleadings and mandated a metropolitan remedy."[26] Thus the sphere of relevant state action was limited to the actions of school boards. The actions of other federal, state, and local governmental authorities to create and maintain residential segregation did not together constitute enough proof to demonstrate a violation of equal protection and mandate a remedy. The Supreme Court opted to treat school district boundaries as if they were sacrosanct as it struck down the interdistrict plan in *Milliken*.[27]

Justice Thurgood Marshall, whose work at the NAACP Legal Defense Fund laid the groundwork for the organization's victory in *Brown v. Board of Education*, labeled the Detroit ruling a "major step backward" in the fight for racial justice. Newspapers around the country hailed the decision as a victory for anti-busing forces and a crushing defeat for civil rights. "Busing Enemies Are Delighted, Advocates Disgusted but Hopeful," read a headline in the next day's edition of the *Washington Post*.[28] The *Los Angeles Times* noted that *Milliken* "seems to signal an end of an era."[29] In histories of the *Brown* decision and its progeny, the Detroit case bookends the period of renewed efforts by federal courts to implement meaningful school desegregation that began with the court's 1968 ruling in *Green v. New Kent County*.[30] But as other scholars have noted, busing was not the only remedy theoretically available to those who sought to racially reform American public education during the 1970s.[31] Indeed, as this book's second chapter shows, busing was only one part of the remedy prescribed by the district court judge in the Denver school desegregation case.

In *Milliken*, the majority opinion reiterated language from *Swann*, stating that "the scope of the remedy is determined by the nature and extent of the constitutional violation."[32] But in his dissent, Justice Marshall indicated that the right to equal educational opportunity was not one tied solely to desegregation as the proper remedy. Segregated schools were both separate and unequal, and the remedies demanded by such inequities were not limited to busing or school-pairing schemes. In his dissent, Marshall argued, "We deal here with the right of all our children, whatever their race, to an equal start in life and to an equal opportunity to reach their full potential as citizens."[33] Indeed, throughout the 1960s and 1970s, the right to equal educational opportunity was an elastic concept that was widely used but rarely defined. Despite the loss in *Milliken*, in the 1970s, advocates for other minority-group students seized upon an expansive idea of equal protection that was not exclusively yoked to segregation as a violation or desegregation as a remedy. Others would make the case in court that equal protection was a far more capacious concept and that it created a right that all students could claim.

The Right to Bilingual Education

An early front in the battle to leverage the Fourteenth Amendment in public schooling was the issue of bilingual education. In the early 1970s, the U.S. Commission on Civil Rights released a series of reports that emphasized the widespread and persistent nature of continuing educational inequities in the southwestern United States. The reports revealed the stark disparities between educational outcomes for children of various minority groups, including African Americans, American Indians, and Mexican Americans. In nearly every comparison of the five states studied—California, New Mexico, Arizona, Colorado, and Texas—outcomes for Mexican American and black students were worse than those of their white peers. Black children were slightly more likely to finish high school, and Mexican American children had higher reading levels, but in both measures the rates were much lower than those of white students. As Mario Obledo, the director of the Mexican American Legal Defense Fund (MALDEF), put it, "These truths stand as massive indictments against the present educational system." He continued, "In essence, what this system has done is to smother the soul and spirit of an entire people."[34]

But although the federal government measured and publicized such disparate outcomes by race, to what extent could the courts hold state actors responsible for fixing them? This was the central question faced by advocates for minority students who sought to use litigation to challenge educational inequalities. As one U.S. Commission on Civil Rights report put it, "The failure of the school to adapt to the different language and cultural heritage of Mexican American students is a significant contributing factor in the cycle which results in lower participation and achievement on the part of Chicano pupils."[35] Could this be evidence that school policy was discriminatory and therefore deserving of a remedy under the Fourteenth Amendment's equal protection clause?

Some district court judges answered this question affirmatively, stoking the hopes of MALDEF lawyers that a Fourteenth Amendment claim could be viable. Lawsuits challenging the segregation of Mexican American students from the early 1970s sometimes resulted in court-ordered reforms in school curricula and pedagogy targeted at reversing this trend, in particular the implementation of bilingual-bicultural programs that included the study of students' cultures and the languages they spoke at home.[36] But for these decisions to have wider resonance, they had to be upheld by higher courts upon appeal.

Lawyers for MALDEF viewed *Keyes v. School Dist. No. 1* as presenting an opportunity to press the courts to accept a broader view of equal protection. The organization joined Denver's school desegregation lawsuit as it entered the remedial phase after the Supreme Court remanded the case back to the district court. During this stage of litigation, the district court would draft its plan to eliminate separate and unequal schooling in the city. The Mexican American Legal Defense Fund asked the court to include a bilingual-bicultural program, contending that "the reason for the dismal performance of Chicano children in the Denver public schools is their 'incompatibility' with the instructional program as presently provided to them."[37] In short, MALDEF lawyers wanted the court to recognize that the schools' curricula alienated Mexican American students, leading to lower grades and higher dropout rates. This, they argued, constituted a deprivation of equal educational opportunity under the Fourteenth Amendment, and it merited a court-ordered remedy.

The district court agreed, but the Tenth Circuit Court of Appeals did not. In 1975, it struck the bilingual-bicultural components from the city's desegregation plan. As the court wrote, "The clear implication of arguments in support of the court's adoption of the Cardenas [*sic*] Plan is that minority students are entitled under the fourteenth amendment to an educational experience tailored to their unique cultural and development needs."[38] Such a claim about the reach of the Fourteenth Amendment's equal protection clause could not withstand such scrutiny, even though pedagogues might recommend it. As the judges concluded, "Although enlightened educational theory may well demand as much, the Constitution does not."[39] Even as educational reform movements targeted the insidious ways that schools perpetuated inequalities between and among minority students and their white peers, the court in *Keyes* rejected attempts to claim more substantive remedies under the equal protection clause.

The inclusion of a bilingual-bicultural program was not the only way that the students' lawyers sought to argue for an overhaul of the way the city's schools taught and treated students of color. Their lawyers also argued that school officials treated schools that had large black and Mexican American populations differently and held them to lower standards, allowing a two-tiered system of education to exist. But this, too, turned out to be a losing argument. When the plaintiffs' lawyers argued that the district provided inferior options to students in its schools with majority black and Mexican American populations compared to the college preparatory programs at its predominantly white high schools, the courts—for a time—considered that this might be a violation of the spirit of equal protection of the law. But in the end, the courts deferred to the school district officials who testified that they were only meeting the needs of "culturally deprived" students—who just happened to be students of color. The courts defined "separate and unequal" in a way that limited the ways advocates for those students could make legal claims about unconstitutional inequalities. The decision linked the right to equality of educational opportunity affirmatively to school desegregation, marking other reforms as the province of local policy rather than constitutional law.

In *Keyes*, the courts accepted arguments that the different educational programs offered by majority-minority schools in Denver—as opposed to the college preparatory curriculum offered by majority-white schools—was merely a reflection of the district's desire to provide an "appropriate" education for each child. The courts accepted this rationale not as proof that the district was providing unequal educational opportunities purposefully but instead as evidence that the district was in fact proactive in attempting to equalize education. That such differences could be predicated on the race and class status of children was not just a convenient way for the district to evade accusations of racism; it was also representative of a genre of sociological and education research that crafted racially neutral ways to identify the "difference" supposedly inherent in the black or brown child.[40] This marking of difference came with a bevy of new names: The child was "culturally" or "educationally" deprived, or—in language that would survive the 1960s and 1970s—"disadvantaged" or "underprivileged." The terminology used blended assumptions about the racial and class status of the children labeled as such.[41] The "cultural deprivation" theory proliferated in the mid-1960s, and adherents included progressive pedagogues who argued that such ideas could be used to equalize American education through "compensatory education" meant to make up for the deficiencies created by students' home environments.[42] Despite their scientific-sounding names, these labels all underscored the same idea that educating these children would be more difficult than educating their white and presumably middle-class peers. Such classifications justified the differential treatment of black and Mexican American students even when they worked in ways that exacerbated rather than ameliorated inequalities.[43]

Exchanges from the trial transcript of *Keyes* illuminate the ways that cultural deprivation theory was wielded by opposing sides and how it became synonymous with ethnic and racial difference. Officials from the Denver public schools wove ideas about culturally deprived children and race into their testimony to justify differential curricula between city high schools during the *Keyes* litigation. Denver Schools Superintendent Louis Kishkunas compared poor Mexican American and African American children unfavorably to Eastern European immigrants who came to the United States in the late nineteenth century. As Kishkunas explained, "The Jewish people . . . were just as poor as the day is long, but they still had a culture, they had a culture of expectation; they had a certain faith in education, which was picked up by their children."[44] Black and Mexican American children, in contrast, he said, "don't have the same faith [and] the same expectations for schools."[45] The difference in achievement rates between white and black and Mexican American students in the city's schools was therefore attributable to differences in culture, which overlapped with race and ethnicity. These differences, he argued, justified the fact that college preparatory programs existed at white high schools, whereas such offerings were scarce at the majority black and Mexican American schools. In this telling, culture rather than race or class explained the academic achievement of children of color.

In *Keyes v. School District No. 1*, the black plaintiffs in the case lived in a middle-class neighborhood of Denver, and they originally filed the lawsuit because they felt that the schools' curricula were not challenging their children. Among the original plaintiffs, Wilfred Keyes was a chiropractor, and Rachel Noel's husband was a doctor. They represented Denver's educated black middle class. As the *Keyes* case shows, the position and interests of black Denverites often diverged substantially from those of the city's Mexican American population. But these discrepancies went ignored, and race was conflated with class and culture as the courts determined whether differences in the quality of education offered to children within the district could be the target of an equal protection claim. "Black" or "Mexican" meant poor and culturally deprived; the inverse was implicitly true for "white." Lawyers for the children argued against Kishkunas's claim that cultural differences explained the lower academic achievement rates of black and Mexican American children. Bilingual-bicultural education experts, including José Cárdenas, testified that that such children were indeed different from their middle-class white counterparts but that this difference was neither bad nor good.[46] They made this argument as part of their case that curricular reform and bilingual-bicultural education were necessary components of school reform in Denver, but the court's eventual ruling rested on the premise that such litigation could only accomplish so much. Those kinds of reforms—the ones aimed at the "culturally deprived" children in schools—were not a problem for the Fourteenth Amendment. They were for the legislatures to decide.

A desegregation lawsuit filed against the school district of Austin, Texas, was an example of how entangled ideas about race, segregation, and achievement could be in litigation. In the case, the school board argued that the special problems posed by Mexican American children in the district merited their segregation within city schools. When faced with a desegregation suit brought by the Department of Justice, the school board's lawyer argued that many Mexican American students were the children of migrant workers, who pulled them out of school in the spring to follow seasonal work. The segregation of Mexican American students therefore allowed teachers to provide "extra attention and help" to surmount the "formidable" task of teaching these children, who were saddled with "retarded educational development." The court commended the district on its use of progressive educational reforms but stated that they could not be substituted for a desegregation plan, clarifying, "Lest we be misunderstood, we congratulate the [district] for some of its progressive educational techniques including the use of inter-cultural experiences, team-teaching, and instruction in the cultural background and heritages of racial and ethnic groups." Such accommodations were optional, and the district was free to pursue them on its own. The court added, "Further, the AISD [Austin Independent School District] may provide for bi-lingual instruction, accelerated education, and remedial education for retarded students."[47]

At the same time, the court drew a firm line between the district's programs that targeted the needs of the children of migrant workers and those that targeted racial segregation in the schools, concluding that they "may not be used as a substitute for adequate desegregation."[48] According to this logic, desegregation and bilingual instruction were not connected by any common concerns emanating from the Fourteenth Amendment under equal protection.

By marking such inequalities as outside the reach of the Fourteenth Amendment, the courts placed the issue before legislatures and local school boards. This left basic issues of educational inequity in the hands of political coalitions, which were increasingly unwilling to cooperate on civil rights issues during the 1970s. At the same time, some issues managed to capture bipartisan support during these years. Foremost among them was bilingual education. The concept of bilingual-bicultural education, championed by Chicano activists in Denver and elsewhere, was in part a response to a history of educational practices that favored assimilation. One of these assimilative tools was language. Historically, American schools had not been English-only institutions, but many were by the 1960s. By adopting English-only policies in the early twentieth century, American states and school districts made decisions shaped by the politics of nativism, labor upheavals, and restrictive immigration policy.[49] Decades later, the political winds shifted, providing opportunities to undo the legacy of English-only education. In California, for example, Republican governor Ronald Reagan signed a bill in 1967 repealing the state's English-only law in order to court Latino voters who might be disaffected by school desegregation lawsuits and policies.[50]

New laws providing for bilingual education were partial victories for those who sought more dramatic civil rights reforms in the schools through the implementation of bilingual-bicultural programs. These stood apart from bilingual-only programs, which were meant to be temporary measures that funneled children into English-only classrooms once they achieved fluency. Bilingual-bicultural education advocates, in contrast, staked their claim on the central importance of cultural pluralism in the classroom as the way to create equal educational opportunities for all children. Like black activists who demanded that schools incorporate black history and culture into their curricula, supporters of bilingual-bicultural education wanted to fundamentally restructure how and what children were taught in schools. And just as importantly, bilingual-bicultural programs were not targeted toward students who primarily spoke Spanish. After all, Mexican Americans in the United States had a long history of migration across the southwestern border.[51] Among persons of Mexican descent in the United States in the 1960s, 85 percent had been born in the United States, even though they were often painted as recent immigrants who were unassimilated.[52] Chicano efforts to institute bilingual-bicultural programs focused on teaching in both Spanish and English to cultivate dual fluency as a means of preserving elements of Mexican American identity, culture, and history in the classroom.

The major successes in the 1970s came in the way of bilingual education that focused on assimilation and the teaching of English language skills. Bilingual education was not a novel idea in the 1960s. Between the 1840s and 1880s, bilingual education flourished in American communities with large populations of immigrants.[53] In the first decade of the twentieth century, the nation's school-aged population included a polyglot mix of foreign nationals.[54] But many of the same forces that pried shut the levers of immigration from nations outside the Americas likewise discouraged bilingual education practices, necessitating its rediscovery in the last third of the twentieth century.[55]

In Congress and the Supreme Court, new developments created opportunities for children who spoke languages other than English at home. The Bilingual Education Act of 1968, which eventually became Title VII of the 1965 Elementary and Secondary Education Act, offered tens of millions of dollars in federal funding to provide bilingual education for low-income children.[56] The law was made possible by the confluence of increased attention to "disadvantaged" students by academics and non-profit organizations, grassroots Chicano activism, and a growing federal role in education policy.[57] Questions about the purpose of education undergirded discussions about how schools should teach children with limited or no English skills. Should programs be tailored to teaching English to these children so that they could quickly be sent into classrooms with native speakers, thus emphasizing assimilation and potentially perpetuating cultural isolation? Or was it better to teach all subjects in languages other than English and make the student's entire educational experience bilingual?[58] Furthermore, should bilingual programs be available to students who already had English-language fluency?

Senator Ralph Yarborough of Texas introduced the federal bilingual education law in 1967, and he framed the law as a logical extension of the War on Poverty.[59] Bilingual education would boost academic achievement among Mexican Americans in the Southwest and Puerto Ricans in the Northeast, thereby preparing more young people for college and the workforce. In sum, bilingual education became a form of compensatory education aimed at Spanish-speaking and other language minority students.[60] The 1968 Bilingual Education Act, through its association with the War on Poverty, implied that speaking another language was a disability by grouping it together with other factors that created disadvantage for students within the nation's schools. The ultimate goal was to prepare these children to assimilate into classes where English was spoken exclusively. This differed foundationally from the vision of Chicano Movement activists who envisioned bilingual-bicultural education as a way to create equitable educational opportunities for Mexican American children by linking students to a shared history and culture.

The assimilationist vision of bilingual education found more support from federal actors once Richard Nixon took office. Less than a month after Nixon's inauguration, Secretary of Health, Education, and Welfare Robert Finch promised that the Nixon administration would back an expansion of federal funds for bilingual education.[61] On May 25, 1970, Office of Civil Rights Director J. Stanley Pottinger sent a memorandum to school districts with student populations that were more than 5 percent foreign-born. The memo noted that students who were not American citizens had the right to equal educational opportunity, and that right included the teaching of English when necessary. Furthermore, the memo warned districts away from funneling non-English-speaking students into lower "tracks," classifying them as mentally retarded based on English language skills alone, or denying them access to college preparatory classes.[62] These were all issues that black and Chicano activists pointed to as perpetuating racial inequality in public schools, but it was students without English language fluency who gained the favor of the federal government under Nixon administration policies.

New laws funding and sanctioning the use of bilingual education as a compensatory program became critical to a number of lawsuits that appeared in federal courts in the early 1970s and that, like *Keyes*, argued that bilingual and bilingual-bicultural education were required to provide equal educational opportunity under the Fourteenth Amendment. One such case came out of Portales, New Mexico, and it is often cited as a major victory for supporters of bilingual-bicultural education. Portales, a small town located about a dozen miles west of the Texas border and closer to Amarillo than Albuquerque, had a student population that included a minority of Mexican American students who primarily spoke Spanish. With the aid of the Chicano Youth Association, students filed a class-action lawsuit against the public schools, alleging a deprivation of equal educational opportunity. Until 1970, there had been no Spanish-surnamed teachers in the schools. Educational outcomes for Mexican American children were abysmal, and drop-out rates were higher than for white students. The district provided no bilingual education services for Spanish-speaking pupils, and testing showed that many of the Mexican American students lacked the English language fluency needed to thrive in an English-only classroom.[63] Despite the funds made available by state and federal legislation, the Portales school district did not apply for money to implement a bilingual education program for its students.[64] The reluctance of the district to pursue opportunities to provide bilingual education meant that Mexican American students would be denied the programs available to public school students elsewhere in the state. Access to equal education therefore hinged upon the willingness of a majority of school board members to pursue funding and implement bilingual programs.

At trial, the plaintiffs brought in experts who testified that, without a bilingual-bicultural education program, the Portales schools could not provide equal educational opportunities to all of its students. It was not enough for federal law to provide funds when they relied on the voluntary adoption of programs by school officials. In places where those officials were hostile to the implementation of a bilingual program, the district's students could be deprived of the same educational opportunities given to their peers who came from English-speaking homes. Citing the district rulings in *Keyes*, the judge agreed that "it would be a deprivation of equal protection for a school district to effectuate a curriculum which is not tailored to the educational needs of minority students." The judge ordered the district to develop plans for a remedial program that would provide bilingual-bicultural education to the district's Mexican American students.[65]

Importantly, the judge issued the ruling in *Serna v. Portales* in 1972, when the Supreme Court had not yet weighed in on *Keyes*. This was also before the Tenth Circuit threw out the Cárdenas Plan in 1974, which would have mandated bilingual-bicultural programs in Denver schools. The school district appealed the ruling, and in *Serna* the Tenth Circuit upheld the bilingual-bicultural plan—but not because of Fourteenth Amendment concerns. The court declined to address the equal protection issue. New Mexico's compulsory education law made it mandatory for children to attend school, but the state law compelling schoolteachers to instruct students in English ensured those students would not receive an "adequate education" as required by the 1964 Civil Rights Act.[66] And so the Tenth Circuit affirmed the district court finding on the basis of statute—not on a deprivation of the right to equal educational opportunity. Even though the result was a court order instituting a bilingual-bicultural program, *Serna v. Portales* was a narrow decision that rested on federal law rather than the constitutional rights of public school students.

A Supreme Court case out of California shaped the Tenth Circuit's decision to avoid the Fourteenth Amendment question in *Serna*. Rather than offer its own interpretation of whether the right to equal educational opportunity included access to bilingual-bicultural programs, the Tenth Circuit anticipated that the Supreme Court would rule definitively on the question in an upcoming term. The case before the Supreme Court, *Lau v. Nichols*, involved parents and guardians of thirteen Chinese American students who sued the San Francisco schools in March 1970, arguing that their children had been deprived of the equal protection of the laws. The schools taught in English, a language these students and thousands of others in the district did not speak fluently. Roughly 2,000 Chinese American students sat in their classrooms every day without understanding what their teachers said. The school board blamed the recent overhaul of the U.S. immigration system through the 1965 Hart-Celler Act for the presence of Chinese-speaking students, but lawyers for the students pointed out that five of the named plaintiffs had been born in the United States and were part of San Francisco's long-established Chinese American community.[67]

The position of Chinese American students in the city's public schools was the result of a longer history of anti-Chinese discrimination in California that dated back to the Gold Rush. With the arrival of tens of thousands of Chinese immigrants in the 1850s and 1860s, the California state legislature began legislating discrimination through the school laws. In 1872, it deleted from the state school law the requirement of localities to educate Chinese students and passed a law that required English-only instruction in public schools.[68] In 1871, the San Francisco school board closed its only Chinese school.[69] When the state legislature repealed the English-only law in 1967, it provided the option of bilingual instruction but did not require schools to provide services for students with limited English language skills.[70]

The federal district court and the Ninth Circuit were both unfriendly to the arguments made on behalf of Chinese American students. They disagreed that the students could seek a remedy through an equal protection claim, which they banished to the realm of de jure segregation. In the words of the Ninth Circuit's decision, the students' plight was, rather, due to "deficiencies created by appellants themselves in failing to learn the English language."[71] The burden of learning the English language therefore fell on the shoulders of schoolchildren. The court also delineated the demands of the Fourteenth Amendment from concerns about progressive educational theory and practice. In language that presaged the Tenth Circuit's decision in *Keyes* to throw out the Cárdenas Plan, the Ninth Circuit declared in *Lau*, "However commendable and socially desirable it might be for the School District to provide special remedial educational programs to disadvantaged students in those areas . . . we find no constitutional or statutory basis upon which we can mandate these things be done."[72] The plaintiffs, undeterred by their loss, appealed the case to the Supreme Court.

In separate amicus briefs to the Supreme Court, the Puerto Rican Legal Defense Fund and a joint brief of MALDEF, the League of United Latin American Citizens, the Association of Mexican American Educators, and the American GI Forum made the case that, by refusing to provide students with bilingual education, schools deprived those students of their right to equal educational opportunity under the Fourteenth Amendment. The MALDEF brief specifically referenced the "damage" argument presented by the NAACP Legal Defense Fund in *Brown v. Board of Education*, stating that "Spanish-speaking children are subjected to a dual effect: first, the school's failure to meet their language needs, and second, the psychological damage brought about as a result of the school's failure to meet their language needs." Students' self-esteem suffered, and Mexican American children perceived their contributions to the classroom as "valueless."[73]

In *Lau v. Nichols*, the U.S. Supreme Court sided with the Chinese American plaintiffs. In its ruling, the Supreme Court created a mixed legacy for students in American public schools. On the one hand, it resulted in the declaration that it was not enough for schools to treat all students the same. The Supreme Court stated in its decision that "there is no equality of treatment merely by providing students with the same facilities, textbooks, teachers, and curriculum; for students who do not understand English are effectively foreclosed from any meaningful education."[74] At the same time, the Supreme Court declined to use the equal protection clause of the Fourteenth Amendment as a firm basis for its decision. It relied instead upon the 1964 Civil Rights Act, which forbade discrimination on the basis of race, color, or national origin, and the May 25, 1970, memo from the Department of Health, Education, and Welfare on bilingual education.[75] Other courts quickly dismissed arguments that *Lau* required bilingual-bicultural education under the Fourteenth Amendment's equal protection clause, which is what many advocates sought. This meant that the case provided two important precedents. First, *Lau* relied upon statute rather than a constitutional right, and second, it focused solely on cases where a student's English language skills were so limited that they prohibited him or her from participating in everyday school activities.

A similar case came from Arizona underscored the important distinction between bilingual-bicultural education as a constitutional right or as a legislatively created entitlement. The parents of Mexican American and Yacqui Indian children sued the Tempe school district, arguing that the schools could not meet their children's needs. Under the right to equality of educational opportunity, they asked for affirmative action hiring of Mexican American and American Indian teachers, bilingual instruction, and the integration of their history and culture into the schools' curricula. But in rejecting the plaintiffs' claims, the Ninth Circuit declared that "the Constitution neither requires nor prohibits the bilingual and bicultural education sought by the appellants. Such matters are for the people to decide."[76] This 1978 ruling, *Guadalupe Organization, Inc. v. Tempe Elementary School District No. 1*, was later cited to dismiss the claims of those who sued on behalf of Blackfeet children who attended school on a reservation in northwest Montana.[77] Children in public schools did not have the right to bilingual-bicultural education. They only had claims to bilingual education services through federal and state legislation and in circumstances in which English language deficiency could be demonstrated. The MALDEF attorney Carlos Alcala called this turn by the courts "the last ditch defense [of bilingual education] rather than the glitter of the front."[78] Alcala viewed equal protection litigation as a promising line of argumentation that could be used to expand the rights of Latino students and increase the quality of education they received. But in *Keyes* and *Lau*, the federal courts foreclosed this use of the Fourteenth Amendment.

The Right to Education

The equal protection argument, which proved to be a difficult path for those seeking bilingual-bicultural education, was not the only means by which students could claim Fourteenth Amendment rights at school. In the early 1970s, a lawsuit out of Texas forced the courts to confront another Fourteenth Amendment strategy that relied on the concept of fundamental rights. Rather than relying on the equal protection clause, fundamental rights litigation rested upon the Fourteenth Amendment's declaration that states cannot "deprive any person of life, liberty, or property, without due process of law." Within the liberty protections of the due process clause lay implicit guarantees of certain fundamental rights—including, perhaps, the right to education.

In earlier cases, the Supreme Court drew upon the due process clause to identify such implied rights. For example, in *Meyer v. Nebraska*, a 1923 decision, the Supreme Court declared that the due process clause

> denotes not merely freedom from bodily restraint, but also the right of the individual to contract, to engage in any of the common occupations of life, to acquire useful knowledge . . . and generally to enjoy those privileges long recognized at common law as essential to the orderly pursuit of happiness by free men.[79]

Later landmark cases, including *Griswold v. Connecticut* and *Loving v. Virginia*, relied upon the due process clause to establish, respectively, the right of married persons to privacy over matters involving birth control and the right of interracial couples to marry.[80] By the early 1970s, the Supreme Court acknowledged several such fundamental rights, although in no place did it enumerate them all.[81] The Supreme Court's language in other cases—including *Brown v. Board of Education* and *Tinker v. Des Moines*—indicated that education was certainly considered a crucially important government interest and, therefore, perhaps a right that students could claim. In *Brown*, for example, the unanimous ruling declared that "education is perhaps the most important function of state and local governments," making it sound like public schooling might be vital to the nation's very survival.[82]

Following this line of reasoning, in the late 1960s, new litigation made the case that education itself is one of the fundamental rights protected by the Fourteenth Amendment's due process clause. The lawsuit that forced the Supreme Court to address the question was the 1973 case *San Antonio v. Rodriguez*. The case emerged out of a series of protests by Mexican American students and parents in the Edgewood school district of San Antonio, Texas, which had a student population that was both poorer and less white than nearby districts. The city of San Antonio encompassed seven school districts that contained residential areas that varied in terms of wealth and racial composition. Significant disparities in school funding existed between the districts, due largely to the difference in property values. Edgewood, which included part of the central city, was by far the poorest.[83] In May 1968, students staged a walkout and boycott of schools in the district.[84] Weeks earlier, students had submitted to the superintendent a formal letter outlining their grievances, which went unaddressed. The walkout was the culmination of brewing discontent among students, who protested the school's curriculum, the use of teachers, and the poor physical conditions of school facilities. Among the demands was the unusual request that authorities conduct an audit of the district's finances: Parents and students charged that the facilities were so poorly maintained that the funds must have been misspent.[85] On May 16, 300 students marched from Edgewood High School to the Central Administration Building, singing and bearing protest signs demanding "Better Education Now."[86] Willie Velasquez, an organizer for the Chicano nationalist political party La Raza Unida, gave a speech in which he emphasized the importance of educational quality. "With the education you get at Edgewood, most of you are going either to Vietnam or wind up as a ditchdigger," Velasquez told the energized crowd.[87] A school boycott followed, and roughly 80 percent of the school's student population participated, as did a few teachers. Janie Hilgen, a twenty-one-year-old teacher, walked out in solidarity with her students. Given the rapid approach of finals week, Hilgen taught her students on the curb in the midst of the boycott so they would not fall behind.[88] In response, school district officials suspended two students and two teachers who supported the boycott.

In the summer of 1968, parents of students in Edgewood filed a lawsuit against the district with the assistance of a local lawyer, Arthur Gochman.[89] In January 1969, a three-judge panel heard the case, which challenged the constitutionality of a Texas state law.[90] *San Antonio v. Rodriguez* is generally considered to be a case that centers on socioeconomic class despite its deep roots in the racial politics of the late 1960s and early 1970s.[91] The case asserted a violation of equal protection of the laws on behalf of Mexican American parents and their children in the San Antonio public schools, which received only a fraction of the funding that nearby white districts reaped from property taxes.[92] State law capped property tax rates, meaning that low-income districts would never be able to catch up to wealthier districts by electing to raise tax rates for their own communities. The students' lawyers argued that the state's funding scheme, coupled with its laws, discriminated against poor minority children, thereby violating the Fourteenth Amendment's equal protection clause. The lawyers likened discrimination on the basis of socioeconomic class with discrimination on the basis of race. In its decision, the district court sided with the children and their parents on the basis that education was a "fundamental right" and that wealth was a "suspect class"—both which would elevate the test used by the courts to strict scrutiny. In such a circumstance, the state must establish that the law or laws involved were based upon a compelling state interest, and in *Rodriguez*, the district court found that the state of Texas's lawyers had made no such case.[93] The Texas school financing scheme was therefore unconstitutional under the Fourteenth Amendment.

Once the Supreme Court agreed to hear the appeal of *Rodriguez*, oral arguments in the case took place on October 12, 1972—the same day the Court heard arguments in *Keyes v. School Dist. No. 1*. With its reliance on an equal protection theory that challenged discrimination on the basis of wealth, *Rodriguez* found a formidable opponent in Justice Lewis Powell, who associated such claims with communism.[94] Powell wrote the majority opinion in *Rodriguez*, in which he was joined by four other justices. Wealth was not a suspect class, and education was not a fundamental right. Neither argument could be used to invoke the authority of the Fourteenth Amendment. The opinion described the poor as "a large, diverse, and amorphous class" that could not be adequately analogized to any other recognized protected class such as groups identified by their race or national origin. As to the fundamental rights question, the majority recognized the powerful language used in other decisions to describe public education's relationship to democratic governance but ruled that "the importance of a service performed by the State does not determine whether it must be regarded as fundamental for purposes of examination under the Equal Protection Clause."[95] Education could be important to democracy—vital, even—but that did not give it the status of a fundamental right under the Constitution.

The majority's opinion did not stop there. Powell's opinion virtually extinguished any hope that fundamental rights reasoning could be used to make claims for educational equity. The Court declared, "Education, of course, is not among the rights afforded explicit protection under our Federal Constitution. Nor do we find any basis for saying it is implicitly so protected." In response to assertions by the plaintiffs' lawyers that education was necessary to the exercise of other fundamental rights like free expression and voting, the court declared that the government could not be assumed to "guarantee to the citizenry the most effective speech or the most informed electoral choice." The majority opinion left those hoping to leverage the Fourteenth Amendment to ensure equality of education with diminished expectations, as the decision conceded that, in the future, it might be possible to demonstrate that "some identifiable quantum" of education was necessary to the exercise of other protected rights. But the plaintiffs had not established the Texas case to be such an instance.[96] Even if the quality of education that students in Edgewood received was inferior, that did not make the state's funding scheme unconstitutional.

After the Supreme Court handed parents and students in Edgewood a defeat, local activists planned a new protest to demand better funding for their schools. This time, a motorcade took protesters to the grounds of the state capitol at Austin, where intrepid participants strung a Mexican flag up the flagpole.[97] From their rally outside the building, young people eventually entered the capitol and flooded the rotunda while chanting "Equality now!" and demanding a meeting with the governor. Governor Dolph Briscoe eventually met with a small group.[98] Pressure from students and parents forced the Texas state legislature to consider alternatives to its school financing scheme.

Amid continued protest, the fiscal crisis in the Edgewood district was compounded by the withdrawal of federal funds connected to Great Society programs, including Model Cities. In 1975, the state offered some relief, but this could not fix the long-term underfunding of Edgewood schools.[99] More sweeping changes to Texas's system of school finance would have to wait. While *Rodriguez* was in the process of being appealed to the Supreme Court, a similar case challenging the state school financing scheme was filed in California. This case, *Serrano v. Priest*, was filed in state court rather than federal court, although it relied upon the same Fourteenth Amendment arguments presented in *Rodriguez*—but with the crucial caveat that it relied upon the education clauses of the California state constitution in addition to the Fourteenth Amendment. The case was filed on behalf of the parents of Mexican American students in Los Angeles in 1968.[100] In 1971, the California supreme court sided with the plaintiffs in finding that wealth was a suspect class and that education was a fundamental right.[101] The use of the state constitution in *Serrano* came to be a model that litigants in other states followed in the decades after the Supreme Court issued its ruling in *Rodriguez*.

In 1984, MALDEF filed a new lawsuit challenging Texas's funding scheme, this time in state court. Using the same line of argumentation as *Rodriguez*, the new case, *Edgewood Independent School District v. Kirby*, relied on the protection of state law. The Texas state constitution mandated that the legislature "establish and make suitable provision for the support and maintenance of an efficient system of public free schools." The "gross inequalities" evident in Texas's school funding scheme violated the spirit of the state constitution, the Texas supreme court eventually ruled in 1989.[102] The *Kirby* case was modeled after *Serrano*, and it was part of a new generation of school finance litigation that took place in the wake of *Rodriguez*. After witnessing the victory in *Serrano* and the loss in *Rodriguez*, litigants brought suit in other state courts, including New Jersey, Connecticut, and West Virginia.[103] Between 1975 and 1992, there were state supreme court rulings using the same logic as *Kirby* in twenty-seven states. Of these cases, twelve ended in rulings that declared present school finance schemes to be unconstitutional.[104] In more than half of school finance equalization cases, plaintiffs prevailed in making the case that state constitutions and state law prohibited such inequities in public school finance.[105] State courts thus became the new front for organizations like MALDEF in the 1980s and after owing to the limitations placed on Fourteenth Amendment jurisprudence by the Burger Court during the 1970s.

These state supreme court decisions demonstrated the potential of state-centered strategies. At the same time, they also created a patchwork of legal protections for students in relation to their right to an education. In other measures of equity, students in Edgewood schools continued to suffer the effects of unequal education after *Rodriguez*, not just in regard to education funding but in other measures of educational quality as well. The Children's Defense Fund, for example, singled out the Edgewood school district for the high number of suspensions of Spanish-surnamed students. Out of the districts surveyed, Edgewood ranked twentieth because of the high number of students suspended, just behind much larger districts like Austin, Fresno, Sacramento, and Corpus Christi.[106]

The ruling in *Rodriguez* also opened a door that allowed legislatures to use access to education as a political tool. If the Constitution did not protect education as a right, perhaps the state could exclude groups that the majority did not wish to educate with taxpayer funds. A few years after *Rodriguez*, the Texas legislature tested the state's ability to further an anti-immigration political agenda through education policy. Efforts to punish those who crossed the border without proper papers culminated in the passage of a 1975 state law that required school districts to provide a free education only to children who were citizens or legally admitted aliens.[107] The law did not explicitly ban undocumented children from the schools. Instead, it allowed districts to refuse to educate undocumented children or to require that they pay tuition. Some districts chose to exclude undocumented children from the schools entirely, while a handful of others chose to charge tuition.[108] Many districts avoided implementing the law and continued providing a free education to all children, perhaps fearing the trouble of deciphering the immigration status of parents. Furthermore, the laws positioned school administrators as arbiters of who was or was not legally present, making them quasi-immigration officials. At first, officials in the Tyler Independent School District declined to enforce the law. In 1977, the district relented and began charging $1,000 tuition, a sum so large that no family would be able to pay it on their own.[109]

Using exclusion from public schools to punish groups was not a new tactic; it was adopted by some Southern states and localities after *Brown v. Board of Education*. Officials in Little Rock, Arkansas, took a similar stance when they closed Central High School the year after the Little Rock Nine desegregated it. The superintendent and school board claimed such measures were necessary because desegregation caused disruption and conflict in the school, but the Supreme Court declared that their action could not be justified because it undermined an desegregation order.[110] The Louisiana state legislature, in an attempt at legal innovation, allowed school districts under desegregation orders to automatically convert into private schools that would continue to benefit from state funding.[111] In Prince Edward County, Virginia, the local schools closed rather than comply with the court's order to desegregate, and the public schools remained shuttered for five years. The Prince Edward School Foundation provided private education for white students, maintaining racial segregation and flouting the Supreme Court's ruling while denying a state-supported education to black children entirely. In a 7-2 ruling in *Griffin v. School Board*, the Supreme Court ordered Prince Edward County to resume offering public education for all students, but it did not do so on the basis of an individual right to education guaranteed by the Constitution. Instead, the ruling focused on the fact that the school closures were clearly linked to resistance to desegregation. As the ruling stated, "Whatever nonracial grounds might support a State's allowing a county to abandon public schools, the object must be a constitutional one, and grounds of race and opposition to desegregation do not qualify as constitutional."[112] The ruling in *Griffin* left open the possibility that states and local governments might choose to stop providing public education for other, perfectly constitutional reasons. *Rodriguez* appeared to confirm this idea.

Once the Tyler, Texas, schools began charging tuition, MALDEF sued on behalf of undocumented students in the district. They first faced the local district court, which sided with the plaintiffs. The judge ruled that the law violated the equal protection clause because it did not even pass the rational basis test—the least stringent of all levels of judicial review. Furthermore, the Texas legislature unconstitutionally encroached upon the federal government's control over immigration policy.[113] The Fifth Circuit affirmed the district court opinion, and in May 1981 the Supreme Court agreed to take the case.

In 1982, the justices handed down their decision in *Plyler v. Doe*. By a one-vote majority, the Supreme Court ruled that the state of Texas's attempt to charge undocumented children tuition for attending public schools violated the Fourteenth Amendment's equal protection clause. In the decision, Justice William Brennan's majority opinion wrestled with the contradictions of previous lawsuits involving education and equality, including *Rodriguez*.[114] Even if education was not a fundamental right protected by the Constitution, the justices were clearly uncomfortable with the idea that a state could categorically deny education to any group it wished. But what, then, was the basis for the finding of a constitutional violation? The opinion noted two ways that the law went awry of the spirit of equal protection. The first criticized the state's rationale for the law. Because the statute targeted children who had no control over their own immigration status, "It is thus difficult to conceive of a rational justification for penalizing these children for their presence in the United States." The majority also noted that education plays a crucial role in preparing young people to participate and compete in the global labor market, and while undocumented workers lived as an "underclass," their immigration status was not immutable. Congress might later choose to grant legal status to some or all of the persons affected by the law. Even if this did not happen, it was difficult to conceive of a state interest that could pass muster with the equal protection clause when class-based legislation took such a serious toll on an individual's future prospects. "Illiteracy is an enduring disability," the decision declared. "The inability to read and write will handicap the individual deprived of a basic education each and every day of his life."[115]

The majority opinion in *Plyler* downplayed the grandiose language with which previous decisions described the importance of public education to government interests. Although it quoted from decisions, including *Brown v. Board of Education*, that noted the crucial part education played in nurturing and supporting democracy, the majority repeatedly emphasized how education created good workers and was essential to economic growth. An uneducated underclass of undocumented adults would burden the state in other ways, undermining the economic argument for excluding children from school. In other words, education supported capitalism, which was an important enough goal to justify striking down state laws that excluded particular groups from the schools. In this way, *Plyler* represented how, in the 1970s, the Supreme Court pivoted from championing the necessity of public education to the nation's vitality to arguing that education's importance lay in creating "economic productivity." The anemic language of *Plyler* was, in a sense, the culmination of legal arguments over the application of the Fourteenth Amendment's equal protection clause to public education during the 1970s.

Disability, Education, and the Constitution's Demands

In August 1967, Victor Rivera was a relatively unremarkable teenaged camp counselor in California's Sequoia National Forest.[116] A sophomore at Santa Ana Valley High School, Rivera consistently earned high marks in his classes. But his life changed dramatically after he dove into a shallow creek and fractured his neck, an accident that partially paralyzed him. Rivera eventually recovered some use of his arms, but he used a wheelchair for the rest of his life.[117]

Rivera subsequently fought two battles: the first to recover physically so that he could leave the hospital, and the second to return to school once he was released. With his mother divorced and money tight at home, the Santa Ana school district's refusal to assist Rivera with transportation to and from school meant that he was unable to return to Santa Ana Valley High School. Instead, district officials referred him to Carl Harvey School, which operated to serve only those students with disabilities. Rivera balked at this offer; he had plans to graduate high school, earn a university degree, and become an attorney, but Carl Harvey did not offer a college preparatory curriculum. No one contested this point: The assistant superintendent even admitted that "the education is not the same."[118] But the Santa Ana school district refused to accommodate Rivera, citing the costs of his "special case."

Victor Rivera's situation was unusual in that he suffered extensive injuries after a tragic accident, but his exclusion from his former school resembled the experience of many other young people in the United States. School districts across the nation legally excluded students with "disabilities," a term that encompassed a wide variety of conditions. In the early 1970s, in every state except Michigan and Iowa, an amendment to the compulsory attendance laws permitted schools to exclude children with "physical, mental, or emotional disabilities."[119] Rivera's former school was not obligated to continue educating him, and the only option available would not provide him with the credentials he needed to apply to college.

Rivera's struggle caught the attention of the *Los Angeles Times*, which published a series of reports about his fight with the school district. His story—that of a bright young man with a promising future who fought back against bureaucratic intransigence—made his condition relatable, if tragic. And it had something of a happy ending. Insisting on earning his diploma at his old high school, he first relied on rides from volunteers. But the unreliable nature of voluntary assistance forced him to seek a long-term solution. He later told the *Times*, "I almost gave up because I felt physically discriminated against" by the school. School board officials eventually relented and offered to pay for taxi fare to bring Rivera to and from school. Eventually, students at Santa Ana Valley High School staged a benefit concert to raise money for a van with a wheelchair ramp. Funds collected by the students and contributions from readers who followed Rivera's plight in the *Times* were enough to secure the vehicle. Hundreds of children and teenagers sent in their weekly allowances in one- or two-dollar amounts.[120]

In May 1969, television cameras and newspaper photographers captured Rivera's "black, brown, and white classmates, all raising their hands in a victory salute and yelling," as the young man boarded the van for the first time.[121] A driver's education teacher donated time to teach Rivera's mother, Josefine Almanza, to drive.[122] In 1970, Rivera earned his high school diploma. He enrolled in Santa Ana College and later transferred to the University of California, Irvine. Rivera took pre-law courses and became an advocate for the rights of students with disabilities as a member of the Disabled and Incapacitated Students of Santa Ana College. But he never became an attorney. In 1977, Rivera died at age twenty-five after undergoing surgery.[123] A month after his funeral, Almanza wrote a letter to the *Los Angeles Times*, thanking readers for all they had done on her son's behalf.[124]

It took a heroic effort on the part of his family and classmates to get Victor Rivera his high school diploma. Undoubtedly his tragic story and his relentless insistence on returning to school made him a media sensation. But he was only one of the many young people who faced exclusion from school because of a disability. The Children's Defense Fund sought to provide a voice for those children and teenagers. In 1974, the newly founded Children's Defense Fund published its first report, *Children out of School in America*. The report was an exhaustive study of school attendance in the United States, and it concluded that roughly 2,000,000 young people between the ages of seven and seventeen did not attend school in any capacity. On average, nearly 5 percent of school-aged children in each state were out of school. The highest percentage was Mississippi, which did not have a compulsory attendance law. In that state, nearly 8 percent of children did not attend school.[125]

By the early 1970s, the federal government estimated that more than 1,000,000 American children were legally excluded from school because they were labeled as being disabled in one sense or another.[126] Even as students in public schools gained other constitutional protections, many continued to be deprived of a basic education by the state. Developments in constitutional law had done little to change that fact by the early 1970s. Indeed, the same year that the Children's Defense Fund published *Children out of School in America*, the Supreme Court issued its ruling in *San Antonio v. Rodriguez* and declared that education was not a fundamental right.

Parents of disabled children in Pennsylvania decided to take the state's schools to federal court, claiming that the exemption for "mentally retarded" children from compulsory education laws was a violation of the Fourteenth Amendment's equal protection and due process clauses. The state's rationale that such children would not benefit from an education was false and led to their arbitrary exclusion, the lawsuit claimed.[127] Furthermore, the lawyers for the Pennsylvania Association for Retarded Children (PARC) made the case that education was a fundamental right under the Constitution—the same argument that the U.S. Supreme Court would dismiss the following year in *Rodriguez*.[128] While the case ended with a settlement in which the state agreed to provide free public education for all Pennsylvania children regardless of disability, the lawsuit boosted efforts to use the courts to end the exclusion of children from public schools on the basis of disability.

Another key case in disability law came from Washington, DC, where more than 10,000 school-aged "exceptional" children were excluded from the public schools. The "exceptional" label was applied as a catch-all term for conditions that included children with physical handicaps in addition to those labeled "mentally retarded," "emotionally disturbed," and "hyperactive." Among the seven plaintiffs, all of whom were African American, were a fourth grader who was excluded for being a "behavior problem," an epileptic teenager, and a thirteen-year-old who became partially paralyzed during a bout with a childhood illness. Not only had school officials excluded these children from school, but there were also no hearings or other procedures associated with the process.[129]

Parents first attempted to challenge the exclusion of their children as part of *Hobson v. Hansen*, the 1967 lawsuit that challenged student tracking in Washington, DC, but Judge Skelly Wright excluded the issue from being litigated as part of the case even as he noted that it constituted a "human tragedy."[130] The parents and guardians of excluded children continued to lobby the school board to educate their children, but the district claimed it did not have the funds to provide special education services to such children. In response, they filed a new lawsuit, *Mills v. Board of Education of the District of Columbia*, in 1971. In the 1972 decision, Judge Joseph C. Waddy—who earlier in his career was a partner in the law firm of Charles Hamilton Houston, a lion in civil rights lawyering—declared that the doctrine of equal educational opportunity extended to all students, including those with disabilities. Waddy ordered the schools to "provide to each child of school age a free and suitable publicly-supported education regardless of the degree of the child's mental, physical or emotional disability or impairment."[131]

A flurry of high-profile stories publicizing the exclusion of children with disabilities from school created legislative opportunities at both the state and federal level. Between 1971 and 1972, supporters of education for children with disabilities flooded state legislatures with hundreds of new bills, many of which passed and became law.[132] Section 504 of the 1973 Rehabilitation Act prohibited those institutions receiving federal funds from discriminating against individuals on the basis of disability—a provision that mirrored the 1964 Civil Rights Act, which gave Congress the authority to restrict funds from those who discriminated on the basis of race.

In late November 1975 Congress approved a new act that sought to ensure equal educational opportunities for students with disabilities. Spurred by the work of organizations including the Association for Retarded Children and the Children's Defense Fund, the bill easily passed both houses of Congress with a nearly unanimous vote.[133] The new law, the Education for All Handicapped Children Act, would eventually become the Individuals with Disabilities Education Act (IDEA), and its passage proved to be a watershed moment in the history of education.[134] No longer would public education be a privilege accorded to only some students with disabilities; schools had to provide education to all children if it offered it to any of them. With its firm guarantee of educational access for children regardless of disability, the law used the power of Congress to guarantee a public education for children who had previously been marginalized, segregated, or excluded entirely from the public school system. The law closed the loophole that existed in state laws permitting the exemption of students with disabilities from compulsory education laws.

The Education for All Handicapped Children Act provided that all children should receive a "free, appropriate public education" despite physical or intellectual disabilities. It also gave children with disabilities and their parents and guardians procedural guarantees that would protect children's access to public schools and the opening to seek judicial relief from the exclusion of their children from school. The act provided federal funds to ensure that students with disabilities would be placed in the "least restrictive environment" appropriate to guarantee their access to public education. In a 1978 case, *Stuart v. Nappi*, the U.S. District Court for the state of Connecticut, citing the *Goss v. Lopez* decision, found that, under the Education for All Handicapped Children Act, a student with severe learning disabilities who had been expelled was still entitled to a free public education from the state.[135]

The idea that education was of preeminent importance, and that children should have access to it, took on a life of its own after the 1960s. As the legal scholar Michael Rebell explained, "Although *Brown* is known for outlawing racial segregation in the schools, the landmark decision also inspired a broad range of judicial involvements in promoting institutional reform that is now deeply rooted in both state and federal jurisprudence."[136] These efforts to establish a positive right to education were most successful at the state level, where discussions centered upon state laws or constitutional provisions that created compulsory education.

The creation of a system of truly universal education that no longer provided school districts with exemptions for educating children with disabilities generated new debates about whether these provisions required equity or adequacy. Was a state required to offer equal educational opportunities to all children across the state, or did it just have to meet a basic level of adequate education, with variation above that standard perfectly acceptable?

As in other cases, however, where parents and advocates attempted to use the federal courts to make substantive educational equity claims for members of minority groups, a Supreme Court decision from 1982 narrowly drew the standards that would dictate whether a state was in compliance with IDEA. At the center of this case was Amy Rowley, who in 1976 was set to begin first grade in Peekskill, New York. Rowley was hearing impaired, and the previous year she had flourished in a mainstreamed kindergarten class with the assistance of teachers trained in sign language interpretation and, eventually, a hearing aid. But the hearing aid could not distinguish among a large number of voices and was practically useless in the midst of classroom cacophony. For Rowley to understand her teacher, she needed to be spoken to individually and without background noise. The sign language interpreter bridged the gap between what her hearing aid captured and what was said in class.[137] Before she began first grade, the school did not include the use of a sign language interpreter in her Individualized Education Plan, claiming that Rowley would do just fine with the hearing aid. But her parents, who were also deaf, insisted that she still required the assistance of a sign language instructor in order to achieve her highest potential. With the exclusive use of a hearing aid, her parents feared that she would be left behind her peers.[138]

Clifford and Nancy Rowley were savvy advocates for their daughter. They knew that federal law granted Amy certain rights and protections, and they immediately appealed the school's decision to withhold a sign language interpreter to the Office of Civil Rights in the Department of Health, Education, and Welfare. Their plea relied on Section 504 of the 1973 Rehabilitation Act, which stipulated that "no qualified individual with a disability in the United States shall be excluded from, denied the benefits of, or be subjected to discrimination under" a program receiving federal funding. When the Department of Health, Education, and Welfare found the school district compliant, they appealed the district's decision all the way to the state commissioner of education on the basis of IDEA, arguing that Amy was not receiving an "appropriate" education under the law.[139] There, too, they lost. Finally, they sued in the local district court, which found in the Rowleys' favor in December 1979. The judge determined that without the assistance of an interpreter, Amy only understood roughly 60 percent of the words spoken to her in a classroom. With an interpreter, this would be nearly 100 percent. Amy's education could not be considered equal and did not satisfy IDEA if the accommodations provided by her school meant that she would remain behind her peers without an interpreter.[140]

In his ruling, District Court Judge Vincent Broderick parsed IDEA to find the proper interpretation of the law as it aligned with the equal protection clause. An "appropriate" education, he wrote, could "mean an 'adequate' education" in which a student received the minimum accommodations that allowed him or her to pass to the next grade level. It could also be interpreted to mean, the judge noted, "one which enables the handicapped child to achieve his or her full potential." Judge Broderick determined that the proper interpretation of the law lay somewhere between those two extremes and that students with disabilities should receive the "opportunity to achieve his full potential commensurate with the opportunity provided to other children."[141] In Amy's case, this meant that she should have the use of an interpreter.

The school district appealed the case to the Second Circuit Court of Appeals, which agreed with Judge Broderick's decision. But when the U.S. Supreme Court heard the case, *Hendrick Hudson Central School District v. Rowley*, a majority of the justices joined in an opinion written by William Rehnquist that overturned the lower-court decisions. Amy Rowley's situation did not entitle her to an interpreter. Once again, the court struggled to reconcile its history of emphasizing the importance of education while denying any substantial right under the Constitution. The Individuals with Disabilities Education Act called for states to ensure a "free appropriate public education," but the majority opinion seemed to indicate that this only had to be "meaningful," dodging the issue of what a "meaningful" education looked like.[142] The implication, however, was that the lower standard identified by Judge Broderick—that a student be given enough assistance that he or she could pass to the next grade—was the proper interpretation of IDEA.

Justice Byron White wrote a dissent in *Rowley*, in which Thurgood Marshall and William Brennan joined. The majority's refusal to interpret IDEA in a robust manner was at odds with the language of the law itself, White argued. The opinion pointed to the fact that the services provided by Amy Rowley's school almost certainly ensured she would fall short of her potential as a student. "Amy Rowley, without a sign-language interpreter, comprehends less than half of what is said in the classroom—less than half of what normal children comprehend," the dissent pointed out. "This is hardly an equal opportunity to learn, even if Amy makes passing grades."[143]

By the early 1970s, thanks in part to the work of the Children's Defense Fund in cataloguing the range of children who were systematically excluded from school, legislation to protect those with disabilities from discrimination became possible under the guise of equal educational opportunity. Getting access to education was an important gain for students with disabilities, but it was not the only issue that their advocates sought to challenge through the courts. Historically, ideas about intellectual or cognitive disability had been linked to scientific racism.[144] As with the labeling of immigrants from Southern and Eastern Europe as more likely to be "feebleminded" in the early twentieth century, conceptions about race and ethnicity continued to shape how children were classified within schools.[145] Until the 1950s, experts considered intelligence to be fixed at birth and the IQ test to be the proper measure. But new research published during the 1950s and early 1960s pointed to the importance of early childhood experiences in shaping intelligence, demonstrating its malleability.[146]

By the late 1960s, powerful critiques of the usefulness of intelligence testing itself emerged. In particular, critics challenged the ubiquitous use of the IQ test to sort children at school. Biases inherent in the testing materials disadvantaged children of color, leading them to score lower than their white peers. This, many argued, looked like thinly veiled institutional racism that legitimated the continuing segregation of children of color. Even after the gains made during the 1960s, advocates for minority children worried about the influence of racial and ethnic discrimination on the classification of children of color in American schools.

Such associations between race and intellectual ability were not easily disentangled in the twentieth century even as civil rights challenges increasingly targeted racial inequality in education. In some places in the United States, the category of "educable mentally retarded" was most often applied to racial minorities, who were then set apart in segregated classrooms where they were more likely to learn "life skills" than traditional academic subjects. The practice of forming separate classes for the educable mentally retarded in California traced back to 1921, when a state law encouraged testing and segregated placement for the "feebleminded" or "mentally defective" children.[147] In Los Angeles, for example, Edmund Bradley claimed that, as late as the early 1970s, the city's school district had identified 10,000 children as such, and that 90 percent of those students were in black or Mexican American neighborhood schools. He called this the "academic assassination" of the city's black and Mexican American children.[148] Statewide, roughly 85,000 children were separated from their peers in classes for the educable mentally retarded.[149]

The California Department of Education was no stranger to the accusation that state's schools were hasty to label children of color as "educable mentally retarded" and segregate them from their peers. In 1971, a sociologist at the University of California, Riverside, made headlines by declaring that her research showed that three-quarters of all students classified as "educable mentally retarded" had been wrongfully designated as such.[150] According to a new test she developed that examined the "adaptability" of young people through holistic examinations, Jane Mercer found that many black and Mexican American students passed her test despite scoring low on IQ tests. In a study of more than 250 students, she found that, when using a different test, the number of children classified as "educable mentally retarded" matched the ethnic and racial proportions of the schools.[151] But the state department of education mandated IQ testing even after officials were aware of the biased nature of the tests. In 1969, the state legislature passed a law demanding a study of the issue.

A lawsuit, initially filed in November 1971, became a class-action suit representing all black children classified as "educable mentally retarded" in California. It took eight years, but in 1979 the court ruled in favor of the plaintiffs. In the *Larry P. v. Riles* decision, the court threw out California's system of student classification, which the court ruled violated the equal protection clause. The court found it in violation of Title VI of the 1964 Civil Rights Act, the Rehabilitation Act of 1973, and the Education for All Handicapped Children Act because

> defendants have utilized standardized intelligence tests that are racially and culturally biased, have a discriminatory impact against black children, and have not been validated for the purpose of essentially permanent placements of black children into educationally dead-end, isolated, and stigmatizing classes for the so-called educable mentally retarded.

These actions, the court ruled, revealed "an unlawful segregative intent." Furthermore, the court labeled IQ testing as having "a history of racial prejudice, of Social Darwinism, and of the use of the scientific 'mystique' to legitimate such prejudices."[152]

The *Larry P.* case shows how important it is, in retrospect, to consider the education cases of the 1970s together. Concepts like "disability"—

and, as *Keyes* showed, "cultural deprivation"—had political meanings that shaped the ability of American schoolchildren to receive a quality education. Even after federal law enshrined the right of students with disabilities not to be excluded from school, without a corresponding right to a high-quality education comparable to the one the state provided to a student's peers, young people could easily find themselves at a great disadvantage. Particularly in the case of students with disabilities, classifications held a power that could easily perpetuate other forms of discrimination, including those based on race, gender, English language fluency, and immigration status.

* * *

In the 1970s, cases that relied upon the Fourteenth Amendment failed to expand the reach of constitutional arguments over equity in education beyond the issue of de jure segregation. The Burger Court limited interpretations of the reach of the equal protection clause even when lower courts were receptive to the idea that young people had a right to a particular standard of education. In the 1970s, advocates for students with limited English language skills and young people with disabilities made far greater strides through state legislatures, state courts, and Congress. This narrative appears to vindicate arguments for a restrained judiciary put forth most forcefully by political scientist Gerald Rosenberg, who made the case in his book *The Hollow Hope* that gains made in school desegregation cases came largely in spite of—rather than because of—Supreme Court cases. According to Rosenberg, the best social movement strategy is one that focuses on state and local governance and not on litigation.

And yet, it is worth examining the fate of the Fourteenth Amendment in education litigation during these years. As previous chapters show, advocates for young people often sought out litigation on constitutional grounds owing to their inability to find effective solutions through legislative means. Furthermore, gains at the state level created a patchwork of protections, meaning that crossing a state line translated to a student having more or fewer rights. Rights granted by legislatures are also more insecure than those protected by the Constitution. They are far more likely to be repealed by subsequent legislatures or through administrative action.

On the limits of legislation, the case of the Department of Education in the early 1980s is revealing. In August 1982, the Reagan administration announced its intention to loosen Department of Education guidelines on the instruction of students with disabilities. The changes would have given schools more leeway in implementing the law and would have allowed them to provide fewer accommodations to such students. The proposal was met with outrage from parents of students with disabilities, who remembered how, less than a decade earlier, many children like theirs were not educated at all. As one parent explained, "We can't trust our states and localities yet." The Reagan administration eventually relented, but only in the face of tremendous social pressure from angry parents and guardians across the nation.[153]

In his dissenting opinion in *San Antonio v. Rodriguez*, Justice Thurgood Marshall forcefully made the case that the courts should serve to protect the interests of minority-group students. In his emphatic dissent, Marshall insisted that the purpose of public education was, in part, to equalize opportunity for all young people in the United States. "In my judgment, the right of every American to an equal start in life, so far as the provision of a state service as important as education is concerned, is far too vital to permit state discrimination on grounds as tenuous as those presented by this record," Marshall wrote. "Nor can I accept the notion that it is sufficient to remit these appellees to the vagaries of the political process which, contrary to the majority's suggestion, has proved singularly unsuited to the task of providing a remedy for this discrimination."[154] Making gains through legislatures typically required bipartisan support—something that advocates for bilingual education and schooling for children with disabilities were able to muster in the early and mid-1970s. But this was less often possible when it came to the issue of racial justice in education, as Marshall knew firsthand from his years with the NAACP Legal Defense Fund and, later, as a federal judge and Supreme Court justice. A narrow definition of the Fourteenth Amendment's protections for young people at school restricted the tools available for those who sought to undermine persistent racial disparities in education, especially in the realm of school discipline, as the next chapter explores.

5

Tinker's Troubled Legacy

Discipline, Disorder, and Race in the Schools, 1968–1985

In May 1974, the *New York Times* published an exposé detailing allegations of the illegal use of corporal punishment at Jordan Mott Junior High School in the Bronx. Tipped off by one of the school's guidance counselors who claimed that he repeatedly reported the beatings to the school board and was ignored, the *Times's* piece noted that children at the school were beaten with a two-and-a-half foot long and quarter-inch thick paddle called "the smoker."[1] At other times, according to the report, administrators beat children with leather belts or, presumably when no physical implement was within immediate reach, whaled on them with "their fists."[2]

Such physical punishments were not reserved for dangerous or outrageous behavior, as students at the school attested. Students at Jordan Mott were beaten for infractions that ranged from tardiness to disrupting class. One former student later testified before the city's school board that she received "five licks with the smoker" for being late to school and forgetting her books at home. She also noted that the school's two deans, who were in charge of disciplining students, meted out the paddlings with "fixed smiles on their faces." It was, she said, "like they were doing it for entertainment."[3] Other students reported that the deans sometimes resorted to humiliation as a tactic in lieu of physical punishment. When they felt that a paddling would not physically hurt enough, the disciplinarians turned to shame and embarrassment. The worst such instance, as students recalled it, was when two boys who misbehaved were forced to hold hands all day as their punishment; they were told that they would be beaten if they did not follow orders.[4]

The school's guidance counselor, Irving Sandrof, told the *Times* reporter that he was motivated to expose the story by his sense of unease that such physical punishments, which directly violated the school district's prohibition on corporal punishment, went on in plain sight. Everyone who worked at the school knew what was happening, and presumably many parents did, too. Sandrof suggested that the beatings were overlooked by school district officials because the school primarily served black and Puerto Rican students. To him, it seemed far less likely that such egregious violations of policy would happen at a school in an upper-class, white neighborhood 100 blocks south in Manhattan. The two deans had been at the school for only five years, and the community school board head eventually commended the deans even as the board disciplined them, crediting the two men with bringing order to "the worst school in the district, with kids hanging out the windows, constant riots, hall muggings, and student harassment of teachers." The community school board president, St. Clair Marshall, told the *Times* of the triumph of the administrators and their paddling regime, "We now have a climate for learning, and academically we have made tremendous improvements."[5]

The paddling scandal in the Bronx exemplified how, even as the courts acknowledged students' constitutional rights, serious concerns remained about the persistence of racial discrimination in American public education. As the previous chapter demonstrates, in the 1970s federal courts adopted narrow conceptions of the scope of equal protection as it applied to students in public schools. The Supreme Court also refused to recognize education as a fundamental constitutional right. Both of these developments in American constitutional law limited the kinds of court-ordered remedies available to lawyers and advocates who argued that children of color continued to face racial discrimination at school. This chapter examines landmark litigation involving students' rights and school discipline and focuses primarily on cases that involved administrators' power to suspend students and use corporal punishment and students' right to privacy. As the courts considered questions about the extent of students' constitutional rights in these realms between the late 1960s and the mid-1980s, they did so in a political and social context that took a distinctly punitive turn. Increasingly in these years many Americans agreed that unruly students constituted a major social problem that required harsher discipline. This chapter explores how such discourses about race, youth, and disorder shaped the contours of students' constitutional rights.

The Punitive Turn in American Politics

Central to the Supreme Court's landmark ruling in *Tinker v. Des Moines*—the free speech decision that served as the foundation of students' constitutional rights—was the authority of school administrators to punish students for disorderly or disruptive conduct. But who determined who was marked as "disorderly" and therefore fell outside the law's protection? As the courts fashioned the shape of students' constitutional rights around ideas of order and disorder, those same concepts became central to national political discourses outside the courtroom and the classroom. Disorder came to have a political meaning and power in the late 1960s and 1970s as the courts articulated the extent of students' rights.

Disorderly students did not deserve the special protection of the law; the need for order superseded concerns about a child's right to bodily integrity. This narrative was used to justify the use of corporal punishment on poor black and Puerto Rican students in the Bronx. Students at Jordan Mott deserved to be paddled because they were exceptionally unruly and would not respond to methods of punishment reserved for other children, or so the logic went. The sense of difference inherent in this argument—that certain kinds of children needed harsher discipline than what would be appropriate at a school filled with middle-class white children—was at the heart of concerns about the ways that American education continued to perpetuate racial discrimination in the desegregation era and beyond.

In the late 1960s, public opinion coalesced around increased concerns about crime, and public dollars and government programs soon followed.[6] These efforts to combat crime were often tied both explicitly and implicitly to ideas of youth and race. Years earlier, President John F. Kennedy's pronouncement that an increase in youth crime rates since 1950 necessitated the passage of federal legislation resulted in the 1961 Juvenile Delinquency Act.[7] Although discourses about juvenile delinquency usually avoided direct discussions of race, efforts to target youth crime more harshly punished children and teenagers of color than whites. While white offenders could benefit from the model of the disaffected, misunderstood teenager—a new category in the postwar era, embodied by the actor James Dean—black and Latino youth were more likely to be labeled as dangerous troublemakers whose reformation warranted a punitive approach.[8]

As the 1960s progressed, concerns about juvenile delinquency took on new forms and resonance alongside fevered reports about the spiking crime rate and summers wracked by civil disorders. Barry Goldwater chose a "law and order" theme for his platform in the 1964 presidential election but was crushed by Lyndon Johnson in a landslide.[9] Nonetheless, the concept only gained potency as new reforms focused on reducing crime arrived filtered through the War on Poverty. "Urban" crime specifically troubled American policymakers in these years, and in response they proffered federal solutions to the problems that they claimed plagued city neighborhoods that had high numbers of minority residents. This led to a shift in resources from fighting poverty to crime with increased policing and monitoring of young people of color.[10] The historian Heather Ann Thompson uses the term "the criminalization of urban space" to refer to the collective effect that law and policy had on American cities in the last third of the twentieth century, as public funds allowed increased surveillance of residents of poorer, racially isolated neighborhoods and more harshly punished certain crimes.[11]

New anti-crime programs adopted under the Nixon administration focused specifically on young black men. In part, these efforts sought to target criminals in the making. The effect was, unsurprisingly, to pull a disproportionate share of them into the criminal justice system.[12] The focus on specific populations as prone to criminal activity was, as historians have demonstrated, a product of postemancipation American politics and, later, mid-twentieth-century social science research. The "criminalization of blackness," as historian Khalil Gibran Muhammad terms this phenomenon, took many forms. After emancipation, Southern states used vagrancy laws, which criminalized idleness, to push African American men into prisons, where they worked in convict labor camps.[13] At the same time, during the early and mid-twentieth century, the work of white intellectuals buttressed the conceptualization of black inferiority and a belief in the inborn propensity for criminal behavior.[14]

The linkages between race and criminality were not limited to the experiences of black Americans, nor were the effects of the War on Crime. With the growing migration of Mexican nationals, Mexican Americans, and Puerto Ricans to urban centers in the two decades following World

War II, their presence challenged the color line and the myriad ways it was literally and metaphorically policed. The legal "whiteness" of persons of Mexican descent and the American citizenship of Puerto Ricans did not insulate them from racialized notions of criminality.[15] Longstanding tensions between police departments and Latino communities contributed to the unrest that sometimes accompanied the protests of the late 1960s.[16] Perhaps more perniciously, "commonsense" ideas about race and culture often shaped the treatment of persons of Mexican descent, in particular, as people who were inferior to whites.[17]

The Moynihan Report, published in 1965, drew upon newer strands of thinking about the relationship between race, culture, and socially deviant behavior. The report, formally titled "The Negro Family: The Case for National Action," was not intended for the American public, but its findings were publicized widely in the wake of the Watts Riots. The Moynihan Report characterized African American neighborhoods as places of poverty, crime, and disorder, and it placed some of the blame on the structure of the black family.[18] Key to Moynihan's larger argument was the role of black children and teenagers, who served as both recipients of social decay as well as transmitters of its worst effects to the world beyond the ghetto. Moynihan's arguments drew upon social science research, and he explicitly linked race to the culture of poverty.

According to the Moynihan Report, slavery destroyed the black family by separating husbands and wives, whose marriages were disregarded by slave owners. The emergence of a matriarchal culture among African Americans jeopardized the futures of young black men in a society that valued male-headed households. Dominant mothers caused the gap in achievement between black and white students, the report argued.[19] Black women were far more likely to work in white-collar positions and had higher levels of educational attainment. Black women were also almost equally as likely to attend college as black men, whereas for whites, there were twice as many men as women enrolled. Rather than seeing this as a reflection of the strength and achievements of black women, the report argued that these disparities were evidence of the breakdown of the traditional black family structure envisioned as a single-family household headed by a male breadwinner. The relative success of black women was indicative of the failure of black men.

But the Moynihan Report did not merely lament the position of poor black children—it also warned that residential segregation would spread pathologies of disorder to middle-class African Americans. According to Moynihan, "The children of middle-class Negroes often as not must grow up in, or next to the slums, an experience almost unknown to white middle-class children. They are therefore constantly exposed to the pathology of the disturbed group and constantly in danger of being drawn into it."[20] Even education, good parenting, and a middle-class upbringing could not save African American children from the scourge of criminality. It was not just the poor who should concern policymakers, but all black youth. They were potentially vectors of cultural decay regardless of social class. Being young and black in America made a person primed to engage in anti-social behavior.

To some, the riots of the mid- and late 1960s proved the danger of the tangle of culture and pathology. The rioting began in 1964 when black residents of Harlem in New York City rebelled after a white police officer shot a reportedly unarmed black teenager. Unrest quickly spread to Bedford-Stuyvesant and lasted for six nights. The following summer witnessed the conflagration of Watts in Los Angeles. Then came the 1966 riots in the supposedly sleepy towns of Benton Harbor, Michigan, and Waukegan, Illinois. By 1967, it seemed to some that every major city in America was either aflame or on the verge of combusting, and in 1968 Richard Nixon made the racially loaded "law and order" politics a hallmark of his campaign for the presidency.[21] While law enforcement was primarily a function of local governments, Nixon's embrace of "law and order" as a presidential campaign slogan provided a way for angry and anxious whites to channel those sensibilities into national politics, catapulting Republicans into the White House and Congress.[22] Rather than taking the form of an angry mob, the politics of law and order channeled white rage into politics focused on policing and the criminal justice system.

The Kerner Commission's investigation and report on civil disorders in the United States recorded 164 such incidents in the first nine months of 1967, indicating the national scope of the crisis.[23] While the riots in Newark, New Jersey, and Detroit, Michigan, were perhaps the most well-known, disorders erupted in numerous suburbs and smaller cities across the country. The civil disorders of the mid- and late-1960s were arguably a new form of racial violence, even if political violence itself was an American tradition. This, in part, helps explain how the riots of the 1960s came to be so politically powerful. The race riots of the early twentieth century were largely examples of white-on-black violence, where white mobs rushed into black neighborhoods, burning structures and murdering people in cities from Wilmington, North Carolina, to Tulsa, Oklahoma.[24] Indeed, the race riots of the 1960s and 1970s were in fact less violent than those than came before if they are measured by the targeting of property rather than persons.[25]

Even "law and order" politics were not new, although they took on new meanings with deeply racial undertones in the late 1960s. "Law and order" was once a slogan adopted by moderate whites to counter the violent Massive Resistance campaign perpetrated by steadfast opponents of desegregation after the 1954 *Brown v. Board of Education* decision. Such was the case in Little Rock, Arkansas, where white women in the city formed a group dedicated to "free public school education and to law and order."[26] Indeed, school desegregation had never been an entirely peaceful process, although it was usually whites who bore responsibility for the disorders that accompanied the arrival of black schoolchildren at all-white schools. Efforts to desegregate schools throughout the nation were marked by violence both outside and inside schools, and before the late 1960s it was usually the fault of unruly whites. The immediate aftermath of the 1954 *Brown v. Board of Education* decision was fraught with violent acts during the Massive Resistance campaign in the South.[27] Angry, screaming whites famously blocked the entrance of the Little Rock Nine into Central High School in 1957. The Reverend Fred Shuttlesworth and his wife, Ruby, were attacked and beaten for attempting to register their daughters at an all-white school in Atlanta.[28] And Ruby Bridges, a six-year-old in New Orleans, faced a threatening mob during her first day at school in Louisiana. The disorders accompanying desegregation were not isolated incidents. Other forms of racial violence perpetrated by whites marked the two decades following World War II, which the historian Arnold Hirsch labeled an "era of hidden violence" characterized by bombings, shootings, and riots intended to drive black families out of white neighborhoods or intimidate them from attempting to integrate an area in the first place.[29]

Racial violence and rioting therefore constituted a thread that ran throughout American culture and politics in the twentieth century, but the punitive measures taken toward those perpetuating the disorders represented a break from the past. The riots of the 1960s and the attendant push for "law and order" prompted a flood of anti-riot and anti-crime legislation, which contributed to the dramatic rise in the nation's prison population in the late twentieth century.[30] "Mass incarceration," as historians term the unprecedented rise in incarceration in the last third of the twentieth century, stemmed from changes in laws that made penalties harsher and redefined certain crimes as particularly abhorrent. Even appearing to be "suspicious" on the street could lead to arrest, as exemplified by the new "stop-and-frisk" laws pioneered by the state of New York in 1964. Stop-and-frisk laws supposedly protected the safety of law enforcement officers, who had the authority to perform a limited search of a person's outer clothing even if the person was not suspected of a crime. In practice, this meant that officers could virtually stop and search any persons they deemed suspicious at will under the guise of personal safety. Other states and cities soon followed suit.[31] Stop-and-frisk policies enhanced the ability of law enforcement officers to search persons that they deemed suspicious. For this reason, the policy is often called a legalized form of racial profiling.[32] Four years after New York enacted its stop-and-frisk law, the U.S. Supreme Court upheld such laws in the 1968 *Terry v. Ohio* case.[33] The New York state legislature further ratcheted up its anti-disorder legal arsenal by passing a law that made it a crime to resist arrest—even if the arrest itself was unwarranted.[34]

The concern about law and disorder leached into discussions about the future of civil rights protections. As Congress considered a law to prohibit discrimination in housing during the winter and spring of 1968, civil disorders again came to the forefront of discussion. In March, Republican Strom Thurmond, the segregationist senator from South Carolina, and Ohio Democrat Frank Lausche introduced an amendment to the Civil Rights Act, which supporters hoped would target housing discrimination, that would make it a crime to cross state lines with the intent to start a riot. The language first introduced by Thurmond and Lausche would have created "a presumption that a defendant had traveled in interstate commerce with the intent of inciting a riot if the riot broke out within 15 days after he entered a state."[35] Instead of merely being a state or local crime, "inciting a riot" would now be a federal offense. Lausche made a grand show of proving that this provision of the law was central to his support for the fair housing measure, shouting, "I want an antiriot bill," as he strode up and down the Senate floor. The amendment was changed to require that the state prove intent to incite a riot, and the bill quickly passed the Senate on March 5 with the anti-riot measure attached.

One month later, Martin Luther King, Jr., was assassinated in Memphis, Tennessee, as he visited the city in support of the Sanitation Workers' Strike. Once again, civil disorders flared across the nation. Newspapers decried the "unruly youth" and "gangs of roaming young Negroes" who participated in the riots, including incidents near schools and historically black colleges.[36] Amid calls for calm from civil rights leaders and President Johnson, media portrayals focused on the central role of young people in the unrest. It was in the tense aftermath that Lyndon Johnson, in one of the last major legislative acts of his presidency, signed the Civil Rights Act—also known as the Fair Housing Act. But the fair housing section was only one part of the law, even if it is remembered as the primary contribution of the legislation. The Civil Rights Act also included the anti-riot Title X, which was christened the "Civil Obedience Act of 1968."

In the speech he delivered upon signing the bill into law, Johnson condemned both the persistence of racial inequality and racism as well as the nation's apparent descent into chaos. Johnson declared, "Of course all of America is outraged at the assassination of an outstanding Negro leader," adding that "America is also outraged at the looting and the burning that defiles our democracy." Johnson attempted to cast the civil disorders as anathema to the legislative work on civil rights that Congress had achieved over the previous four years. This America could embrace both black freedom and civil obedience. As Johnson gave the speech, National Guard members patrolled segregated black neighborhoods just a few miles away in the nation's capital.[37]

Like Johnson's lamentation at the violent response to deeply embedded racism, the Kerner Commission Report echoed the dual condemnation of white-created racism and black-led civil disorder. It also identified young men as those who both experienced the American racial regime's worst oppression but were likewise responsible for inciting the nation's civil disorders. The report lamented that the "nation is moving toward two societies, one black, one white—separate and unequal," and it emphasized the way that racism poisoned black neighborhoods. But it also laid responsibility for the "coercion and mob rule" that marked the long, hot summers of the 1960s at the feet of young black men. The report expressed concern over the state of "the black ghettos, where segregation and poverty converge on the young to destroy opportunity and enforce failure. Crime, drug addiction, dependency on welfare, and bitterness and resentment against society in general and white society in particular are the result."[38] Segregated black neighborhoods were pressure cookers that harmed young African Americans, who then turned their fury outward toward police and property. There was no conspiracy that led to the civil disorders; rather, disorder and violence erupted because of the terrible conditions endemic to the lives of young African Americans.[39]

In sum, the poor, opportunity-deprived environments created a propensity toward criminality that barreled the nation toward the violent unrest that marked the civil disorders of the late 1960s. A central problem, according to the commission's report, was the American system of public education, which failed young African Americans. According to the Kerner Commission, "The hostility of Negro parents and students toward the school system is generating increasing conflict and causing disruption within many city school districts."[40] This was evidenced by the participation of many young black men who had not finished high school in civil disorders. Concerns about conditions at schools and why dropout rates were so high among African American students undergirded these assertions. The Kerner Report joined in a chorus at the end of the 1960s that seemed to come to a consensus that the nation's problems were twofold: persistent racial discrimination, and the threat to law and order that it nurtured, particularly among young black men.

The consensus about the linkages between race and disorder were shared not only across the political aisle but also across the color line. The punitive turn in American politics was not limited to whites; it also infused black municipal politics in the 1970s, contributing to support for harsher punishments, especially for drug-related crimes.[41] Increasing residential segregation in central cities, compounded by poverty and a rise in the crime rate, made harsher penalties for lawbreakers attractive to a new generation of black city leaders and neighborhood residents. As James Forman, Jr., explains, "Far from ignoring the issue of crime by blacks against other blacks, African American officials and their constituents have been consumed by it."[42] The politics of order and disorder were therefore not only embraced by white Americans but by black Americans as well, even as the effects of such punishments weighed disproportionately on black men. Faced with stereotypes of "ghetto" residents and the reality of urban crime, support for harsher punishments rose among some blacks just as it did among whites.

At Jordan L. Mott Junior High School, the focus of the Bronx paddling scandal, the school was under the control of the recently organized Community School District 9. The principal, William E. Green, was a thirty-four-year-old black man who explained that the school was "in complete chaos" when he became principal but that things became "much better" under his control.[43] Indeed, all of the administrators charged with illegally using corporal punishment at the school were black men. The decentralization of New York City schools into community districts was intended to localize control over the schools—a process that studies of the conflicts over the Ocean Hill–Brownsville district demonstrate generated, rather than ameliorated, disagreements about how and by whom children should be taught.[44] In the case of students at Mott, it gave the schools' administrators the sense that they had the license to punish students as they saw fit, in part because they assumed that parents as well as many students would see harsher punishments as the only way to keep the school's students under control.

Disorder and Discipline at School

In the decade that followed the publication of the Kerner Report, Americans regularly told pollsters that their primary concern about public education was discipline. Gallup began tracking opinions about American public education in the late 1960s, as student protests and disruptions related to racial justice and anti-war activism peaked in schools and civil disorders broke out in the streets. In nearly every annual survey, discipline beat out school funding, drug use, and even busing and desegregation as the worst problem in education. The same survey revealed that those polled also felt that the quality of education had declined.[45] T. H. Bell, the commissioner of education in the Nixon and Ford administrations, made public his views that school discipline was out of control, laying the blame on "moral habits" and "social behavior" that Americans inculcated in children at home.[46] The Senate Subcommittee on Juvenile Delinquency summed up its survey of several hundred school districts by describing "brutal assaults on teachers and students as well as rapes, extortions, burglaries, thefts, and an unprecedented wave of wanton destruction and vandalism" that "seriously threatens the ability of our educational system to carry out its primary function."[47]

Reading the words of the Senate subcommittee, it is no surprise that Americans were suddenly so attuned to a new and seemingly intractable discipline problem that threatened public education. But were things truly getting worse in the mid-1970s, as politicians claimed? Evidence—including federal reports—suggested that the perception of school violence made the problem seem more pervasive than it actually was. As the 1970s progressed, Americans were more likely to report to pollsters that discipline was their main concern than they had in previous years.[48] And yet, data collected by academics who studied the issue and self-reports from schools sent to the federal Department of Health, Education and Welfare (HEW) showed that disruptions and school crime actually declined during those same years or, at most, leveled off from their height in the tumultuous late 1960s and early 1970s.[49] Student behavior did not appear to be getting worse, but this did not change the public perception of the problem.

The discipline problem attracted national attention, and HEW published a report on the issue in December 1977. Among the pertinent findings of the report, "Violent Schools—Safe Schools," was that schools were not, by and large, afflicted with major problems of violence and crime. Despite its title, which seemed to suggest otherwise, the report declared that "principals' assessments of the seriousness of violence and vandalism in their schools for the years 1971–1976 showed no overall change. In fact, they suggested some improvement in urban areas."[50] The report revealed that, by its standards, only 8 percent of American public schools had "serious" problems with discipline. But when pointing to what factors distinguished those schools that were likely to have serious problems from those that did not, the data showed that it was not an issue of schools being in urban, suburban, or rural areas. Rather, the variable with the most influence on a school's climate was its leadership: "A central conclusion of this study is that strong and effective school governance, particularly by the principal, can help greatly in reducing school crime and misbehavior." Those principals whose styles were judged "fair, firm, and, most of all, consistent" were most successful in cultivating a positive school environment and reducing crime and violence.[51] One of the key takeaways from "Violent Schools—Safe Schools" might have been the need for better training of school administrators, but media attention focused instead on misbehaving students.

Newspapers labeled the perceived nationwide discipline issue as "disastrous." In early 1977, before HEW issued its report and made its conclusions public, Indiana Democrat Birch Bayh, the chairman of the Senate Subcommittee on Juvenile Delinquency, stated that "the survey of public elementary and secondary school districts produced a ledger of violence confronting our schools that read like a casualty report from a war zone or vice squad annual report."[52] Zeroing in on the issue of student assaults on teachers, the *New York Times* similarly echoed Bayh's "war zone" language the following year with its splashy headline on an article related to safety in the city's schools titled "Casualties in the Classroom."[53]

Concerned that public opinion was out of step with the reality of life in American classrooms, the Children's Defense Fund (CDF) sought to change the perception that what students needed was harsher discipline. Under the leadership of Marian Wright Edelman, the CDF sought to create a competing narrative that positioned all children as worthy of an education—especially those considered troublemakers. Instead of pushing "problem" students out onto the streets, Americans should use education to provide new paths and opportunities for those students. Harsh disciplinary policies like suspensions and expulsions, which deprived students of educational opportunities and set them up to fail, were inherently contrary to the mission of the CDF.

In 1974 the CDF's first publication, *Children out of School in America*, revealed that, in many school districts, minority students were far more likely than their white peers to be suspended from school. This issue was especially acute at the junior high and high school level. Black secondary school students were three times as likely as white students to report having been suspended. Only 4.1 percent of white junior high and high school students reported having been suspended, whereas the figure for black students was more than three times higher—12.8 percent. Puerto

Rican students had the second highest rates, with 9.4 percent reporting suspensions. For Mexican American students, the number was 7.1.[54] These figures corroborated data reported by school districts in five states that also showed disproportionate rates of suspension by race. Of the 402 school districts surveyed, half responded that they had suspended 5 percent or more of the district's black students during the 1972–1973 school year. Only 23 percent of districts reported suspension rates for white students as 5 percent or higher. Of those districts with high suspension rates of black students, 100 districts reported suspension rates of 10 percent or higher for their black student populations.[55]

One of the primary goals of the CDF's next report on school suspensions was to push back against media narratives that cast schools as out-of-control places requiring strict, draconian regimes.[56] Edelman and her staff worked to recast the image of American students and persuade American adults to reject the punitive turn in education policy. The CDF's analysis of school data revealed that most suspensions were for "nondangerous, nonviolent offenses which do not have a seriously disruptive effect on the educational process."[57] Two-thirds of suspensions were for the general offense of "breaking school rules." Instead of reserving the harshest punishments for fighting or seriously disrupting school, administrators regularly sent students home for being truant or tardy, smoking, or violating the dress code. Only 3 percent of the suspensions were due to what was deemed criminal activity.[58]

The CDF's analysis used newly collected data from the Office of Civil Rights along with the organization's internal research, and it covered districts that enrolled more than half the nation's public school population. The report showed that black students were twice as likely as white students to report being suspended in the past year. The numbers were not consistent across school districts or even within them. Students in some districts were far more likely to be suspended than others. In the most worrisome cases for advocates of civil rights reforms, a few districts suspended more than half of their black student populations at some point during the school year. And twenty of the surveyed school districts officials reported suspending between one-third and one-half of their black student populations.[59] Joliet Township High School, located in a small city on the far outskirts of Chicago, had the most striking suspension rate. In the 1972–1973 school year, administrators reported to the Office of Civil Rights that they suspended 64 percent of the school's black students but only 25 percent of the white student population.[60] The Proviso school district, located just west of Chicago, reported the second highest suspension rate of black students the same year, at 53 percent. But the high-suspending districts identified by the CDF were not clustered in one state or region: They included schools in California, Ohio, New Jersey, and Kentucky.[61] "Some will claim that disproportionate suspension of black children simply reflects their disproportionate misbehavior," the report warned. "All the evidence we have seen . . . makes plain that disproportionate suspension of blacks reflects a pervasive school intolerance for children who are *different.*"[62]

Despite a burgeoning number of victories in students' rights cases at the federal level and increased attention to racial disparities in suspensions by civil rights and child advocacy organizations, lawyers who sought to target racial discrimination in school discipline through the courts faced a number of difficulties. The numbers alone, no matter how stark the disparities, were not enough to prove that racial discrimination was intentional on the part of school officials. One way to confront the problem of intentional discrimination was to pursue discipline reform as part of a desegregation lawsuit. The maintenance of a de jure segregated system showed intentional racial discrimination on the part of school districts, so it might be possible to challenge seemingly discriminatory disciplinary policies as part of the litigation. Such was the effort of Department of Justice lawyers who sued the Wilcox County, Alabama, schools for maintaining a segregated school system more than a decade after *Brown v. Board of Education.*[63] But as in many other desegregation cases, with their endless hearings and cadre of experts, the concerns about racially discriminatory disciplinary policies never earned the same attention from the courts as charges of employment discrimination against black teachers or concerns over desegregation schemes.[64] Grouping concerns about racial discrimination in school discipline with the other complex issues in desegregation suits meant that they could take a backseat to other concerns about racial balance in schools and the employment of minority teachers.

More often, these cases were considered "second-generation" school desegregation cases and were litigated separately. The Children's Defense Fund supported the plaintiffs in one such case from Newburgh, New York. Black students in the Newburgh public schools had been engaged in years of protest against racial segregation and discrimination when the lawsuit was first filed in 1974. The city itself was a hotbed of protest and racial strife in the late 1960s, and the schools figured centrally in the conflict. The city was a relatively small one—roughly 25,000 inhabitants—with only one public high school. In response to the city's growing minority population that included blacks and Puerto Ricans, the city manager pioneered the use of work requirements for welfare recipients, claiming euphemistically that "migrant-type citizens" abused the system.[65] A "minor" civil disorder broke out in July 1967 and another flared in July 1971.[66] In 1972, city police blockaded a black neighborhood in town after they alleged that a group of black teenagers pelted cars with rocks and bottles.[67] In 1969, an multiracial group of 600 students participated in a boycott of the schools led by the Black Student Association in an effort to extend busing services and have the schools recognize the birthdays of Martin Luther King, Jr., and Malcolm X.[68] The city's sole high school was located in a "white" part of town, and many black students had to walk miles to school even though the district bused in white students from nearby towns.[69] Other concerns of the students echoed those elsewhere: The school's staff had few black or Puerto Rican teachers, and white teachers excluded black students from extracurricular activities.[70] The lawsuit claimed that school officials meted out suspensions in racially discriminatory ways; in particular, it claimed that students had been suspended for criticizing district policy. These claims came under the First Amendment, asserting that such practices had a "chilling effect" on the students' right to free speech.[71] The case resulted in a consent decree in which the district agreed to eliminate the gross disparities between the suspension rates of white students and black and Latino students.[72]

Another lawsuit from the early 1970s was less successful. In a case from Florida, a large-scale fight between black and white high school students led to the suspension of forty-nine students, only one of whom was white. The blame for the fight, all participants seemed to agree, did not lie with any single racial group. The mass suspensions of black students were, their lawyers argued, a clear example of racial discrimination. But the court accepted the administration's logic that they disproportionately suspended black students because they stayed on campus after the fighting subsided, whereas white students fled and were not easy to identify. Despite the starkly different treatment of black and white students, the court sided with the school and found no evidence of intentional racial bias.[73]

A few years later, the National Association for the Advancement of Colored People (NAACP) Legal Defense Fund brought another case in Florida that arose from similar circumstances. After two years of desegregation, a "general melee" between black and white students broke out on campus, for which the administration and the court did not solely blame either group. And yet, black students were apparently punished more harshly than whites in the disciplinary actions that followed. More than 100 black students received suspensions, and several faced expulsion.[74] Legal Defense Fund lawyers made a range of claims in an attempt to strike at racially discriminatory discipline policies. They argued that the school's disciplinary practices violated the principles of due process of law and that the suspensions and expulsions violated First Amendment protections of free speech and peaceful assembly, as many of the suspensions came from a walkout of black students. Furthermore, they argued that the disciplinary tactics had become "badges of slavery," drawing on the authority of the Thirteenth Amendment. The district court refused to accept the argument that the disproportionate discipline of black students indicated a pattern of intentional discrimination, pointing to incidents where those punishments had been given to white students in the past.[75]

Another way to challenge discriminatory disciplinary policies did not directly come through the courts, but through the administrative power of federal agencies. The Children's Defense Fund report on student suspensions attracted attention from the media, and in September 1975, HEW announced it would launch an investigation into the charges that schools regularly disciplined black students more harshly than white students. The Children's Defense Fund wanted HEW to demand more detailed data than the federal government had already collected, including rates of discipline by race. Most of the information on public schools came from the Elementary and Secondary School Survey, which began in 1968. Edelman and her fellow advocates for children of color pointed to Title VI of the 1964 Civil Rights Act, which forbade the federal government from funding programs that discriminated on the basis of race, color, and national origin. The Elementary and Secondary Education Act of 1965 also included language on this point.[76] If the federal government had its own data showing that minority students faced disproportionate rates of discipline, the agency would be compelled to do something about it if racial discrimination was the cause.

Title VI was the key to compliance with the desegregation mandate of *Brown* with its threat of withholding federal funds, and it could potentially also be used to punish districts that practiced other forms of racial discrimination beyond segregation. But, of course, targeting forms of racial discrimination that were not as obvious as de jure segregation would be a challenge, even with major civil rights legislation on the side of advocates. In 1971, the Supreme Court issued a ruling that potentially made it easier for lawyers to target less obvious forms of racial discrimination. In *Griggs v. Duke Power Co.*, the Supreme Court found that, even though a particular policy (in this case, the requirement of a high school diploma) did not have a discriminatory intent on its face, its effect made it more difficult for minority job candidates to secure employment even though the policy did not result in better job performance.[77] This conflicted with Title VII of the 1964 Civil Rights Act, which prohibited private employers from practicing racial discrimination in hiring. Employers could not mask their desire to exclude groups based on race, color, or national origin through policies that appeared neutral but in fact perpetuated otherwise illegal discrimination.

Griggs was an employment law case, but the idea that facially neutral policies resulted in illegal racial discrimination was ripe for application to other areas of civil rights law. This area of civil rights law became known as "disparate impact," and owing to the language of the Fourteenth Amendment, it required proof of discriminatory intent just as lawsuits claiming de jure segregation did. The usefulness of disparate impact to combat racial discrimination in school discipline was limited by the ways in which lawsuits were allowed. In 2001, the U.S. Supreme Court restricted the ability of individuals to bring disparate impact suits, ruling in *Alexander v. Sandoval* that the 1964 Civil Rights Act did not include a "private right of action."[78] In short, only federal agencies could bring disparate impact claims—not individual persons who felt their children's schools meted out discipline in a racially discriminatory manner.[79]

Lawyers for children in the Dallas, Texas, public schools turned to statistical analysis and expert testimony to make their case. A school desegregation case, *Tasby v. Estes*, resulted in the implementation of a desegregation order in 1971 that included busing students to new schools. For many black students, this meant they now attended previously white schools as a minority. Within the span of a couple of years, parents complained that administrators were quicker to discipline black students than their white peers. As the desegregation case was caught up in the appeals process at the Fifth Circuit, lawyers filed a new lawsuit based solely on the issue of disparate rates of discipline by race. *Hawkins v. Coleman* challenged the higher rates of suspension and corporal punishment for black children. The case emerged out of a fight between a white and black student at a recently desegregated junior high school that ended in suspensions for both young men. The mother of the black student sued, alleging that the white student repeatedly harassed and provoked her son.[80] Data provided to the court showed that, across the district, black students were more likely to be suspended or paddled than white students; when broken down, the problem was worse where black students constituted a new minority in a previously all-white school. In 1974, federal judge Sarah Hughes agreed, in part owing to the testimony of Superintendent Nolan Estes, who admitted during the trial that institutional racism permeated the district's disciplinary policies and practices.[81] The finding of "institutional racism" was rather unusual—many complained that they did not even know what the term meant—but in response, the district adopted an "affirmative action" program to comply with the ruling.[82]

These cases targeted single school districts, and consent decrees do not create precedent, leaving their effects felt only at the local level. The expense and difficulty of bringing such lawsuits was one that vexed civil rights lawyers earlier in the twentieth century, before *Brown v. Board of Education*. In those days, Thurgood Marshall would travel the South, litigating teacher pay equalization cases one at a time—an expensive and time-consuming pursuit for those looking to make sweeping change. As concerns about school safety grew in the late 1970s, advocates turned to other pressing issues, including the use of corporal punishment and student privacy.

Corporal Punishment and the Rights of Children

While the Children's Defense Fund focused on racial discrimination in suspensions, this was not the only form of school discipline that could be subject to abuse, especially when it came to the treatment of minority students. The early 1970s also witnessed a civil rights challenge to the practice of corporal punishment in American public schools. With new Fourteenth Amendment protections for suspensions and expulsions, activists pressed the courts to extend constitutional protections to the realm of physical discipline. They turned, in part, to the Eighth Amendment to the Constitution, which states, "Excessive bail shall not be required, nor excessive fines imposed, nor cruel and unusual punishments inflicted." Its language does not identify any particular actors, nor does the amendment stipulate that such prohibitions only apply to punishment for a crime. Read broadly, the amendment could be interpreted to include teachers and principals in public schools. And so, during the 1970s, the Eighth Amendment became part of the struggle to eliminate corporal punishment in American public schools.

Similar to concerns about the disproportionate rates of suspensions and expulsions of children of color, the efforts to put an end to corporal punishment were linked to civil rights issues of justice in education, as demonstrated by the Bronx paddling scandal. Reports from the Office of Civil Rights found, for instance, patterns of disparate outcomes in American public schools for students of color in the late 1970s. Florida school districts, in particular those surrounding some of the state's largest cities, led the nation in disproportionate rates of corporal punishment. Broward County schools, which included Fort Lauderdale, led the nation in "excess corporal punishment." Second was Hillsborough County public schools, which encompassed Tampa. Dade County, which includes Miami, was third.[83] It is perhaps not a coincidence, then, that the Supreme Court's eventual ruling on corporal punishment came from the Sunshine State.

As with the challenge to the use of suspensions, lawsuits explicitly charged that corporal punishment was subject to abuse and racially discriminatory use in schools. A year before the Bronx paddling scandal broke, lawyers sued a school district in Ohio for the paddling of children by school administrators under the Eighth and Fourteenth amendments to the Constitution. A junior high school student, Leatha Benita Sims, was at the center of the case. Her lawyers claimed that in addition to the punishments being excessive under the Eighth Amendment, administrators unfairly targeted black students for discipline.[84] But such lawsuits faced a twin challenge: First, they had to prove discriminatory intent on the part of school officials, and second, they had to persuade a judge that the constitutional prohibition of "cruel and unusual" punishments applied to school officials. In *Sims v. Waln*, the court denied Sims's lawyers' claim that there was racial discrimination in how these punishments were meted out; it also dismissed the claim that there was any violation of the Eighth Amendment. These questions about the reach of the Eighth Amendment—who did it restrain from action, and who did it protect?—became a contested point that eventually propelled the issue to the Supreme Court.

Sims was only one case of many filed on behalf of students who were physically punished in their schools. The incidents that spurred the litigation were often related to a sense that corporal punishment was used arbitrarily by teachers and other school officials to punish students in a manner that exceeded the gravity of the student's infraction. Despite the regulations that usually governed the practice, corporal punishment was subject to abuse. In a case from Vermont, a mathematics teacher slapped a student across the face.[85] In Dallas, students alleged that in addition to paddling, a teacher hit a student with a shoe.[86] In each of these cases, the courts dispensed with any Eighth Amendment arguments by declaring that it only applied to criminal, and not civil, cases. The amendment existed to prevent "cruel and unusual" punishments of convicts, not schoolchildren.[87]

This interpretation of the Eighth Amendment was relatively new. In the late eighteenth century, slaves, convicts, and schoolchildren could all find themselves publicly punished at the whipping post. But by the middle of the nineteenth century, incarceration replaced corporal punishment for criminals.[88] The penal reform movement did not abolish corporal punishment, but it largely replaced it in prisons and jails. By the mid-twentieth century, Delaware was the only state that continued to prescribe whippings for certain crimes.[89] The practice of convict leasing, which grew in the South after the abolition of slavery, constituted a new form of brutal and legal physical punishment. In the convict lease system, those persons convicted of crimes—usually black men, often on tenuous charges—became an unfree labor force for the profit of industry and the state.[90]

By the early 1960s, the Supreme Court made it clear that the Eighth Amendment's prohibition on cruel and unusual punishment applied to the states, giving prisoners a legal tool to challenge beatings at the hands of prison guards.[91] One important case came from Arkansas. The state penitentiaries held thousands of prisoners in Cummins Farm and Tucker Farm, where inmates toiled in the fields filling baskets with tomatoes, cucumbers, and okra. Prison rules stipulated that physical punishments were recommended for a specific range of misbehaviors from "homosexuality" to insubordination, but prisoners claimed that they were beaten for all kinds of offenses, often viciously. For example, in November 1965, nearly 100 years after the ratification of the Thirteenth Amendment, which abolished slavery but expressly sanctioned the legality of convict labor, a field warden whipped white prisoner William Jackson with a leather strap "for not picking enough cotton."[92] In 1968, the Eighth Circuit ruled that the whippings in Arkansas prisons ran afoul of the Eighth Amendment, in part because "corporal punishment is easily subject to abuse in the hands of the sadistic and the unscrupulous."[93] Prison officials could not be trusted to employ such physical punishments because of the likelihood of abuse and the violation of prisoners' constitutional rights.

And yet, despite a century and a half of penal reform and the willingness of courts to recognize the inherent dangers in allowing corporal punishment in prisons, the practice remained perfectly legal in many schools. This was not for lack of effort on the part of opponents. By the early 1970s, American parents had been contesting the practice in court since the early nineteenth century. The earliest such case was decided in 1833 in Pennsylvania, in favor of the teacher.[94] The most notable case from the 1830s was *State v. Pendergrass*, in which the state supreme court of North Carolina found that a teacher who whipped a student stood in the place of the parent, or *in loco parentis*, and had the power to physically punish students just as parents retained the right to spank their children.[95] This decision introduced *in loco parentis* to American law and enshrined it in the realm of education.[96] "One of the most sacred duties of parents, is to train up and qualify their children, for becoming useful and virtuous members of society," the judge declared in *Pendergrass*. He continued,

> This duty cannot be effectually performed without the ability to command obedience, to control stubbornness, to quicken diligence, and to reform bad habits; and to enable him to exercise this salutary sway, he is armed with the power to administer moderate correction, when he shall believe it to be just and necessary.[97]

Of course, should the parent or teacher acting in his stead "endanger life," disfigure the child, or cause lasting injury, such an action would not be considered reasonable. Rather, the standard was whether the pain was permanent or temporary.

As the whippings at Arkansas prison farms invoked the specter of American slavery, the use of corporal punishment in schools had racial undertones. The *Brown* decision increased support in some quarters for corporal punishment. In Virginia, for example, state legislators enshrined in law the power of teachers to physically punish students.[98] Seven other states followed suit and expressly legalized corporal punishment by statute between 1958 and 1970.[99] In Washington, DC, where the school board banned the practice after a teacher used it "to an excessive and unwarranted degree," the board again debated the issue after the 1962 Thanksgiving Day Riot, which broke out following a football game between a black public high school and an all-white prep school.[100] By the 1970s, school administrators had long traded the whips and switches of an earlier era for the paddle. Only two state legislatures, Massachusetts and New Jersey, prohibited the use of corporal punishment in schools, and Maryland's state school board banned the practice in 1971.[101] The Massachusetts prohibition on the practice only became law in March 1972, but this followed an ugly spate of local publicity about the use of physical punishment.[102] Since 1969, the public schools in Boston had been under a consent decree in which school officials were temporarily banned from the practice due to a lawsuit in which students claimed to have been slapped, shoved, and punched by teachers. In one instance, a teacher ripped the earring from the earlobe of a teenaged girl.[103]

In some places, the use of corporal punishment actually increased in the 1970s. In Dallas, the number of students paddled each year quadrupled during the first year of desegregation. In January 1971, the district reported 335 instances of corporal punishment; in January 1972, during the first year of desegregation, that same figure was 2,147, which is more than six times the previous rate of use.[104] Nearly 25,000 students received physical punishments in the latter year, an effect that Superintendent Nolan Estes attributed to "the increase in unrest resulting from school desegregation."[105] Despite the superintendent's acknowledgment of the problems of "institutional racism" in Dallas schools, he nonetheless vigorously defended the use of corporal punishment.

In 1971, the National Education Association (NEA) decided to launch its own study of the issue. The organization's Report of the National Task Force on Corporal Punishment followed in 1972. Although the report declared that "no teacher consciously wants to inflict pain, either physical or psychological, upon a young person," it also concluded that "teachers and other educators use corporal punishment almost exclusively where conditions for dealing with disruptions are so poor that the school staff has reached a point of total frustration."[106] Citing studies that indicated that corporal punishment was an ineffective disciplinary tactic, the report recommended that every public school in America phase out physical punishments, with exceptions for moments when physical restraint was necessary to protect the safety of others. Quoting the Concerned Parents Committee of Covina, California, the report warned of "the kind of arbitrariness, racial prejudice, assumption of student guilt, and general disregard of individual rights that characterizes 'difficult' schools."[107] Concerns about racial discrimination were embedded in assumptions about the obstinacy and unruly nature of certain young people as the only punishment they could understand.[108]

In order to coordinate the efforts of opponents to corporal punishment, the American Civil Liberties Union (ACLU) hosted a conference that drew participants from fifty organizations and agencies in the spring of 1972.[109] Members of local groups from across the nation, representing local and national groups in places that ranged from rural Kentucky to Montgomery, Alabama, and Pittsburgh, Pennsylvania, met in New York.

One of the goals of the meeting was to establish a system to collect data from across the nation on corporal punishment in schools. It was difficult to arouse public support for statewide bans on the practice if so little information was available about how and when it was used and which children were most vulnerable to its abuse.

Despite the recommendations of the NEA and the work of groups like the ACLU, corporal punishment did not wither on the vine during the 1970s. Indeed, many teachers liked the practice. When given a chance to voice their views on the issue, they continued to support it in large numbers. The NEA report downplayed the organization's own research on its membership, which found that in 1969 nearly half of all teachers surveyed approved of the use of corporal punishment in secondary schools, including two-thirds of all elementary school teachers.[110] Other studies also indicated that the NEA was at odds with the sentiments of its own members and teachers at large. A study of thousands of school officials, teachers, students, and parents in Norfolk, Virginia, found that, among all groups, teachers supported the practice with a near two-thirds majority, followed closely by school administrators, of whom 61 percent approved of it. In stark contrast, more than half of parents and students felt that it was not an effective way to discipline students.[111] In Los Angeles, where corporal punishment was banned by the board of education in 1975, the teachers' union negotiated an end to the ban just three years later.[112] In Pittsburgh, nearly three-quarters of the city's public schoolteachers signed a petition asking for the reinstatement of corporal punishment. Teachers in some areas claimed that the ability to physically punish students was necessary in an era of "increasing classroom unruliness," which critics called part of the "law and order backlash."[113]

The case on which the Supreme Court would settle the issue of whether corporal punishment in schools violated the Constitution came from Florida. In 1971, the lawyers for two students at a Miami junior high school filed a lawsuit alleging that, by paddling the young men with a wooden stick, the school administrators had violated their constitutional rights under the Eighth Amendment. The details of the case included appalling instances of abuse of the practice. James Ingraham was one of a group of students punished collectively for being "slow to leave the stage of the school auditorium when asked to do so by a teacher." The students were herded off to the principal's office, where they lined up to take their licks with the paddle. But Ingraham refused to submit to the punishment because, he claimed, the paddling was unfair. Unlike the other students, he had not dallied on the stage. The principal then pulled the assistant principal and another staff person into his office, where they held Ingraham down on the desk as the principal administered— instead of the usual five—"at least twenty licks."[114] When Ingraham arrived home that night, his mother took him to the hospital, where a physician examined the boy's extensive bruising and recommended that he stay home and rest for a week before returning to school.[115] When the scandal at Mott Junior High School in the Bronx broke, the Ingraham case was before the Fifth Circuit Court of Appeals, which sided with the students.[116]

Other students in the case testified to a reign of terror in the school's halls sustained by the assistant principals, who were charged with keeping order and disciplining students. Florida state law permitted schools to use corporal punishment, although it forbade practices that were "degrading or unduly severe."[117] The Dade County school district further delineated its policy, limiting school officials to administering five "licks" with a flat, wooden paddle that measured less than two feet long, four inches wide, and a half-inch thick.[118]

But the punishments students described regularly flouted district rules about where, when, and how students should be subject to corporal punishment. Students described brutal beatings, and the district did not challenge the veracity of these stories. Roosevelt Andrews, another plaintiff in the case, testified that his encounter with Assistant Principal Solomon Barnes was similarly out of line with the supposed infraction. Spotted by Barnes in the hall during a passing period, the assistant principal claimed that Andrews would be tardy for his next class and ordered him into the boys' bathroom with a number of other students. Barnes forced the students to line up at the urinals before whacking them one by one with the paddle and sending them back to class. When Andrews, now alone in the bathroom with Barnes, claimed that he had not actually done anything wrong and would have made it to class in time had the assistant principal not called him into the bathroom, he was pushed between the toilets and struck across the leg, arm, neck, and back with the paddle.[119]

Another student testified that one of the assistant principals carried a paddle with him as he patrolled the school's halls, while another carried brass knuckles. Others noted that punishments for claiming innocence were more brutal than accepting an unjust paddling, recalling a student who had been "thrown across" the principal's office for protesting what he felt was an undeserved punishment. One student claimed that the assistant principal had broken a bone in his hand with the paddle; another testified that at various times he had been smacked across the head, beaten with a leather belt, and was once hit so forcefully with the paddle that he coughed up blood.[120] The school district did not attempt to refute these facts.[121]

Students were paddled regularly—an estimated average of eight students punished per day—for all kinds of infractions. They were paddled for being too noisy, sitting in the wrong seat in the auditorium, having untucked shirts, or not "assuming the position" quickly enough while preparing to be paddled for another offense. Corporal punishment was used for infractions small and large. The district argued that it was a less onerous punishment than suspension or expulsion and was therefore a preferable method of disciplining students. In its initial ruling, the Fifth Circuit took the concerns of students and their parents seriously. The judges ruled that, while corporal punishment was not cruel or unusual per se, the way administrators at Miami's Drew Junior High School meted it out was "often severe, and of a nature likely to cause serious physical and psychological damage."[122]

Upon rehearing two years later, the Fifth Circuit reversed itself, echoing *Pendergrass* in noting that the "paddling of recalcitrant children has long been an accepted method of promoting good behavior and instilling notions of responsibility and decorum into the mischievous heads of school children." The court's logic departed from the concept of *in loco parentis*, emphasizing the right of administrators to physically punish students in relation to the need to maintain order and encourage proper conduct as opposed to the natural rights of parents over children. Indeed, newer court cases involving corporal punishment actually circumscribed the rights of parents. In a case out of North Carolina, a district court judge responded to the claim that the school violated a mother's rights as a parent by paddling her child against her wishes by denying that any such deprivation occurred. In the 1975 decision, the court declared, "There can be no doubt about the state's legitimate and substantial interest in maintaining order and discipline in the public schools." Furthermore, the court cited *Tinker v. Des Moines* and *Goss v. Lopez* to note that it should be "self evident, that to fulfill its assumed duty of providing an education to all who want it a state must maintain order within its schools."[123] The legacy of these decisions, in this interpretation, was a victory not for students but for administrators, who now had the blessings of constitutional law to maintain order in their schools through physical force.

In 1977, the U.S. Supreme Court agreed with the Fifth Circuit's ruling in *Ingraham v. Wright* in a five-to-four decision. Students in public schools were not shielded by the Eighth Amendment from corporal punishment. Pointing to a long history of the practice grounded in the common law, the Court declared that students did not even need due process protections before being paddled. Corporal punishment was, in the majority's ruling, a less serious punishment than suspension or expulsion, which deprived a student of education. Furthermore, the decision asserted that the Eighth Amendment only applied to criminal matters, and this was a civil case.[124]

But what of administrators who—without safeguards like due process for students—abused the practice? The majority opinion declared that, because public schools were largely subject to community control through school boards, if the practices of school officials were out of line with local community standards, then the system was poised to correct them. Furthermore, students could sue school officials who went too far, providing another means of avoiding the abuse of children.[125]

In deciding *Ingraham v. Wright* in favor of school officials, the Supreme Court prioritized the keeping of order in the classroom, declaring that it was a "substantial" state interest. If administrators could argue that a practice contributed to the maintenance of order, students' constitutional rights were diminished. Ignoring the arguments that paddling was ripe for abuses within schools, the Court deferred to local authorities. Writing in a dissent, Justice Byron White disagreed that the Eighth Amendment clearly applied only to punishments for crimes and stated that, in drawing this artificial limit on the amendment, the Court created a bizarre set of standards that allowed for punishments of schoolchildren that would not be sanctioned for a murderer if the same actions took place in a prison. In short, "The record reveals beatings so severe that if they were inflicted on a hardened criminal for the commission of a serious crime, they might not pass constitutional muster."[126]

Justice White also doubted that students would be able to successfully sue and recover damages for wrongful or excessive punishments, noting that it was not clear if Florida law even allowed students to bring suit against school officials. Most states allowed the practice of corporal punishment, excepting only New Jersey, Massachusetts, and Maine. In New York, the law only prohibited school officials from using "deadly force" when administering corporal punishment; anything lesser was acceptable according to the law, making it difficult for parents to sue abusive teachers and administrators. With the Supreme Court's rejection of the "cruel and unusual" argument, lawyers turned to other areas of constitutional law to carve out protections for students. After *Ingraham*, other circuit courts (excepting the Fifth) adopted the "shock the conscience" standard borrowed from cases involving police brutality to determine whether students could bring lawsuits under a substantive due process claim.[127]

The way states handled drawing the line between child abuse—which is illegal everywhere—and corporal punishment—which continued to have the sanction of law in many states—relied upon variable boundaries. In Florida, for example, the state legislature vacillated on whether it would even permit individual school districts to ban corporal punishment. But those school officials who overstepped their authority and used excessive force could find their names printed in a registry of child abusers compiled by the Florida Department of Health and Rehabilitative Services. The determination of whether a paddling constituted abuse was left to the courts, which relied on a general "you bruise, you lose" rule. When students sued after receiving bruises that lasted a week, a panel of judges found the injury to be indicative of the use of "excessive force," while the dissenting judge observed that such a judgment could never be standardized since some children bruise more easily than others.[128]

Punishment and the Right to Privacy

Ingraham v. Wright was litigated in an era that followed dramatic changes in other areas of American constitutional law. Even as the majority opinion in *Ingraham* distinguished between issues of criminal procedure and students' rights, arguing that the former was not applicable to the latter, the justices did later rely on criminal procedure to determine the extent of students' rights. Key rulings extended protections to those suspected of crimes, particularly in the area of search and seizure. With harsher penalties and more policing the hallmarks of the War on Crime, concerns like those of the Fourth Amendment became increasingly important for students in American public schools. The unchecked ability of teachers and school administrators to search a student's person or belongings would make students far more likely to be accused of breaking a school rule or committing a crime, which could end in an arrest and legal consequences.

As in *Ingraham v. Wright*, the courts confronted other questions about the extension of principles of criminal law to the realm of school discipline. The Fourth Amendment to the Constitution prohibited state officials from the "unreasonable search and seizure" of a person and his "house, papers, and effects," but did this encompass teachers and principals? They were assuredly state actors, but was their relationship to children more like that of a parent or that of a police officer?[129] In matters of discipline, the court hedged; school officials had the right to discipline children, even paddle them, but had to provide hearings if a child was to be suspended or expelled from school. As unfair as a child might find it, the Constitution did not prohibit a parent from rifling through her drawers or snooping under the bed for contraband. Furthermore, the reliance on *Tinker v. Des Moines* and *Goss v. Lopez* seemed to create a robust right for school officials to maintain order, even when that might seem to conflict with the rights that students did not shed at the schoolhouse gate. How an issue like the authority to search students' belongings would fit into the regime of students' constitutional rights was increasingly important as the War on Crime marched onward. One facet of the War on Crime was that states adopted reforms allowing juvenile court judges to "waive" cases into adult court for non-violent offenses—a move that was more frequently used for drug charges than for other offenses.[130]

The landmark decision on search and seizure at schools, *New Jersey v. T.L.O.*, began in 1980 with a high school freshman's bad luck. A teacher discovered the student, whose initials the case name bore, smoking cigarettes in the girls' bathroom with a friend. When the student complained that she had not been smoking at all, the assistant vice principal asked to see her purse, where he found—along with an incriminating pack of cigarettes—loose rolling papers. Suspicious that the rolling papers indicated drug use, the assistant vice principal dug further into her purse and was presented with the trappings of a small-time drug dealer. Along with cash, marijuana, and a pipe, the assistant vice principal found an index card listing the names of her customers and "two letters that implicated her in marihuana dealing" in a zippered pocket.[131] The student's lawyers sued the school, arguing that the search violated the students' right to privacy and ran afoul of the Fourth Amendment.

The stakes for the student were high; not only was she punished by the school for what was discovered in her purse, but the assistant vice principal also called the police and reported the student. She was then charged with delinquency in juvenile court. She received a ten-day suspension from school, earning three days for smoking and seven for marijuana possession. The charges against her in juvenile court would have been more serious. New Jersey's Controlled Dangerous Substances Act, which was adopted in 1970, prescribed up to six months in jail and up to a $500 fine for possession of less than twenty-five grams of marijuana, although the juvenile court to which she was referred was allowed to offer more lenient sentencing than she would have received in criminal court.[132] She was eventually declared delinquent by the court.[133]

In oral argument before the Supreme Court, New Jersey Deputy Attorney General Allan Nodes emphasized the need for school officials to have extended authority to search students. "In many ways, teachers take the place and perform the function of parents," Nodes told the justices, invoking the idea of *in loco parentis*. He also emphasized the importance of maintaining order, arguing, "We must have discipline in the schools—and [it] can't be maintained by teachers who are encumbered by the same rules as police officers."[134] In an amicus brief that supported broad disciplinary authority for teachers and principals, the Reagan administration likewise described school crime as reaching "epidemic proportions," referring to the "Violent Schools—Safe Schools" report to make its point.

The Supreme Court forged a middle path with its ruling, protecting both the authority of school officials to search students' personal things within limits. The search of the student's purse and the subsequent "rummaging around" that produced evidence of drug dealing were reasonable, the majority opinion determined. It dispensed quickly with arguments for the *in loco parentis* authority of officials, declaring, "If school authorities are state actors for purposes of the constitutional guarantees of freedom of expression and due process, it is difficult to understand why they should be deemed to be exercising parental rather than public authority when conducting searches of their students."[135] As *Tinker v. Des Moines* and *Goss v. Lopez* established, and *Ingraham v. Wright* affirmed, state compulsory education laws complicated old theories about parental delegation of authority—and thus that the kind of power held by school officials was more like a parent and largely excluded from constitutional scrutiny—that had long been inscribed in law through *in loco parentis*. After all, by taking away the right to keep children uneducated, the state assumed a different kind of purpose in educating its populace, more aligned with ideals of citizenship and participatory democracy. Children did have a substantial interest in their own privacy, but at the same time, the courts balanced that interest with the "substantial interest of teachers and administrators in maintaining discipline in the classroom and on school grounds." Furthermore, the Supreme Court emphasized that new societal conditions perhaps increased the importance of such tasks. Citing "Violent Schools—Safe Schools," the majority decision declared, "Maintaining order in the classroom has never been easy, but in recent years, school disorder has often taken particularly ugly forms: drug use and violent crime in the schools have become major social problems."[136]

Justice Thurgood Marshall wrote a harsh partial dissent accusing the majority of creating a standard that deviated from a clear previous line of cases that relied upon the probable cause standard, creating a standard for school officials that was vague and "Rorschach-like." Marshall charged that

> the Court today holds that a new "reasonableness" standard is appropriate because it will spare teachers and school administrators the necessity of schooling themselves in the niceties of probable cause and permit them to regulate their conduct according to the dictates of reason and common sense.

He added that reason and common sense were central to his under-standing of probable cause. Marshall warned that this new, amorphous standard could actually hurt both school officials and students, giving some teachers the sense that no searches were warranted and others the idea that they could rifle through students' belongings whenever they liked. Marshall concluded, "The sad result of this uncertainty may well be that some teachers will be reluctant to conduct searches that are fully permissible . . . while others may intrude arbitrarily and unjustifiably on the privacy of students." Marshall would have excluded the evidence beyond the initial finding of the pack of cigarettes, which confirmed the teacher's accusation that the student was smoking. The further, more invasive search of the student's purse was therefore beyond the scope of the assistant vice principal's authority.[137]

In footnote 4, Marshall noted the words of Justice Potter Stewart from a 1971 Fourth Amendment case: "In times of unrest, whether caused by crime or racial conflict or fear of internal subversion this basic law and the values that it represents may appear unrealistic or 'extravagant' to some. But the values were those of the authors of our fundamental constitutional concepts."[138] In this case, *Coolidge v. New Hampshire*, the plaintiff claimed that the police had exceeded their Fourth Amendment authority in the search of his home after a fourteen-year-old girl disap-peared on a snowy night; her body was found, discarded on the side of a highway, eight days later when the snow melted. Justice Marshall's invocation of Stewart's words emphasized the importance of the neu-trality of the law. In moments of heightened anxiety—whether over the brutal murder of a child or concerns about out-of-control high school students—state actors might be inclined to violate the constitutional rights of individuals, feeling that the urgency of a situation merited the setting aside of traditional procedures. But such examples could not be justified by urgency or context; the rule of law superseded these con-cerns. By overreaching in times of panic, the courts set too harsh a stan-dard for times of peace.

In the 1980s and 1990s, schools began to adopt "zero-tolerance" poli-cies modeled on the "get tough" ethos of the War on Drugs. In certain cases, students faced automatic expulsions for certain infractions of school rules; these policies also mandated that schools call in police in certain situations, which meant that students would likely be arrested.

All of these developments, both inside and outside the schools, raised the stakes of students' rights to privacy and fairness in disciplinary procedures.[139] Under a zero-tolerance policy, not only would T.L.O have likely faced automatic expulsion from school, but the school also would have been required to call the police.

Under the "reasonableness" standard articulated by *New Jersey v. T.L.O.*, the courts largely deferred to school officials, leading one publication to note in 2005 that, in the intervening two decades since that ruling, "the proliferation of zero tolerance policies, warrantless searches, and drug testing of public school students suggests that the rights to privacy and due process are not held in the same esteem."[140] By 2009, another case heard by the Supreme Court demonstrated just how pervasive this authority to search students' persons and belongings had become when the Court weighed whether the strip-search of a thirteen-year-old girl violated her Fourth Amendment right to privacy. Acting on information from another student that the girl had prescription and non-prescription pills that she gave to other students, the school's assistant principal asked the school nurse to search the girl's clothing. The nurse had the girl remove all outer garments, and then pull out her bra and underpants, exposing her genitals. An eight-justice majority ruled that, owing to the facts of the case, the strip search was unreasonable and a violation of the Fourth Amendment.[141] But the Court did not explicitly ban all future strip searches of students; school officials could infer that if they believed the practice was warranted by circumstances, they would retain the authority to look under students' clothing. Justice Clarence Thomas, the lone dissenter, filed an opinion stating that the court should return to *in loco parentis* and not intervene in school affairs as it restricted the ability of school administrators to "maintain discipline" and protect the "health and safety" of students.[142]

Despite the authority that the Supreme Court granted to school officials to maintain order in their schools, government reports continued to describe the state of American education in woeful terms. Newly elected president Ronald Reagan quickly appointed Terrel Bell to the administration's top education post. Though Reagan campaigned on a promise to dismantle the Department of Education, which was separated from Department of Health, Education, and Welfare and became its own entity in the last months of Jimmy Carter's presidency, Bell instead used his position to form a commission that in 1983 produced a seminal report on the state of American public education. In *A Nation at Risk*, the commission warned of a "rising tide of mediocrity" swelling in American schools, threatening "our very future as a Nation and a people."[143]

A Nation at Risk did not explicitly name a golden age of American public schooling, but it implied a narrative of dramatic decline in the past two decades. The report echoed Bell's attitudes from his years as education commissioner under Nixon and Ford. "Our society and its educational institutions seem to have lost sight of the basic purposes of schooling, and of the high expectations and disciplined efforts to attain them," the report darkly noted, concluding that schools had been "called on to provide solutions to personal, social, and political problems that the home or other institutions either cannot or will not solve."[144] Instead, *A Nation at Risk* suggested that American public education should focus on promoting "excellence." While the report generated a great deal of criticism in its wake, it represented the elevation of a new narrative of public schooling that framed the years that witnessed the largest successes of advocates for students of color as the nadir of educational quality.[145] Rather than focus on efforts to identify and remedy inequities within the system, the report instead cast education as essential to economic progress and worker productivity, and it positioned public education as a key weapon of the Cold War. The Department of Education under Reagan therefore pursued national policy based on the perceived failure of public schools while operating under a president with a political philosophy that opposed federal intervention. As with the crisis of discipline in the 1970s, the crisis of educational quality in the 1980s held appeal even where it lacked a sound evidentiary basis.

* * *

Fifteen years after the U.S. Supreme Court issued its ruling in *Ingraham v. Wright*, establishing that the use of corporal punishment in American public schools did not violate the Eighth or Fourteenth Amendments, researchers from the University of Alabama published a study on the punishment of children in an unnamed south Florida school district. The study's data set came from the 1987–1988 school year and examined the disciplinary records of more than 4,000 students.[146] The study showed the combined effect of *Goss v. Lopez* and *Ingraham v. Wright*: Students were far more likely to receive an "internal suspension" or corporal punishment than a suspension from school when disciplined. Suspensions and expulsions, with their due process protections for students, evidently became a less attractive option for school discipline than options that fell outside the purview of constitutional law.

The study also found that the most serious offenses were quite rare, and school officials most often wrote referrals for students for minor incidents. It found that "the majority of disciplinary problems were those that have vexed teachers and administrators for many years—defiance of school authority, fighting, bothering others, and truancy."[147] But when broken down by race, the researchers observed that the kind of punishment a student received varied greatly depending on whether that student was identified as white, black, or Latino. Almost 60 percent of white students who were punished received an in-school suspension while only a third of white students received corporal punishment. The numbers were nearly exactly reversed for black students, of whom 54 percent received corporal punishment and only 23 percent an in-school suspension. Black students were also more likely than white students to receive the "more serious" punishment of out-of-school suspension (44 percent of black students versus 35 percent of white students).[148] By this reckoning, black students received school referrals more often than students of other races and ethnicities, and they were also subjected, on the whole, to harsher punishments by school officials. This was most evident when it came to corporal punishment. Furthermore, the researchers concluded that "data from disciplinary files indicate that corporal punishment was administered most frequently for defiance of school authority, fighting, and bothering others." But when they compared rates of corporal punishment to those incidents, they found an irregularity. "A review of the data indicates that white pupils were referred for these acts more frequently than black pupils and, thus, should have received higher rates of corporal punishment."[149]

The University of Alabama study did not make any broad conclusions but, instead, assembled the raw data and suggested possible explanations for the discrepancies in the way black and white children were disciplined at school. The authors concluded that, while it was possible that black students had engaged in more serious misbehavior, the data could not support such a conclusion, nor could the reports of faculty and staff. The study ended with the note that the most likely culprit was "some form of bias" on the part of the school officials who meted out punishment. That they assigned harsher penalties to black students than white students for the same infractions seemed the most obvious explanation.

Other evidence backed up the Florida study. A nationwide survey found that in 1988, there were more than 1,000,000 incidents of corporal punishment in American public schools. In nearly a third of these cases, black children were paddled, despite the fact that black students made up only 16 percent of the student population.[150] Over the course of the year, more than 5 percent of black children reported being paddled, while the figure for white and Latino children was less than half of that.[151] In summing up the findings, the report on the survey stated that "if a student who misbehaves is male or black, he is more likely to be paddled than a student who misbehaves and is female or white, even if they do the same thing. There is no evidence, however, that blacks break school rules more often than whites."[152]

The safeguards put in place by the courts to protect students' rights to be in school and not be excluded for arbitrary reasons depended upon, in many circumstances, the snap judgment of school officials. In the realm of corporal punishment, where not even a simple hearing was required by the courts, this was especially true. Assistant principals doled out paddlings on the spur of the moment in many schools; they were therefore unlikely to reflect upon the conscious or unconscious biases that might lead them to be more quick to the "smoker" with a black student than a white one for the same offense. And the law permitted this. With the limit of students' rights weighed against the authority of officials to keep order, being labeled as "disorderly" or "disruptive" put a child on the wrong side of the law.

Corporal punishment was not the only realm in which disparate outcomes based on race became more pronounced after the 1970s. Rates of suspensions and expulsions of children of color in secondary schools rose after the Children's Defense Fund began tracking national data in 1973. A 2013 study published by the Civil Rights Project at the University of California, Los Angeles, examined national rates of suspension and expulsion in comparison to those found by the CDF. The report detailed disturbing findings. In the 2009–2010 school year, the suspension rate for white students remained roughly the same as it had forty years earlier; it increased to 7.1 from 6 percent. For Latino students, the suspension rate soared in that same time period. While Latino students had suspension rates that were roughly on par with whites in the early 1970s, by the 2010s that rate had doubled. For black students, the situation was much worse. The University of California, Los Angeles, report found that, for black students, who were suspended at twice the rate of white students in the early 1970s, the rate had more than doubled once again in the intervening forty years. Roughly one out of every four black students in American middle schools and high schools was suspended in the 2009–2010 school year.[153] Most alarmingly, 31 percent of black male middle school students received suspensions, and more than one-third of all black male students with disabilities received suspensions during the same time period.

When viewed in context of the contested history of students' rights, these figures are less astounding. The War on Crime, with its focus on identifying and harshly punishing those who committed crimes, weighed most heavily on people of color as evidenced by the disproportionate rates of incarceration of minorities. As American politicians of all stripes embraced "tough on crime" positions, concerns about disruptions and crime in public schools strengthened the authority of administrators to maintain order. This punitive approach to students, supported by the courts, complicated efforts to make schools places that furthered the cause of racial justice rather than places that exacerbated racial inequities. As the previous chapter showed, advocates for minority-group children repeatedly failed to make rights claims that would establish meaningful civil rights reforms in the schools. When it came to ensuring that disciplinary policies would be fair and just, they were no more successful. Landmark rulings like *Ingraham v. Wright* and *New Jersey v. T.L.O.* were not explicitly about race, but the Supreme Court's language legitimized concerns about a national problem of disorderly students that profoundly shaped the experiences of children of color in schools. It is possible to imagine a regime of students' rights that values both student safety and equal access to educational opportunity for all children. In a system that values the former far above the latter, it should be less surprising that racial inequities persist.

Epilogue

In 1989, the UN General Assembly adopted the Convention on the Rights of the Child (CRC), which laid out a series of principles intended to protect children. The CRC was the culmination of decades of work on the issue of children's rights that began with the League of Nations in 1924. According to the Convention, children deserved both protection and autonomy so they might develop into individuals with the capacity to fully contribute to society, and their families deserved the support that would allow children to thrive. The wide-ranging principles included protections against child trafficking, statelessness, and sexual exploitation, and it offered special protections for refugees and children with disabilities. The CRC also included the right to be free from discrimination and positive rights including "freedom of thought, conscience, and religion," freedom of association and assembly, and a right to education.[1] In some ways, it echoed fundamental principles of American constitutionalism. And yet, in important other ways—like asserting a positive right to education—it departed from that tradition.

"We believe this is a popular issue favored by a majority of Americans," said one official in the George H. W. Bush administration, who predicted an easy path to ratification for the treaty.[2] Who could be opposed to a document intended to improve the lives of children around the world? Yet Bush stalled on bringing the treaty to the Senate. The ratification of the CRC would have been largely a symbolic measure, as local, state, and federal law would determine whether its provisions were put into effect.[3] Nonetheless, the CRC became a target of conservative culture warriors, who asserted that the very idea of the rights of children threatened the cohesion of the family.[4] The United States eventually signed the CRC in 1995 under President Bill Clinton, but the Senate refused to ratify it.[5] This sets the United States apart in the international community, as every other UN nation-state has ratified the treaty.

Those who oppose ratification sometimes assert that the U.S. Constitution offers all the rights that young people need. They claim that the CRC would only duplicate extant rights. But this is, as this book demonstrates, simply untrue. The U.S. Constitution has not been interpreted to protect a right to education, and those who seek to undo the legacy of systemic racism in public schooling have limited legal tools. Indeed, the fact that all Americans do not have the right to quality public education remains a contemporary issue in the United States. In the first two decades of the new millennium, students and their advocates have confronted new challenges at school and others, like racial discrimination, that have persisted for decades. And yet there remains an important relationship between the rights of students and the experience of going to school in America. American education continues to be shaped by the decade and a half between the late 1960s and the mid-1980s in which the courts defined and limited the scope of students' constitutional rights, particularly as judicial decisions chipped away at claims to educational quality and focused instead on administrators' authority to maintain order at school.

Despite the Supreme Court's narrow interpretation of the Fourteenth Amendment's equal protection clause, some advocates continue to bring students' rights litigation when legislatures and school boards have failed to provide adequate educational opportunities to students. In September 2016, the public interest firm Public Counsel filed a lawsuit on behalf of students in Detroit public schools alleging that the district's schools did not even provide basic literacy to its majority-black student population. Noting that, in the plaintiffs' schools, "illiteracy is the norm," the initial complaint declared that "the State simply provides buildings—many in serious disrepair—in which students pass days and then years with no opportunity to learn to read, write, and comprehend."[6] Local news reports detailed the dilapidated conditions of physical school buildings as well as the poor quality of instruction offered to students within their walls. Leaky ceilings, black mold, inadequate heat in the winter, inadequate air conditioning in the summer, and a lack of appropriate textbooks and school supplies were characteristic of many of the city's schools. One high school student plaintiff described the poor instruction in schools as being "like babysitting, not school."[7] The lawsuit, *Gary B. v. Snyder*, asserted a "fundamental right of access to literacy" guaranteed by the Fourteenth Amendment. In June 2018, Federal District Judge Stephen Murphy III dismissed the lawsuit, stating that the Constitution did not protect a fundamental right to literacy.

Read against the history of students' constitutional rights since the 1960s, the *Gary B.* case appears to be a predictable result of the Supreme Court's Fourteenth Amendment jurisprudence in the realm of education. When the court offered narrow interpretations of the equal protection clause and rejected the concept of a fundamental right to education, the majority did so alongside the argument that legislatures were the proper venue for these debates—not the courts. But the example of Detroit reveals just how ineffective local and state governance can be at offering even a "minimum quantum" of adequate education to many of the nation's children. Especially when those children go to school in a district that primarily serves poor students of color in a state with a legislature that is dominated by conservatives. Of course, in the wake of *San Antonio v. Rodriguez*, in which the Supreme Court declared that education was not a fundamental right protected by the Fourteenth Amendment,[8] lawyers turned to state constitutions to claim equitable and adequate education on behalf of students. Michigan provides a clear of example of what can happen in states where this strategy failed. Years earlier, American Civil Liberties Union lawyers filed a "right to read" lawsuit based on Michigan law and the state constitution.[9] It was only after losing this lawsuit that some lawyers turned to the U.S. Constitution as a last resort.[10]

Reading the history of the development of students' rights through the lens of race provides insight into other pressing contemporary issues. In particular, the courts' focus on school safety and the need to maintain order in the classroom has also had disproportionate consequences for students of color. Since the early 2000s, academics, journalists, and educators have raised alarm about the problem of the "school-to-prison pipeline." The term refers to the correlation between poor educational outcomes and the increased likelihood of eventual incarceration; in particular, the literature that discusses the pipeline is concerned with how it affects black, Latino, and Native American students. One way to understand the link between education and incarceration is to identify how the punitive turn in American law and politics that generated the rise in the nation's prison population similarly shaped educational practices and policies. In particular, those who are most vulnerable to be swept into the system of punishment—including young black and Latino men—disproportionately share the burden of the punitive turn in education. As Victor Rios explains in his ethnography, *Punished: Policing the Lives of Black and Latino Boys*, "In an attempt to uphold the law and maintain order, officers often took extreme punitive measures with youths perceived as deviant or criminal."[11] The work of the Children's Defense Fund and the Southern Regional Council to identify and track racial disparities in school discipline during the 1970s identified similar trends among educators and administrators. In their quest to maintain order, stereotypes of "disruptive" students shaped their perception of situations. Importantly, this has not necessarily resulted in a better system of public education. The sociologist Aaron Kupchik has argued that such policies actually make schooling worse for young people. Instead of improving American public education, such policies have had the opposite effect.[12] At one high-suspending school, Kupchik found that the vast majority of student suspensions were for "defiance": "These incidents fall short of actual crime and often short of school rule violations, but they contribute to a chaotic, unruly feeling" in the school, which suggested that a punitive regime was necessary to quell disorder in the school, even when such punitiveness became counterproductive.[13]

The law is not entirely responsible for these developments, nor is it a primary factor in generating the astonishingly disproportionate rates of student suspensions by race. Nonetheless, this book illustrates how a confluence of factors—including changes on the Supreme Court, national politics, social movements, and changing conceptions of childhood and youth—worked together to shape the meaning of students' constitutional rights in the years in which they were primarily forged. It is critical to consider not only practices and policies that engender racial discrimination in education but also how the articulation of students' constitutional rights continues to shape the experience of going to school. That the law allows for and encourages such punitive policies reflects an unintended consequence of the students' rights movement, and it shows how important it is to think critically about the law, especially from the perspective of the people that these policies affect most directly: the students.

* * *

The mass shooting at Marjory Stoneman Douglas High School in Park-land, Florida, in February 2018 sparked nationwide protests both inside and outside American schools. At their core, the March for Our Lives protests expressed the central idea that all students should have the right to go to school without fear of being killed. This concept—that students in American public schools should have the right to learn without fear of bodily harm—is a relatively recent idea, but one that the protests reveal is rooted in the everyday experience of being a student in the era of mass shootings. This is a reality that is difficult for those who attended school before the modern era to understand, although it makes the issue no less pressing for students whose everyday lives are shaped by the astonishing numbers of school shootings that take place each year.

It remains to be seen if this particular event will mark the start of a new era of student activism. But at the massive rally held in in the na-tion's capital on March 24, 2018, the stage was dominated by young peo-ple, including students who survived the shooting at Douglas six weeks earlier. The youngest speaker was eleven-year-old Naomi Wadler, who led a walkout at her elementary school. The protest lasted for eighteen silent minutes: seventeen minutes for the students murdered at Doug-las and an extra minute for a black teenager who died after being shot at an Alabama high school in early March. In her speech, Wadler in-voked a broader concern about the toll that gun violence took on young black women in the United States, declaring that "I represent the Afri-can American women who are victims of gun violence, who are simply statistics instead of vibrant, beautiful girls full of potential."[14] Wadler's speech linked together various critiques of race in America: the invis-ibility of students of color as well as how racial discrimination prevents so many young people from accessing the equal opportunities they are supposedly promised, even—and perhaps especially—at school. Since the 1999 Columbine High School massacre in Littleton, Colorado, nearly 200,000 students have experienced a shooting at school. And gun vio-lence on campus disproportionately affects students of color. Latino stu-dents are twice as likely as whites to have experienced a school shooting, while black students are three times more likely.[15]

A positive right to go to school without fear is, of course, not one recognized by the U.S. Constitution. Of the many ways that Americans think about the purpose of public schooling, not all value the independence of young people that is evident in the extension of constitutional rights protections to high school students. In the last three decades, it appears that a model of education that views students as needing protection from crime and violence at school matters more than anything else. Scholars of contemporary education have noted the rise of zero-tolerance policies, the presence of police officers in schools, the use of drug-sniffing dogs and locker searches, and the installation of metal detectors as elements of this punitive turn in education. It is possible, too, that an inadvertent effect of the student movement against gun violence at school might work to heighten the disciplinary crackdown on all students.

The way to avoid embracing harsher punishments as a panacea is, of course, to listen to the students. In their words, we can understand the foundational stakes of their demands for change and the pressing nature of the matter. The history of the development of students' constitutional rights is one that reveals how important it is to fashion student-centered remedies that are conscious of existing race, sex, and class inequities. What student protesters in the 1960s and 1970s often wanted was an education that respected their experiences and lives, curricula that reflected their cultures, and leadership that acknowledged the particular needs of students. As Barbara Bennett Woodhouse explained, education "promotes autonomy, dignity, and equality"—all values that the American constitutional order claims to embody.[16] And so a lack of dedication to making education more equal and accessible to all young people is a betrayal of fundamental American values. In particular, it demonstrates the poverty of our sense of the rights of children and how the goal of equal educational opportunity for all might be made meaningful.

ACKNOWLEDGMENTS

The only way to end is by thanking my students. In the fall of 2005, I began teaching in Baltimore—a job for which I was woefully underprepared at a school that was tremendously underresourced. My students tolerated my many shortcomings, and they inspired this book. They showed me that the most perceptive critiques of public education can come straight from the mouths of seventh graders and set me down a path to find out what young people in the past had to say. In the end, I wrote this book for them.

Many organizations supported this project along the way. I am grateful to the National Endowment for the Humanities and the American Society for Legal History for providing crucial research funding. A National Academy of Education/Spencer Foundation postdoctoral fellowship gave me the time to write the manuscript. I have been privileged to begin my career at an institution that values the research of scholars in the humanities, and I thank the University of Oklahoma Office of the Vice President for Research, the College of Arts and Sciences, the Humanities Forum, and the Institute for the American Constitutional Heritage for their financial support of this book. The Mellon Foundation and the University of Chicago provided funding that helped me complete initial research out of which the idea for this book grew.

I am grateful, too, to the many people who have commented on this work, offered helpful suggestions, and asked critical questions at various phases of the project, especially the anonymous readers for NYU Press. Thanks to my editor, Clara Platter, whose enthusiasm for the project motivated me to get it done. Thanks, too, to Amy Klopfenstein at NYU Press for her guidance through the publishing process. Jennifer Dropkin's scrupulous copyediting caught many mistakes and smoothed the rough edges of my writing. The University of Chicago's Social History Workshop was where I hashed out early ideas about what the book could be, and I am grateful to the many people at Chicago who forced me to clarify my ideas and sharpen my writing. Special thanks go to Natalie Belsky, Matthew Briones, Sarah L. H. Gronningsater, Patrick Kelly, Amy Lippert, Casey Lurtz, Shaul Mitelpunkt, Emily Romeo, Julie Saville, Diana Schwartz, Jim Sparrow, Amy Dru Stanley, Jackie Sumner, Katie Turk, and Sarah Jones Weicksel. Through our writing group, Chris Dingwall, Sarah Miller-Davenport, and Emily Remus offered thoughtful feedback, friendship, and comic relief. Thanks to Martha Biondi, Winston Bowman, Tomiko Brown-Nagin, Eric Foner, Sally Gordon, Joanna Grisinger, Stephanie Hinnershitz, Mandy Hughett, Amalia Kessler, Felicia Kornbluh, Matthew Lassiter, Sara Mayeux, Chris Schmidt, Rebecca de Schweinitz, Tracy Steffes, and Rebecca Zietlow for their incisive comments and questions on research I presented at conferences. Through the National Academy of Education/Spencer Foundation, I had the opportunity to be mentored through the writing phase by the wonderful and generous historians Ruben Flores, Adam Nelson, Laura Muñoz, and Jonathan Zimmerman.

I am deeply indebted to the archivists and librarians who generously shared their knowledge of collections and provided helpful advice at every opportunity. At the University of Oklahoma I have been fortunate to be surrounded by brilliant and thoughtful colleagues, many who I can now count as friends. I am grateful to Kathy Brosnan, Elyssa Faison, Alisa Fryar, Paul Gilje, Anne Hyde, Mackenzie Israel-Trummel, Ben Keppel, Andreana Pritchard, Rachel Shelden, Allyson Shortle, Melissa Stockdale, Sarah Tracy, Solongo Wandan, Julie Ward, and Jane Wickersham. I owe an especially deep debt of gratitude to Cathy Kelly, who mentored me and provided sage advice at crucial moments during the last several years. Kathleen Tipler and Ana Bracic provided crucial feedback on the fourth chapter, and the members of my writing group, Ronnie Grinberg and Jenn Holland, offered comments and questions on virtually the entire book. Kevin Butterfield has been a perpetual font of ideas, support, and advice. Kevin helped me write the proposal and navigate the publishing process, and he consistently offered encouraging words and helpful feedback throughout the researching and writing of the book. My department chair, Sam Huskey, has been a tireless supporter of my teaching and research, and I am immensely grateful for all he has done on my behalf. Special thanks go to my sharp and careful research assistant, Madison Ewald.

David Chappell backed this project from the start, and I am lucky to have him in my corner. David read and commented on the entire manuscript and offered feedback on several versions of several chapters—a task no one should reasonably be expected to do. The book is richer and more thoughtful for his efforts. Justin Wert also read and commented on the entire manuscript, and I am especially grateful for the many ways he has offered support of my academic career. At a daylong manuscript workshop hosted by the OU Humanities Forum, Michael Grossberg and David Tanenhaus provided extensive feedback on the manuscript. The comments they offered clarified my thinking on the rights of children and teenagers and sharpened my understanding of why the book mattered. I am immensely grateful for all the work they put in to making this book better. Many thanks to Janet Ward, the board members of the Humanities Forum, and Hannah Zinn, who made the workshop possible.

Mark Bradley, Jane Daily, and Adam Green pushed me to ask important questions, do careful research, and consider the broader stakes of my work. I was lucky to have Mark as a kind and thoughtful adviser for both my undergraduate and graduate careers. Jane took me under her wing early at Chicago, and she consistently pushed me to improve my work while offering detailed feedback on everything I wrote. Adam Green has put countless hours into advising and mentoring me, and his thoughtfulness has shaped my thinking about the project over the years. He was especially supportive at a crucial moment when I decided to completely reimagine the project and take on a perhaps unwisely ambitious plan of research and writing.

There is probably no person who has had a greater hand in making this book possible than Carl Smith. Carl brought me into the American Studies program at Northwestern and has served as my mentor ever since. Carl taught me what it means to do historical research, to ask big questions, and to write well. No words here can adequately describe just how important his mentorship and friendship have been to me, and I appreciate how lucky I am to have met him at such a pivotal point in my life.

Throughout the process of writing this book, my family has offered unconditional love and support. My brothers and their families have cheered me on every step of the way and served as welcome distractions, as did aunts, uncles, and cousins, too many to count. My parents, Bill and Teresa Schumaker, taught me to never stop learning. They have always supported me with kindness, love, and good humor. Nobody has done more work in the background to see this thing through than Matthew Barton, who is a committed partner in every sense of the word. Matthew gave me the support I needed to finish this project while patiently reminding me that there is more to life than a book. Thank you for everything.

NOTES

INTRODUCTION

1 On the long history of black student protest, see V. P. Franklin, "African American Student Activism in the Twentieth Century," *Journal of African American History* 88, no. 2 (Spring 2003): 105–109. On black student protest in Chicago, see Dionne Danns, *Something Better for Our Children: Black Organizing in Chicago Public Schools, 1963–1971* (New York: Routledge, 2003). The historians Matthew Countryman and Todd Robinson have noted the importance of black student protest within a larger story that takes place primarily outside the schools, especially in the North. See Matthew Countryman, *Up South: Civil Rights and Black Power in Philadelphia* (Philadelphia: University of Pennsylvania Press, 2007), chap. 6; and Todd Robinson, *A City within a City: The Black Freedom Struggle in Grand Rapids, Michigan* (Philadelphia: Temple University Press, 2012), chap. 4.

2 The best overview of high school student protest in the United States is Gael Graham, *Young Activists: American High School Students in the Age of Protest* (DeKalb: Northern Illinois University Press, 2006). On the involvement of young people in the Black Freedom Struggle, see Rebecca de Schweinitz, *If We Could Change the World: Young People and America's Long Struggle for Racial Equality* (Chapel Hill: University of North Carolina Press, 2011); and Jon Hale, *The Freedom Schools: Student Activists in the Mississippi Civil Rights Movement* (New York: Columbia University Press, 2016). On the importance of high school student protest to the Chicano Movement, see Carlos Muñoz, *Youth, Identity, Power: The Chicano Movement* (New York: Verso, 1989); Mario T. Garcia, *Blowout! Sal Castro and the Chicano Struggle for Educational Justice* (Chapel Hill: University of North Carolina Press, 2011); Armando Navarro, *Mexican American Youth Organization: Avant-Garde of the Chicano Movement in Texas* (Austin: University of Texas Press, 1995); and Guadalupe San Miguel, Jr., *Chicana/o Struggles for Education: Activism in the Community* (College Station: Texas A&M University Press, 2013).

3 Before 1975, rules and legislation regarding the disciplinary rights of students were set by state legislatures or local school boards, and as the American Civil Liberties Union Student Rights Project found in its study of New York City schools in the 1969–1970 academic year, even in districts with liberal protections for students, principals often disregarded them without consequence. See Ira Glasser and Alan Levine, *New York Civil Liberties Union Student Rights Project Report on the First Two Years, 1970–1972* (New York: New York Civil Liberties Union, 1972).

4 *Tinker v. Des Moines Independent Community School District*, 393 U.S. 503 (1969).

5 Recent works on free speech after *Tinker* include Catherine J. Ross, *Lessons in Censorship: How Schools and Courts Subvert Students' First Amendment Rights* (Cambridge, MA: Harvard University Press, 2015); and Anne Proffitt Dupre, *Speaking Up: The Unintended Costs of Free Speech in Public Schools* (Cambridge, MA: Harvard University Press, 2010).

6 See, generally, Richard Kluger, *Simple Justice: The History of* Brown v. Board of Education *and Black America's Struggle for Equality* (New York: Knopf, 1976); and Mark Tushnet, *The NAACP's Legal Strategy against Segregated Education, 1925–1950* (Chapel Hill: University of North Carolina Press, 1987). On criticism of the focus on school desegregation, see Derrick Bell, *Silent Covenants:* Brown v. Board of Education *and the Unfulfilled Hopes for Racial Reform* (New York: Oxford University Press, 2005); Risa Goluboff, *The Lost Promise of Civil Rights* (Cambridge, MA: Harvard University Press, 2010); and Jack Balkin, ed., *What* Brown v. Board of Education *Should Have Said: The Nation's Top Legal Experts Rewrite America's Landmark Civil Rights Decision* (New York: New York University Press, 2002).

7 Justin Driver, *The Schoolhouse Gate: Public Education, The Supreme Court, and the Battle for the American Mind* (New York: Pantheon Books, 2018).

8 On the Farmville student strike, see Jill Ogline Titus, *Brown's Battleground: Students, Segregationists, and the Struggle for Racial Justice in Prince Edward County, Virginia* (Chapel Hill: University of North Carolina Press, 2011).

9 Charles Payne emphasizes the role young people played in leading the movement in Mississippi in *I've Got the Light of Freedom: The Organizing Tradition and the Mississippi Freedom Struggle* (Berkeley: University of California Press, 1995), as does John Dittmer's *Local People: The Struggle for Civil Rights in Mississippi* (Champaign: University of Illinois Press, 1994). On the sit-in movement, see William Chafe, *Civility and Civil Rights: Greensboro, North Carolina, and the Black Struggle for Freedom* (New York: Oxford University Press, 1980); and Barbara Ransby, *Ella Baker and the Black Freedom Movement: A Radical Democratic Vision* (Chapel Hill: University of North Carolina Press, 2003). On the Freedom Rides, see Raymond Arsenault, *Freedom Riders: 1961 and the Struggle for Racial Justice* (New York: Oxford University Press, 2007).

10 On the New Left, see Tom Hayden, *The Port Huron Statement: The Visionary Call of the 1960s Revolution* (New York: Thunder's Mouth Press, 2005); and Todd Gitlin, *The Sixties: Years of Hope, Days of Rage* (New York: Bantam, 1987).

11 On college student protests and the New Left, see Martha Biondi, *The Black Revolution on Campus* (Berkeley: University of California Press, 2012); and Robert Cohen, *Freedom's Orator: Mario Savio and the Radical Legacy of the 1960s* (New York: Oxford University Press, 2009). See also Ibram X. Kendi, *The Black Campus Movement: Black Students and the Racial Reconstruction of Higher Education, 1965–1972* (New York: Palgrave Macmillan, 2012); Joy Williamson, *Black Power on Campus: The University of Illinois, 1965–1975* (Champaign: University of Illinois

Press, 2003); and Robert Cohen and David J. Snyder, eds., *Southern Student Activism in the 1960s* (Baltimore: Johns Hopkins University Press, 2013).

12 Throughout this book, I use several different terms to refer to persons of Mexican descent as well as persons of Latin American descent. I primarily refer to persons of Mexican descent as "Mexican American," which is a reflection of the strong presence of a second generation of Mexican immigrants in the American Southwest in the 1960s. This is especially true in the case of Denver, which is the focus of the second chapter. The term "Mexican American" therefore reflects both the ancestry and American citizenship of such persons. The term "Chicano" is used in the context in which people referred to themselves as such, claiming that particular identity, often by affiliating with the Chicano Movement. The hyphenated term "Mexican-American" is used only to refer to the generation of postwar activists who self-consciously identified as such.

13 Carlos Muñoz, Jr., refers to the East Los Angeles blowouts as an event "that sparked the emergence of the Chicano Civil Rights Movement" in the second edition of his authoritative account of the movement, and Ian Haney López likewise notes the blowouts as marking the rise of the movement. See Muñoz, *Youth, Identity, Power*, 1; and Ian Haney López, *Racism on Trial: The Chicano Fight for Justice* (Cambridge, MA: Belknap, 2003), 4.

14 On the age of majority generally, see Corrine T. Field and Nicholas L. Syrett, eds., *Age in America* (New York: New York University Press, 2015). On age and marriage, see Nicholas L. Syrett, *American Child Bride: A History of Minors and Marriage in the United States* (Chapel Hill: University of North Carolina Press, 2016). On age and voting rights, see Rebecca de Schweinitz, "'The Proper Age for Suffrage': Vote 18 and the Politics of Age from World War II to the Age of Aquarius," in Field and Syrett, *Age in America*, 209–236. On the consumption of alcohol, see Timothy Cole, "'Old Enough to Live': Age, Alcohol, and Adulthood in the United States, 1970–1984," in Field and Syrett, *Age in America*, 237–258.

15 On the history of childhood, see Steven Mintz, *Huck's Raft: A History of American Childhood* (Cambridge, MA: Belknap Press, 2006). On the rise of the idea of the adolescent, see John Demos and Virginia Demos, "Adolescence in Historical Perspective," *Journal of Family and Marriage* 31, no. 4 (November 1969): 632–638. G. Stanley Hall popularized the concept in his book *Adolescence* (New York: D. Appleton, 1904).

16 On the debates over pedagogy in the 1960s, see Jonathan Kozol, *Death at an Early Age* (New York: Houghton Mifflin, 1967); Philip W. Jackson, *Life in Classrooms* (New York: Holt, Reinhart & Winston, 1968); Neil Postman and Charles Weingartner, *Teaching as a Subversive Activity* (New York: Delacorte Press, 1969); and Ivan Illich, *Deschooling Society* (New York: Harper & Row, 1971). On the general history of school reform, see David Tyack and Larry Cuban, *Tinkering toward Utopia: A Century of Public School Reform* (Cambridge, MA: Harvard University Press, 1995).

17 For examples of the argument that students in public elementary and secondary schools should not have constitutional rights, see Justice Hugo Black's dissent in *Tinker v. Des Moines*, 393 U.S. 503 (1969); and Justice Clarence Thomas's concurring opinion in *Morse v. Frederick*, 551 U.S. 393 (2007).

18 Barbara Bennett Woodhouse, *Hidden in Plain Sight: The Tragedy of Children's Rights from Ben Franklin to Lionel Tate* (Princeton, NJ: Princeton University Press, 2008).

19 Ibid.

20 On the growth and bureaucratization of urban schools, see David Tyack, *The One Best System: A History of American Urban Education* (Cambridge, MA: Harvard University Press, 1974). The years between 1920 and 1940 represented a dramatic increase in the percentage of teenagers enrolled in and graduating from high school; see ibid., 183.

21 John L. Rury and Shirley A. Hill, *The African American Struggle for Secondary Schooling, 1940–1980* (New York: Teachers College Press, 2011), 63–64.

22 Rubén Donato, *The Other Struggle for Equal Schools: Mexican Americans during the Civil Rights Era* (Albany: State University of New York Press, 1997), 16.

23 Ansley Erickson, *Making the Unequal Metropolis: School Desegregation and Its Limits* (Chicago: University of Chicago Press, 2016).

24 For a list that includes many of the education cases brought by the Mexican American Legal Defense Fund (MALDEF), see San Miguel, *Chicana/o Struggles for Education*, chap. 2. On Puerto Rican activism in New York City, see Sonia Song-Ha Lee, *Building a Latino Civil Rights Movement: Puerto Ricans, African Americans, and the Pursuit of Racial Justice in New York City* (Chapel Hill: University of North Carolina Press, 2014).

25 On the founding of the Children's Defense Fund, see Marian Wright Edelman, *Lanterns: A Memoir of Mentors* (Boston: Beacon Press, 1999).

26 On the establishment of the juvenile justice system and the history of juvenile courts, see David Tanenhaus, *Juvenile Justice in the Making* (New York: Oxford University Press, 2005); Michael Willrich, *City of Courts: Socializing Justice in Progressive Era Chicago* (New York: Cambridge University Press, 2003); and Margaret K. Rosenheim and Adele Simmons, eds., *A Century of Juvenile Justice* (Chicago: University of Chicago Press, 2002).

27 *In re Gault*, 387 U.S. 1 (1967). On the decision, see David S. Tanenhaus, *The Constitutional Rights of Children: In re Gault and Juvenile Justice* (Lawrence: University Press of Kansas, 2011).

28 On the history of the Burger Court, see Laura Kalman, *The Long Reach of the Sixties: LBJ, Nixon, and the Making of the Contemporary Supreme Court* (New York: Oxford University Press, 2017).

29 Payne, *I've Got the Light of Freedom*, 5.

CHAPTER 1. THE RIGHT TO FREE SPEECH

1 In the court transcripts and records, Canzetta Burnside is referred to as "Cansetta" or occasionally "Canzetter," a misspelling of her first name. Testimony of Margaret Burnside, court transcript, October 8, 1964, p. 18, Civil Case #1252, *Burnside v. Byars*, U.S. Dist. Court, Meridian, MS, box 6, National Archives and Records Administration Southeast Division Regional Depository, Morrow, GA (hereafter NARA-Atlanta).

2 Testimony of Neva Louise English, court transcript, October 8, 1964, p. 43, Civil Case #1252, *Burnside v. Byars*, U.S. Dist. Court, Meridian, MS, box 6, NARA-Atlanta.

3 Testimony of Montgomery Moore, court transcript, October 8, 1964, p. 75, Civil Case #1252, *Burnside v. Byars*, U.S. Dist. Court, Meridian, MS, box 6, NARA-Atlanta.

4 Testimony of Neva Louise English, court transcript, October 8, 1964, p. 45, Civil Case #1252, *Burnside v. Byars*, U.S. Dist. Court, Meridian, MS, box 6, NARA-Atlanta.

5 Thomas Bynum, *NAACP Youth and the Fight for Black Freedom* (Knoxville: University of Tennessee Press, 2013); and Rebecca de Schweinitz, *If We Could Change the World: Young People and America's Long Struggle for Racial Equality* (Chapel Hill: University of North Carolina Press, 2011).

6 There is a larger literature on black teachers than on black administrators in Southern schools, although there are ways in which the categories overlap. On the development of black education during the Jim Crow era, see James D. Anderson, *The Education of Blacks in the South, 1860–1930* (Chapel Hill: University of North Carolina Press, 1988). On the role of black teachers in segregated Southern schools, see also Adam Fairclough, *A Class of Their Own: Black Teachers in the Segregated South* (Cambridge, MA: Belknap Press, 2007); and Vanessa Siddle Walker, *The Lost Education of Horace Tate: Uncovering the Hidden Heroes Who Fought for Justice in Schools* (New York: New Press, 2018). On the white ideological influences on black schools, see William H. Watkins, *The White Architects of Black Education: Ideology and Power in America, 1865–1954* (New York: Teachers College Press, 2001).

7 Charles Bolton, *The Hardest Deal of All: The Battle over School Integration in Mississippi, 1870–1980* (Jackson: University Press of Mississippi, 2005), 80.

8 On the Freedom Rides, see Raymond Arsenault, *Freedom Riders: 1961 and the Struggle for Racial Justice* (New York: Oxford University Press, 2007); and Taylor Branch, *Parting the Waters: America in the King Years, 1954–1963* (New York: Simon & Schuster, 1988), chap. 12.

9 John Dittmer, *Local People: The Struggle for Civil Rights in Mississippi* (Champaign: University of Illinois Press, 1994), 100–101.

10 Ibid., 108–109.

11 Ibid., 107.

12 Freedom school curricular materials, Joseph and Nancy Ellin Freedom Summer Collection, box 1, folder 11, McCain Library and Archives, University of Southern Mississippi, Hattiesburg. See also Dittmer, *Local People*, 114.

13 Dittmer, *Local People*, 111.

14 Howard Zinn, *SNCC: The New Abolitionists* (Boston: Beacon Press, 1964), 75–78.

15 On the use of alternative schooling to support student protesters, see the sections on the development of La Escuela Tlatelolco in chap. 2 and the "freedom school" sessions in Columbus, Ohio, in chap. 3, both in this volume.

16 On the Jackson sit-in protest, see Anne Moody, *Coming of Age in Mississippi* (New York: Doubleday, 1968); and M. J. O'Brien, *We Shall Not Be Moved: The Jackson Woolworth's Sit-In and the Movement It Inspired* (Jackson: University Press of Mississippi, 2013).

17 Testimony of Gene Young, *Congressional Record—House*, 1964, p. 13515, Michael J. Miller Civil Rights Collection, box 2, folder 13, McCain Library and Archives, University of Southern Mississippi, Hattiesburg.

18 "Freedom Day in Canton, MS," *CORE-lator*, March–April 1964, Joseph and Nancy Ellin Freedom Summer Collection, box 2, folder 12, McCain Library and Archives, University of Southern Mississippi, Hattiesburg.

19 See Steven Mintz, *Huck's Raft: A History of American Childhood* (Cambridge, MA: Belknap Press, 2006), chap. 15.

20 On the voter registration campaign of Freedom Summer, see Dittmer, *Local People*, chaps. 10–12; Charles Payne, *I've Got the Light of Freedom: The Organizing Tradition and the Mississippi Freedom Struggle* (Berkeley: University of California Press, 1995), chaps. 8–11; Emilye Crosby, *A Little Taste of Freedom: The Black Freedom Struggle in Claiborne County, Mississippi* (Chapel Hill: University of North Carolina Press, 2005); and James P. Marshall, *Student Activism and Civil Rights in Mississippi: Protest Politics and the Struggle for Racial Justice* (Baton Rouge: Louisiana State University Press, 2013). For a detailed account of the events of Freedom Summer, see Bruce Watson, *Freedom Summer: The Savage Season That Made Mississippi Burn and Made America a Democracy* (New York: Viking, 2010); and Taylor Branch, *Pillar of Fire: America in the King Years, 1963–1965* (New York: Simon & Schuster, 1998), pt. 3.

21 Jon Hale, *The Freedom Schools: Student Activists in the Mississippi Civil Rights Movement* (New York: Columbia University Press, 2016); Daniel Perlstein, "Teaching Freedom: SNCC and the Creation of the Mississippi Freedom Schools," *History of Education Quarterly* 30, no. 3 (Autumn 1990): 297–394; and Jon Hale, "'The Student as a Force for Social Change': The Mississippi Freedom Schools and Student Engagement," *Journal of African American History* 96, no. 3 (Summer 2011): 325–347.

22 Charles Cobb, memo, "Summer Freedom Schools in Mississippi," [1963–1964], James Forman Papers, box 41, folder 14, Library of Congress Manuscript Division, Washington, DC.

23 Ibid.

24 Ibid.

25 "Memorandum: On the SNCC Mississippi Summer Project," [ca. 1964], Joseph and Nancy Ellin Freedom Summer Collection, box 1, folder 10, McCain Library and Archives, University of Southern Mississippi, Hattiesburg.

26 Charles Cobb, memo, "Summer Freedom Schools in Mississippi," [1963–1964], James Forman Papers, box 41, folder 14, Library of Congress Manuscript Division, Washington, DC.

27 Ellin wrote of the situation in Hattiesburg, "We do have lots of books for the library, many unusable . . . though there's a shortage of Negro books." See Joseph Ellin to unknown, August 11, 1964, Joseph and Nancy Ellin Freedom Summer Collection, box 1, folder 1, McCain Library and Archives, University of Southern Mississippi, Hattiesburg.

28 Jon Hale conducted a number of oral histories with freedom school students for his article, "The Student as a Force for Social Change."

29 Joseph Ellin to the editor of the *Gazette*, August 1, 1964, Joseph and Mary Ellin Freedom Summer Collection, box 1, folder 1, McCain Library and Archives, University of Southern Mississippi, Hattiesburg.

30 Charles Cobb, interview with John Rachal, October 21, 1996, p. 21, Center for Oral History and Cultural Heritage, McCain Library and Archives, University of Southern Mississippi, Hattiesburg, www.digitalcollections.usm.edu.

31 Charles Cobb, memo, "Summer Freedom Schools in Mississippi," [1963–1964], James Forman Papers, box 41, folder 14, Library of Congress Manuscript Division, Washington, DC.

32 Rayford Lee Bourn to Nancy Ellin, September 9, 1964, Joseph and Nancy Ellin Freedom Summer Collection, box 1, folder 5, McCain Library and Archives, University of Southern Mississippi, Hattiesburg.

33 Larry Stevens, "Holmes County Report," September 15, 1964, James Forman Papers, box 42, folder 5, Library of Congress Manuscript Division, Washington, DC.

34 On freedom school student involvement in direct action campaigns, see Hale, *The Freedom Schools*, chap. 5.

35 Seth Cagin and Philip Dray, *We Are Not Afraid: The Story of Goodman, Schwerner, and Chaney, and the Civil Rights Campaign for Mississippi* (New York: Nation Books, 1988), 291–293.

36 Clayborne Carson, *In Struggle: SNCC and the Black Awakening of the 1960s* (Cambridge, MA: Harvard University Press, 1981), 114–115.

37 Florence Mars, *Witness in Philadelphia* (Baton Rouge: Louisiana State University Press, 1977), 12.

38 Perlstein, "Teaching Freedom," 314.

39 Mars, *Witness in Philadelphia*, 113–114.

40 *Bunside v. Barnett*, original complaint, n.d., Civil Action #1251, *Bunside v. Barnett*, box 6, NARA-Atlanta. The name attached to the case is spelled "Bunside," reflecting a misspelling of Robert Earl Burnside's surname.

41 Affidavit of Robert Burnside, Eula Mae Miller, and Ola B. Morris, September 25, 1964, Civil Action #1251, *Bunside v. Barnett,* box 6, NARA-Atlanta.

42 Testimony of Montgomery Moore, court transcript, October 8, 1964, pp. 74–77, Civil Case #1252, *Burnside v. Byars,* box 6, NARA-Atlanta.

43 Montgomery Moore to parents, September 24, 1964, Civil Case #1252, *Burnside v. Byars,* U.S. Dist. Court, Meridian, MS, box 6, NARA-Atlanta.

44 Anderson, *The Education of Blacks in the South,* 3.

45 On teachers and the movement, see Adam Fairclough, *Teaching Equality: Black Schools in the Age of Jim Crow* (Athens: University of Georgia Press, 2001), chap. 3; and Stephanie Shaw, *What a Woman Ought to Be and Do: Black Professional Women Workers during the Jim Crow Era* (Chicago: University of Chicago Press, 1995). On black teachers who worked behind the scenes to challenge Jim Crow, see Walker, *The Lost Education of Horace Tate.*

46 Moderate white leaders understood the threat posed by *Brown* and worked to circumvent it by addressing the inequities of "separate and unequal." See Anders Walker, *The Ghost of Jim Crow: How Southern Moderates Used* Brown v. Board of Education *to Stall Civil Rights* (New York: Oxford University Press, 2009). On efforts to equalize public education in Mississippi, see Bolton, *The Hardest Deal of All,* chaps. 2 and 3.

47 "Nichols, Ajatha: Oral History," June 4, 2012, Mississippi Civil Rights Project, http://mscivilrightsproject.org.

48 Testimony of Margaret Burnside, court transcript, October 8, 1964, pp. 12–13, Civil Case #1252, *Burnside v. Byars,* U.S. Dist. Court, Meridian, MS, box 6, NARA-Atlanta.

49 Ibid., p. 18.

50 Affidavit of Martha Burnside, November 10, 1964, Congress of Racial Equality, Mississippi 4th Congressional District Records, 1961–1966, micro 793, reel 4, segment 73, Wisconsin Historical Society Library Microforms Room, Madison.

51 Testimony of Margaret Burnside, court transcript, October 8, 1964, p. 4, Civil Case #1252, *Burnside v. Byars,* U.S. Dist. Court, Meridian, MS, box 6, NARA-Atlanta.

52 Original complaint, Civil Action #1251, *Bunside v. Barnett,* U.S. Dist. Court, Meridian, MS, box 6, NARA-Atlanta.

53 Original complaint, *Burnside v. Byars,* October 1, 1964, p. 2, Civil Case #1252, *Burnside v. Byars,* U.S. Dist. Court, Meridian, MS, box 6, NARA-Atlanta.

54 Limitations on the authority of state legislators and the scope of parents' right to privacy in *Pierce v. Society of Sisters* and *Meyer v. Nebraska* (whether students could be compelled to attend public school and whether the state could forbid the teaching of certain subjects in private schools) were important precedents to the court's turn toward students and the question of whether they, too, had rights. The flag salute case, *West Virginia v. Barnette,* and the school prayer case, *Engel v. Vitale,* both indicated that state officials' authority within schools was not absolute and that students had limited, undefined rights under the First Amendment.

Furthermore, the *Brown v. Board of Education* case referenced a right to education when it is made compulsory by the state. See *Meyer v. Nebraska*, 262 U.S. 390 (1923); *Pierce v. Society of Sisters*, 268 U.S. 510 (1925); *West Virginia v. Barnette*, 319 U.S. 624 (1943); *Engel v. Vitale*, 370 U.S. 421 (1962); and *Brown v. Board of Education*, 347 U.S. 483 (1954).

55 A brief description of the rights of parents can be found in the sixteenth chapter of the first volume of Blackstone's *Commentaries*, titled "Of Parent and Child." See William Blackstone, *Commentaries on the Laws of England*, vol. 1, ed. William G. Hammond (San Francisco: Bancroft-Whitney Co., 1890), 784.

56 Anne Proffitt Dupre, *Speaking Up: The Unintended Costs of Free Speech in Public Schools* (Cambridge, MA: Harvard University Press, 2010), 9–10.

57 On the development of the common schools, see Johann Neem, *Democracy's Schools: The Rise of Public Education in America* (Baltimore: Johns Hopkins University Press, 2017).

58 Emily Zackin, *Looking for Rights in All the Wrong Places* (Princeton, NJ: Princeton University Press, 2013), 67.

59 Ibid., 71.

60 David Tyack and Robert Lowe, "The Constitutional Moment: Reconstruction and Black Education in the South," *American Journal of Education* 94, no. 2 (February 1986): 236–256.

61 Zackin, *Looking for Rights in All the Wrong Places*, 72.

62 Tracy Steffes, *School, Society, and State: A New Education to Govern Modern America, 1890–1940* (Chicago: University of Chicago Press, 2012), 141–147.

63 *Minersville v. Gobitis*, 310 U.S. 586 (1940).

64 Dissent, Harlan Fiske Stone, *Minersville v. Gobitis*, 310 U.S. 586 (1940).

65 Ibid.

66 *West Virginia v. Barnette*, 319 U.S. 624 (1943).

67 Testimony of Linda Jordan, court transcript, p. 65, October 8, 1964, Civil Case #1252, *Burnside v. Byars*, U.S. Dist. Court, Meridian, MS, box 6, NARA-Atlanta.

68 Testimony of Canzetta Burnside, court transcript, p. 33, October 8, 1964, Civil Case #1252, *Burnside v. Byars*, U.S. Dist. Court, Meridian, MS, box 6, NARA-Atlanta.

69 Workers for COFO and SNCC were often called "freedom riders," even years after the Freedom Rides ended. See Dittmer, *Local People*, 97.

70 Testimony of Canzetta Burnside, court transcript, p. 34, October 8, 1964, Civil Case #1252, *Burnside v. Byars*, U.S. Dist. Court, Meridian, MS, box 6, NARA-Atlanta.

71 Testimony of Linda Jordan, court transcript, p. 61, October 8, 1964, Civil Case #1252, *Burnside v. Byars*, U.S. Dist. Court, Meridian, MS, box 6, NARA-Atlanta.

72 Ibid., pp. 62–63.

73 Testimony of Montgomery Moore, court transcript, October 8, 1964, p. 89, Civil Case #1252, *Burnside v. Byars*, U.S. Dist. Court, Meridian, MS, box 6, NARA-Atlanta.

74 Ibid., p. 91.

75 Testimony of Leroy Peeples, court transcript, p. 106, October 8, 1964, Civil Case #1252, *Burnside v. Byars*, U.S. Dist. Court, Meridian, MS, box 6, NARA-Atlanta.

76 Testimony of A. B. Ernest, court transcript, p. 103, October 8, 1964, Civil Case #1252, *Burnside v. Byars*, U.S. Dist. Court, Meridian, MS, box 6, NARA-Atlanta.

77 Transcript of hearing, p. 21, October 8, 1964, Civil Case #1252, *Burnside v. Byars*, U.S. Dist. Court, Meridian, MS, box 6, NARA-Atlanta.

78 Ibid., p. 125.

79 Ibid., pp. 124–125.

80 MFDP Lauderdale County—Reports (Weekly) by M. Schwerner & Staff, January–July 1964, Mississippi Freedom Democratic Party, Lauderdale County, MS, records, 1964–1966, micro 55, reel 2, segment 52, Wisconsin Historical Society Library Microforms Room, Madison.

81 Notice of appeal, Civil Action #1252, November 23, 1964, *Burnside v. Byars*, U.S. Dist. Court, Meridian, MS, box 6, NARA-Atlanta.

82 Bureau of the Census, "Preliminary Reports: Population Counts for States, Mississippi," *1960 Census of Population* (Washington, DC: Government Printing Office, 1960), table 1.

83 Unita Blackwell, *Barefootin': Life Lessons from the Road to Freedom* (New York: Crown, 2006), 70; Unita Blackwell, interview with Mike Garvey, April 21, 1977, p. 7, Center for Oral History and Cultural Heritage, McCain Library and Archives, University of Southern Mississippi, Hattiesburg, www.digitalcollections.usm.edu.

84 "Preliminary Reports: Population Counts for States, Mississippi," table 1.

85 "School Desegregation in Issaquena and Sharkey," Michael J. Miller Civil Rights Collection, box 2, folder 13, McCain Library and Archives, University of Southern Mississippi, Hattiesburg.

86 Blackwell, *Barefootin'*, 84; and Unita Blackwell, interview with Mike Garvey, April 21, 1977, p. 9, Center for Oral History and Cultural Heritage, McCain Library and Archives, University of Southern Mississippi, Hattiesburg, www.digitalcollections.usm.edu.

87 Unita Blackwell, interview with Mike Garvey, April 21, 1977, pp. 6–7, Center for Oral History and Cultural Heritage, McCain Library and Archives, University of Southern Mississippi, Hattiesburg, www.digitalcollections.usm.edu.

88 Blackwell, *Barefootin'*, 137.

89 "Profiles of Freedom Schools," Joseph and Nancy Ellin Freedom Summer Collection, box 1, folder 11, McCain Library and Archives, University of Southern Mississippi, Hattiesburg.

90 Sandra Adickes, *Legacy of a Freedom School* (New York: Palgrave Macmillan, 2005), 84.

91 Ibid., 85–86.

92 "The Mississippi Student Union Convention—December 1964," COFO News, Michael J. Miller Civil Rights Collection, box 4, folder 4, McCain Library and Archives, University of Southern Mississippi, Hattiesburg.

93 Adickes, *Legacy of a Freedom School*, 87.

94 "The Mississippi Student Union Convention—December 1964," COFO News, Michael J. Miller Civil Rights Collection, box 4, folder 4, McCain Library and Archives, University of Southern Mississippi, Hattiesburg.

95 Liz Fusco recalled that the Mississippi Student Union acted "on their own" and could not be controlled by adults in COFO. See Liz Fusco, "To Blur the Focus of What You Came Here to Know," Michael J. Miller Civil Rights Collection, box 2, folder 15, McCain Library and Archives, University of Southern Mississippi, Hattiesburg.

96 Original complaint filed April 1, 1965, p. 17, Civil Action #1096, *Blackwell v. Issaquena County* case file, U.S. Dist. Court, Jackson, MS, NARA-Atlanta.

97 Martin Nicolaus to unknown, February 16, 1965, Martin and Victoria Nicolaus Papers, 1964–1965, Archives Main Stacks, SC3090, Freedom Summer Digital Collection, Wisconsin Historical Society, Madison, http://content.wisconsinhistory.org.

98 Affidavit of Eugene White, May 6, 1965, Civil Action #1096, *Blackwell v. Issaquena County* case file, U.S. Dist. Court, Jackson, MS, NARA-Atlanta.

99 Affidavit of Roosevelt White, May 6, 1965, Civil Action #1096, *Blackwell v. Issaquena County* case file, U.S. Dist. Court, Jackson, MS, NARA-Atlanta.

100 Orsmond E. Jordan obituary, *Jackson (MS) Clarion-Ledger*, May 5, 2010.

101 Martin Nicolaus to unknown, February 16, 1965, Victoria and Martin Nicolaus Papers, 1964–1965, Archives Main Stacks, SC3090, Freedom Summer Digital Collection, Wisconsin Historical Society, Madison, http://content.wisconsinhistory.org.

102 Affidavit of O. E. Jordan, May 5, 1965, Civil Action #1096, *Blackwell v. Issaquena County* case file, U.S. Dist. Court, Jackson, MS, NARA-Atlanta.

103 Martin Nicolaus to unknown, February 16, 1965, Victoria and Martin Nicolaus Papers, 1964–1965, Archives Main Stacks, SC3090, Freedom Summer Digital Collection, Wisconsin Historical Society, Madison, http://content.wisconsinhistory.org.

104 Affidavit of O. E. Jordan, May 5, 1965, Civil Action #1096, *Blackwell v. Issaquena County* case file, U.S. Dist. Court, Jackson, MS, NARA-Atlanta.

105 The original complaint notes that the number was 200, although Jordan's affidavit states that he and other school officials counted 177 button-wearing students. See original complaint filed April 1, 1965, Civil Action #1096, *Blackwell v. Issaquena County* case file, U.S. Dist. Court, Jackson, MS, NARA-Atlanta; and affidavit of O. E. Jordan, May 5, 1965, Civil Action #1096, *Blackwell v. Issaquena County* case file, U.S. Dist. Court, Jackson, MS, NARA-Atlanta.

106 Original complaint filed April 1, 1965, Civil Action #1096, *Blackwell v. Issaquena County* case file, U.S. Dist. Court, Jackson, MS, NARA-Atlanta.

107 "School Boycott Total Climbs Sharply Today," *Greenville (MS) Delta Democrat-Times*, February 22, 1965.

108 "Negro Students Boycott Schools in Indianola," *Greenville (MS) Delta Democrat-Times*, February 24, 1965.

109 "School Boycott Loses Steam," *Greenville (MS) Delta Democrat-Times*, February 23, 1965.

110 Affidavit of R. W. Ferrell, Mrs. W. R. Rogers, J. R. Carter, J. R. Wade, W. E. Fleeman, Jr., and Superintendent H. G. Fenton, May 3, 1965, Civil Action #1096, *Blackwell v. Issaquena County* case file, U.S. Dist. Court, Jackson, MS, NARA-Atlanta. The numbers are inconsistent in separate accounts. Some claimed as many as 1,000 students participated in the boycott, others more than 400. See "School Desegregation in Issaquena and Sharkey," Michael J. Miller Civil Rights Collection, box 2, folder 13, McCain Library and Archives, University of Southern Mississippi, Hattiesburg.

111 Bolton, *The Hardest Deal of All*, 100.

112 Original complaint filed April 1, 1965, Civil Action #1096, *Blackwell v. Issaquena County* case file, U.S. Dist. Court, Jackson, MS, NARA-Atlanta.

113 *Blackwell v. Issaquena County Board of Education*, 363 F.2d 749 (5th Cir. 1966).

114 Unita Blackwell, interview with Mike Garvey, April 21, 1977, pp. 38–39, Center for Oral History and Cultural Heritage, McCain Library and Archives, University of Southern Mississippi, Hattiesburg, www.digitalcollections.usm.edu.

115 Ibid., p. 40.

116 Affidavit of Eugene White, May 6, 1965, Civil Action #1096, *Blackwell v. Issaquena County* case file, U.S. Dist. Court, Jackson, MS, NARA-Atlanta.

117 Charles Cobb, interview with John Rachal, p. 8, October 21, 1996, Center for Oral History and Cultural Heritage, McCain Library and Archives, University of Southern Mississippi, Hattiesburg, www.digitalcollections.usm.edu.

118 Martin Nicolaus to Jim, February 16, 1965, Victoria and Martin Nicolaus Papers, 1964–1965, Archives Main Stacks, SC3090, Freedom Summer Digital Collection, Wisconsin Historical Society, Madison, http://content.wisconsinhistory.org.

119 Ibid.

120 O. E. Jordan to parents, Exhibit A, affidavit of May 7, 1965, attached to original complaint filed April 1, 1965, Civil Action #1096, *Blackwell v. Issaquena County* case file, U.S. Dist. Court, Jackson, MS, NARA-Atlanta.

121 In 1900, 53 percent of black children between the ages of ten and fourteen attended school. For children aged five to nine, the number was only 27 percent. See Anderson, *The Education of Blacks in the South*, 150–152.

122 On the history of black education in Mississippi, see chaps. 1 and 2 in Bolton, *The Hardest Deal of All*.

123 Fairclough, *Teaching Equality*, 60.

124 Dittmer, *Local People*, 258.

125 Per capita expenditures for black schools in Sharkey and Issaquena Counties were $171.38 through April 1965. For white schools, it was $330.31 for the same time period. See Answers to Interrogatories Propounded by Plaintiffs, p. 5, Civil Action #1096, *Blackwell v. Issaquena County* case file, U.S. Dist. Court, Jackson, MS, NARA-Atlanta.

126 As in other states, Mississippi's compulsory education law was a Progressive reform passed in 1918. See "Good Question! Does Mississippi Need a School Attendance Law?" *Greenville (MS) Delta Democrat Times*, January 9, 1973; and "Segregation Tries Costly to the South," *Atlanta Daily World*, April 17, 1958.

127 Court transcript, p. 121, Civil Case #1252, *Burnside v. Byars*, U.S. Dist. Court, Meridian, MS, box 6, NARA-Atlanta.

128 Unita Blackwell, interview with Mike Garvey, April 21, 1977, p. 39, Center for Oral History and Cultural Heritage, McCain Library and Archives, University of Southern Mississippi, Hattiesburg, www.digitalcollections.usm.edu.

129 Charles L. Zelden, *Thurgood Marshall: Race, Rights, and the Struggle for a More Perfect Union* (New York: Routledge, 2013), 127; and Jack Greenberg, *Crusaders in the Courts: How a Dedicated Band of Lawyers Fought for the Civil Rights Revolution* (New York: Basic Books, 1994), 321.

130 Bolton, *The Hardest Deal of All*, 111.

131 Ibid., 73–75.

132 Ibid., 117.

133 Affidavit, *U.S. v. Natchez*, Civil Action #1120, U.S. Dist. Court, Jackson, MS, *U.S. v. Natchez* case file, NARA-Atlanta; and Dittmer, *Local People*, 354. African Americans in Natchez had been among the first in the state to petition for desegregation in 1955. The publication of the signers' names led to the abandonment of the campaign.

134 Blackwell, *Barefootin'*, 97–100.

135 Transcript of trial, Civil Action # 1160, *United States of America v. Wilkinson County School Dist., et al.*, U.S. Dist. Court, Vicksburg, Wilkinson County and 1209 Yazoo County, box 1160, NARA-Atlanta.

136 Denial of Application for Temporary Injunction, May 11, 1965, Civil Action #1096, *Blackwell v. Issaquena County* case file, U.S. Dist. Court, Jackson, MS, NARA-Atlanta.

137 Order by Judge Harold Cox, May 11, 1965, Civil Action #1096, *Blackwell v. Issaquena County* case file, U.S. Dist. Court, Jackson, MS, NARA-Atlanta.

138 Melvyn Zarr, "Recollections of My Time in the Civil Rights Movement," *Maine Law Review* 61, no. 2 (2009): 370.

139 Marian Wright Edelman, *Lanterns: A Memoir of Mentors* (Boston: Beacon Press, 1999), 67.

140 Ibid., 78–79.

141 Zarr recalled that a great deal of the lawyers' time was spent attempting to get cases transferred from state courts to the federal courts. Melvyn Zarr, phone interview with the author, July 27, 2016.

142 Zarr, "Recollections of My Time in the Civil Rights Movement," 371.

143 "School Desegregation in Sharkey and Issaquena Counties," n.d., Michael J. Miller Civil Rights Collection, box 2, folder 13, McCain Library and Archives, University of Southern Mississippi, Hattiesburg.

144 Testimony of Neva Louise English, Court Transcript, October 8, 1964, p. 48, Civil Case #1252, *Burnside v. Byars*, U.S. Dist. Court, Meridian, MS, box 6, NARA-Atlanta.

145 *Burnside v. Byars*, 363 F.2d 744 (5th Cir. 1966).

146 Ibid.

147 Answers to Interrogatories Propounded by Plaintiffs, July 14, 1965, p. 5, Civil Action #1096, *Blackwell v. Issaquena County* case file, U.S. Dist. Court, Jackson, MS, NARA-Atlanta.

148 Evelyn Brooks Higgenbotham coined "the politics of respectability" in *Righteous Discontent: The Women's Movement in the Black Baptist Church* (Cambridge, MA: Harvard University Press, 1996). Glenda Gilmore revealed how the "respectable" involvement of black women in Progressive politics insulated their work on behalf of civil rights from the virulent racism of the early twentieth century in *Gender and Jim Crow: Women and the Politics of White Supremacy in North Carolina* (Chapel Hill: University of North Carolina Press, 1996). On respectability politics and the Black Freedom Struggle in the mid-twentieth century, see Kevin Gaines, *Uplifting the Race: Black Leadership, Politics, and Culture in the Twentieth Century* (Chapel Hill: University of North Carolina Press, 1996); and Danielle McGuire, *At the Dark End of the Street: Black Women, Rape, and Resistance—A New History of the Civil Rights Movement from Rosa Parks to Black Power* (New York: Knopf, 2010).

149 Bolton, *The Hardest Deal of All*, 105.

150 "Fact Sheet (Background on refugees use of the Greenville AFB)," n.d., Michael J. Miller Civil Rights Collection, box 3, folder 14, McCain Library and Archives, University of Southern Mississippi, Hattiesburg.

151 The *Delta Democrat-Times* noted that most cotton workers in the Delta were "grandchildren or grandparents" and that many workers in their twenties, thirties, and forties left the area in search of better work and higher pay. See "Very Young, Very Old Facing Joblessness," *Greenville (MS) Delta Democrat-Times*, February 11, 1965.

152 "Nov. hearing on 'kickout' law seen," *Baltimore Afro-American*, October 30, 1965; and "Fund Fights Mississippi 'War on Orphans: 7000 Indigent Children Barred from Classes,'" *NAACP and Legal Defense and Educational Fund Report*, October 1965, Joseph and Nancy Ellin Freedom Summer Collection, box 2, folder 17, McCain Library and Archives, University of Southern Mississippi, Hattiesburg.

153 On other forms of non-racial classification that received renewed legal attention during the 1960s and 1970s, including vagrancy and illegitimacy, see Risa Goluboff, *Vagrant Nation: Police Power, Constitutional Change and the Making of the 1960s* (New York: Oxford University Press, 2016); and Serena Mayeri, "Marital Supremacy and the Constitution of the Nonmarital Family," *California Law Review* 103 (2015): 1277–1352.

154 "Fund Fights Mississippi 'War on Orphans: 7000 Indigent Children Barred from Classes,'" *NAACP and Legal Defense and Educational Fund Report*, October 1965,

Joseph and Nancy Ellin Freedom Summer Collection, box 2, folder 17, McCain Library and Archives, University of Southern Mississippi, Hattiesburg.

155 Affidavit of Sezzie Brown, September 14, 1966, Civil Action #1096, *Blackwell v. Issaquena County* case file, U.S. Dist. Court, Jackson, MS, NARA-Atlanta; Deposition of Clyde Richardson, December 28, 1965, pp. 28–30, Civil Action #1096, *Blackwell v. Issaquena County* case file, U.S. Dist. Court, Jackson, MS, NARA-Atlanta; and Affidavit of Dorothy Jean Trass, Gracie Mae Green, Vera Mae Green, and Robert Fitzpatrick, September 14, 1966, Civil Action #1096, *Blackwell v. Issaquena County* case file, U.S. Dist. Court, Jackson, MS, NARA-Atlanta.

156 Motion for temporary restraining order, January 12, 1966, Civil Action #1096, *Blackwell v. Issaquena County* case file, U.S. Dist. Court, Jackson, MS, NARA-Atlanta. Of the fourteen black students who transferred to Fielding Wright, a formerly all-white elementary school, twelve were placed in remedial classes. See the deposition of Clyde Richardson, pp. 28–30, Civil Action #1096, *Blackwell v. Issaquena County* case file, U.S. Dist. Court, Jackson, MS, NARA-Atlanta.

157 "Nichols, Ajatha: Oral History."

158 Alan Schiffman, "Neshoba Project Report," February 1, 1965, Michael J. Miller Civil Rights Collection, box 3, folder 14, McCain Library and Archives, University of Southern Mississippi, Hattiesburg.

159 The figures are based on a court report of May 15, 1967, Civil Case #1396, *U.S. v. Neshoba County Schools* case file, US Dist. Court for the Southern District of Mississippi, Eastern Division, NARA-Atlanta. The reports of harassment are found in the denial of the request for an injunction, dated March 22, 1967, in ibid.

160 *United States v. Neshoba County School District*, Civil Case #1396, *United States v. Neshoba County School District* case file, US Dist. Court for the Southern District of Mississippi, Eastern Division, NARA-Atlanta.

161 Bolton, *The Hardest Deal of All*, 169–170.

162 Blackwell, *Barefootin'*, 143.

163 Liz Fusco, "To Blur the Focus of What You Came Here to Know," Michael J. Miller Civil Rights Collection, box 2, folder 15, McCain Library and Archives, University of Southern Mississippi, Hattiesburg.

164 John W. Johnson, *The Struggle for Student Rights: Tinker v. Des Moines and the 1960s* (Lawrence: University of Kansas Press, 1997), 4–5.

165 *Tinker v. Des Moines Independent Community School District*, 393 U.S. 503 (1969).

166 A number of works on students and free speech identify the precedent created by the *Blackwell* and *Burnside* cases within the context of larger conflicts over students and First Amendment protections. The most comprehensive legal treatment of the cases is Kristi Bowman's "The Civil Rights Roots of *Tinker's* Disruption Test," *American University Law Review* 58, no. 5 (June 2009): 1129–1165. See also David L. Hudson, *Let the Students Speak! A History of the Fight for Free Expression in American Schools* (Boston: Beacon Press, 2011); and James C. Foster, *Bong Hits 4 Jesus: A Perfect Constitutional Storm in Alaska's Capital* (Fairbanks: University of Alaska Press, 2010).

167 Dissent, *Tinker v. Des Moines*, 393 U.S. 503 (1969).

168 COFO [Council of Federated Organizations] newsletter, June 11, 1965, Joseph and Nancy Ellin Freedom Summer Collection, box 1, folder 9, McCain Library and Archives, University of Southern Mississippi, Hattiesburg.

169 On the process of "learning" the state's racial caste system, see Jennifer Rittenhouse, *Growing Up Jim Crow: How Black and White Southern Children Learned Race* (Chapel Hill: University of North Carolina Press, 2006).

CHAPTER 2. THE RIGHT TO EQUAL PROTECTION

1 Reba Yépes, interview with author, July 27, 2016, Denver, CO.

2 This chapter uses the terms "Mexican American" and "Chicano" to refer to persons of Mexican descent. My use of "Mexican American" includes all persons of Mexican descent, including Mexican nationals, as the majority of such persons in Denver during the 1960s were American citizens by birth. My use here of "Chicano" reflects the language used by activists in Denver during this era to describe themselves.

3 On the early stages of development of the Chicano Movement in Denver, see Ernesto Vigil, *The Crusade for Justice: Chicano Militancy and the Government's War on Dissent* (Madison: University of Wisconsin Press, 1999), chaps. 1–4.

4 Tom I. Romero, Jr., "Of Race and Rights: Legal Culture, Social Change, and the Making of a Multiracial Metropolis, Denver, 1940–1970" (PhD diss., University of Michigan, 2004), 9–10.

5 In 1950, the Denver metropolitan population was 612,128; by 1960, that figure had increased to 923,161. The city itself grew by 17 percent in the same period, to a population of 489,217. See Bureau of the Census, "Preliminary Reports: Population Counts for Standard Metropolitan Statistical Areas: Denver," *1960 Census of Population* (Washington, DC: Government Printing Office, 1960).

6 The 1960 census classified Mexican Americans as "white," thus making their presence as a distinct population largely indistinguishable from other white persons in the data. The Denver public school system did count "Spanish-surnamed" students, which provides rough figures of the population in Denver during the 1960s. See Romero, "Of Race and Rights," 10–11; and Bureau of the Census, *Census of Population: 1960*, vol. 1: *Characteristics of the Population*, pt. 7, *Colorado* (Washington, DC: Government Printing Office, 1963), xx.

7 Bureau of the Census, *Census of Population: 1960*, vol. 1: *Characteristics of the Population*, pt. 7, *Colorado*, table 99.

8 "Blackness" and "whiteness," as social constructs, were unstable categories even as they were foundational to the social, political, and economic structures of the South. See Grace Elizabeth Hale, *Making Whiteness: The Culture of Segregation in the South, 1890–1940* (New York: Pantheon, 1998). On the West, see Peggy Pascoe, *What Comes Naturally: Miscegenation Law and the Making of Race in America* (New York: Oxford University Press, 2009); and Ian Haney-López, *White by Law: The Legal Construction of Race* (New York: New York University Press, 1996).

9   "'Poor Performance' Elementary Schools," n.d., Rachel Noel Papers, box 1, folder 10, Blair-Caldwell Research Library, Denver, CO.

10 "Hispanos Push for Unity to Effect School Change," *Rocky Mountain News*, March 24, 1969, Corky Gonzales Papers, Western History Collection, box 1, folder 47, Denver Public Library, Denver, CO.

11 "First Draft Proposal to Establish a Viable Chicano Studies Program and the Development of the School of Tlatelolco" [ca. 1970], Corky Gonzales Papers, Western History Collection, box 3, folder 6, Denver Public Library, Denver, CO.

12 *Shelley v. Kraemer*, 334 U.S. 1 (1948).

13 Frederick Douglas Watson, "Removing the Barricades from the Northern Schoolhouse Door: School Desegregation in Denver" (PhD diss., University of Colorado-Boulder, 1993), 44.

14 On the way federal, state, and local policy and private real estate practices combined to create and maintain neighborhood segregation outside the South, see Arnold Hirsch, *Making the Second Ghetto: Race and Housing in Chicago, 1940–1960* (Cambridge: Cambridge University Press, 1983); Thomas Sugrue, *Origins of the Urban Crisis: Race and Inequality in Postwar Detroit* (Princeton, NJ: Princeton University Press, 1996); Beryl Satter, *Family Properties: How the Struggle over Race and Real Estate Transformed Chicago and Urban America* (New York: Metropolitan Books, 2009); and Richard Rothstein, *The Color of Law: A Forgotten History of How Our Government Segregated America* (New York: W. W. Norton, 2017).

15 Romero, "Of Race and Rights," 299–300.

16 Ibid., 205.

17 Watson, "Removing the Barricades," 8–9.

18 James F. Reynolds, "A Neighborhood Survey in a Residential Section of Denver, Colorado, for the City and County of Denver, Mayor's Commission on Community Relations," 1963, Rachel Noel Papers, box 1, folder 1, Blair-Caldwell Research Library, Denver, CO.

19 On the Park Hill Action Committee's efforts to maintain the neighborhood, see Romero, "Of Race and Rights," chap. 7.

20 The population growth rate of the United States rose sharply during the 1950s and then fell every decade following until the 1990s, primarily as a result of decreasing fertility rates. The nation's population grew 19 percent between 1950 and 1960, 13.3 percent between 1960 and 1970, and 11.5 percent between 1970 and 1980. See Frank Hobbs and Nicole Stoops, Bureau of the Census, *Demographic Trends in the Twentieth Century* (Washington, DC: Government Printing Office, 2002), 13.

21 Testimony of Olberholtzer, *Keyes v. School Dist. No. 1* Collection (hereafter *Keyes* Collection), 1st accession, box 13, folder 1, Norlin Library Special Collections, University of Colorado at Boulder. On the drop in fertility rates during the Great Depression, see Price V. Fishback, Michael R. Haines, and Shawn Kantor, "Births, Deaths, and New Deal Relief during the Great Depression," *Review of Economics and Statistics* 89, no. 1 (February 2007): 1–14.

22 Smith, Stedman, and Whittier Schools had populations that were more than 90 percent black. See Office of Planning, Research, and Budgeting, "Report of Estimated Ethnic Distribution of Pupils, Classroom Teachers and Other Certificated and Classified Personnel," September 26, 1969, Rachel Noel Papers, box 1, folder 7, Blair-Caldwell Research Library, Denver, CO.

23 Elmwood Elementary was 91.6 percent "Hispano" in 1969, while the other schools that were predominantly Mexican American were Elyria (73 percent), Fairmont (80 percent), Fairview (83 percent), Garden Place (65 percent), Gilpin (59 percent), Greenlee (73 percent), Remington (56 percent), Smedley (77 percent), Swansea (67 percent), Westwood (54 percent), and Wyatt (52 percent). See ibid.

24 These numbers leave out Asian American and Native American students, groups that each constituted less than 1 percent of the total student population. These figures are based on the number of schools with white populations that were less than 70 percent in 1969. These schools were Elmwood, Elyria, Evans, Fairmont, Fairview, Garden Place, Gilpin, Greenlee, Hallett, Harrington, Knapp, Mitchell, Moore, Munroe, Newlon, Park Hill, Perry, Philips, Remington, Smedley, Smith, Stedman, Swansea, Valverde, Westwood, Whittier, Wyatt, and Wyman. See ibid.

25 See ibid.

26 See ibid.

27 Testimony of Paul Klite, reporter's transcript, *Keyes v. School Dist. No. 1*, vol. I, *Keyes* Collection, 1st accession, box 31, folder 2, Norlin Library Special Collections, University of Colorado at Boulder.

28 Testimony of Rep. George L. Brown, reporter's transcript, *Keyes v. School Dist. No. 1*, vol. VI, *Keyes* Collection, 1st accession, box 32, folder 3, Norlin Library Special Collections, University of Colorado at Boulder.

29 Watson, "Removing the Barricades," 13–15.

30 Ibid., 19–20.

31 Testimony of Lidell M. Thomas, reporter's transcript, *Keyes v. School Dist. No. 1*, vol. X, *Keyes* Collection, 1st accession, box 33, folder 1, Norlin Library Special Collections, University of Colorado at Boulder.

32 "History of the Mobile Classrooms," memo, R. L. Hedley to Thayne McKnight, March 14, 1984, *Keyes* Collection, box 13, folder 8, Norlin Library Special Collections, University of Colorado at Boulder. The "mobile units" used were not trailers, per se, but more like modular homes with their own foundations. The units had access to heat, air conditioning, and plumbing. William K. Ris, oral argument, October 12, 1972, *Keyes v. School Dist. No. 1*, posted at the *Oyez Project*, www.oyez.org.

33 "All Things Equal: Rachel Noel Changed the Way Denver Goes to School," *Rocky Mountain News*, September 23, 1990, Rachel Noel Papers, box 1, folder 3, Blair-Caldwell Research Library, Denver, CO.

34 Watson, "Removing the Barricades," 42.

35 In late 1967, Park Hill parents complained that it had been seven years since the board began discussing the need for a new school in northeast Denver. In the

meantime, several other schools were built elsewhere in the city. See the minutes, December 14, 1967, archived at the Denver Public Schools Board of Education, Denver School Administration Building, Denver, CO (hereafter Denver School Board Minutes).

36 Research Services, Inc., "Equality of Educational Opportunity in Denver, Colorado," October 1963, Rachel Noel Papers, box 1, folder 5, Blair-Caldwell Research Library, Denver, CO.

37 Ibid.

38 Denver School Board Minutes, December 16, 1965.

39 "Denver Schools Policy 5100," Denver School Board Minutes, May 6, 1964.

40 Watson, "Removing the Barricades," 64–65.

41 Denver School Board Minutes, October 21, 1965. While the school board minutes did not record which article Andrews presented to the board, it was likely either written by J. Skelly Wright, a judge on the DC Court of Appeals, or Robert L. Carter, a lawyer with the NAACP's Legal Defense Fund. On the issue, both argued for the unconstitutionality of de facto segregation per the Fourteenth Amendment. See J. Skelly Wright, "Public School Desegregation: Legal Remedies for De Facto Segregation," *Case Western Law Review* 63, no. 3 (May 1965): 478–501; and Robert L. Carter, "De Facto School Segregation: An Examination of the Legal and Constitutional Questions Presented," *Case Western Law Review* 63, no. 3 (May 1965): 502–531.

42 "Proposal to Denver School Board Concerning Overcrowded Conditions at Stedman School," Denver School Board Minutes, November 18, 1965.

43 Denver School Board Minutes, January 13, 1966.

44 Denver School Board Minutes, January 26, 1966. The Citizens' Council was a network of local organizations founded in the South after the *Brown v. Board of Education* ruling to preserve "states' rights and racial integrity" by fostering resistance to civil rights reforms. See Neil R. McMillen, *The Citizens' Council: Organized Resistance to the Second Reconstruction, 1954–1964* (Urbana: University of Illinois Press, 1971), 12. On the resurgence of the Citizens' Councils in the 1970s, see Stephanie R. Rolph, *Resisting Equality: The Citizens' Council, 1954–1989* (Baton Rouge: Louisiana State University Press, 2018).

45 Watson, "Removing the Barricades," 32.

46 U.S. Commission on Civil Rights, *Racial Isolation in the Schools* (Washington, D.C.: Government Printing Office, 1967); and Denver School Board Minutes, May 4, 1967.

47 Rachel Noel oral history, conducted by Juanita Gray and James Harlan Davis, 1973, tape 2, side B, Western History/Genealogy Department Oral History Project, Denver Public Library, www.denverlibrary.org.

48 Denver School Board Minutes, June 29, 1967. Historian Gerald Horne describes the Watts Riots, which lasted for six days in August 1965 and resulted in thirty-four deaths and more than a thousand injuries, as an "insurrection" against the racial and economic subordination that isolated African Americans in poor, seg-

regated neighborhoods like Watts. See Gerald Horne, *Fire This Time: The Watts Uprising and the 1960s* (Charlottesville: University of Virginia Press, 1995).

49 Jules Mondschein, Commission on Community Relations, "Preliminary Report on Northeast Park Hill," p. 4, July 7, 1967, Rachel Noel Papers, box 1, folder 3, Blair-Caldwell Research Library, Denver, CO.

50 Jules Mondschein, Commission on Community Relations, "Final Report— Northeast Park Hill," August 31, 1967, Rachel Noel Papers, box 1, folder 3, Blair-Caldwell Research Library, Denver, CO.

51 *Report of the National Advisory Commission on Civil Disorders* (the Kerner Commission Report; New York: Bantam, 1968).

52 Denver School Board Minutes, March 21, 1968.

53 Watson, "Removing the Barricades," 94.

54 Ibid., 97.

55 Rachel Noel oral history, conducted by Juanita Gray and James Harlan Davis, 1973, tape 2, side B, Western History/Genealogy Department Oral History Project, Denver Public Library, www.denverlibrary.org.

56 Watson, "Removing the Barricades," 98–99.

57 "All Things Equal: Rachel Noel Changed the Way Denver Goes to School," *Rocky Mountain News*, September 23, 1990, Rachel Noel Papers, box 1, folder 3, Blair-Caldwell Research Library, Denver, CO.

58 Watson, "Removing the Barricades," 107–108.

59 On the Ocean Hill–Brownsville community control experiment, which resulted in racial conflict and a teacher strike, see Daniel Perlstein, *Justice, Justice: School Politics and the Eclipse of Liberalism* (New York: Peter Lang, 2004); and Jerald E. Podair, *The Strike That Changed New York: Blacks, Whites, and the Ocean Hill–Brownsville Crisis* (New Haven, CT: Yale University Press, 2004).

60 Watson was eventually removed from his post by national Black Panther Party leaders, ostensibly for his persistent legal troubles. See Summer Cherland, "No Prejudice Here: Racism, Resistance, and the Struggle for Equality in Denver, 1947–1994" (PhD diss., University of Nevada, Las Vegas, 2014), 92–93.

61 For a fuller account of these events, see Watson, "Removing the Barricades," 100–101; and Cherland, "No Prejudice Here," 127–129.

62 Cherland, "No Prejudice Here," 129–130.

63 Memo, SAC [special agent in charge] Denver to FBI Director, "Crusade for Justice—Extremist Matter—Spanish American," FBI Files, Corky Gonzales Papers, Western History Collection, box 2, folder 2, Denver Public Library, Denver, CO.

64 "Brown Power Unity Seen behind School Disorders," *Los Angeles Times*, March 17, 1968. On the East Los Angeles blowouts, see Carlos Muñoz, *Youth, Identity, Power: The Chicano Movement* (New York: Verso, 1989); and Ian Haney López, *Racism on Trial: The Chicano Fight for Justice* (Cambridge, MA: Belknap, 2003).

65 Carlos Tejeda, "Genealogies of the Student 'Blowouts' of 1968," in *Marching Students: Chicana and Chicano Activism in Education, 1968 to the Present*, ed.

Margarita Berta-Ávila, Anita Tijerina Revilla, and Julie López Figueroa (Reno: University of Nevada Press, 2011), 9–42.

66 "Corky, Commandos Take Podium at School Parley," *Rocky Mountain News*, November 6, 1968, Corky Gonzales Papers, Western History Collection, box 1, folder 47, Denver Public Library, Denver, CO.

67 "28 Persons Arrested During Two Days of Strife," *Denver Post*, March 22, 1969, Corky Gonzales Papers, Western History Collection, box 5, folder 10, Denver Public Library, Denver, CO.

68 "Transfer Approved; Teacher Hub in Controversy," *Denver Post*, March 21, 1969, Corky Gonzales Papers, Western History Collection, box 5, folder 10, Denver Public Library, Denver, CO.

69 Jason Kosena, "West High, 1969," *Denver Post*, March 21, 2009.

70 Ibid. The FBI file indicates that twenty-seven people were arrested that day. Memo, SAC [special agent in charge], Denver to FBI Director, March 21, 1969, Corky Gonzales Papers, Western History Collection, box 1, folder 61, Denver Public Library, Denver, CO.

71 In a three-month period in 1967, three young Mexican American men were shot by Denver police officers. Andrew Garcia, twenty-three years old, and Richard Medina, twenty years old, survived, but Louis Pineda, who was only seventeen years old, died from his injuries. The police officer was cleared of any charges related to his death. Timeline of events, n.d., Corky Gonzales Papers, Western History Collection, box 5, folder 21, Denver Public Library, Denver, CO.

72 "Witnesses Blame Police for West High School Riot," *Rocky Mountain News*, December 3, 1969, Corky Gonzales Papers, Western History Collection, box 6, folder 52, Denver Public Library, Denver, CO.

73 "SDS Urges Support of West Students," *Rocky Mountain News*, March 22, 1969, Corky Gonzales Papers, Western History Collection, box 5, folder 10, Denver Public Library, Denver, CO.

74 "Racial Disturbances Instigated by Crusade for Justice and Black Panther Party, Denver, Colorado, 1969," March 24, 1969, FBI File, Corky Gonzales Papers, Western History Collection, box 1, folder 61, Denver Public Library, Denver, CO.

75 "Chicano Students' Demands at West High," FBI File, Corky Gonzales Papers, Western History Collection, box 1, folder 61, Denver Public Library, Denver, CO.

76 "Racial Disturbances Instigated by Crusade for Justice and Black Panther Party, Denver, Colorado, 1969," March 24, 1969, FBI File, Corky Gonzales Papers, Western History Collection, box 1, folder 61, Denver Public Library, Denver, CO.

77 "Charges against Teacher Are Called Unfounded," *Rocky Mountain News*, March 21, 1969, Corky Gonzales Papers, Western History Collection, box 5, folder 10, Denver Public Library, Denver, CO.

78 "Transfer Approved; Teacher Hub in Controversy," *Denver Post*, March 21, 1969, Corky Gonzales Papers, Western History Collection, box 5, folder 10, Denver Public Library, Denver, CO.

79 Memo, FBI Director to SAC [special agent in charge] Denver, April 11, 1969, Corky Gonzales Papers, Western History Collection, box 1, folder 69, Denver Public Library, Denver, CO.

80 "West High Troubles Cost City $25,000," *Rocky Mountain News*, n.d., Corky Gonzales Papers, Western History Collection, box 5, folder 10, Denver Public Library, Denver, CO.

81 In addition to emphasizing the presence of Crusade for Justice and Black Panther members, including Lauren Watson, the local Black Panther leader, the FBI report on the protests labeled it a "harassment campaign." See "Racial Disturbances Instigated by Crusade for Justice and Black Panther Party, Denver, Colorado, 1969," March 24, 1969, FBI File, Corky Gonzales Papers, Western History Collection, box 1, folder 61, Denver Public Library, Denver, CO.

82 "All Things Equal: Rachel Noel Changed the Way Denver Goes to School," *Rocky Mountain News*, September 23, 1990, Rachel Noel Papers, box 1, folder 3, Blair-Caldwell Research Library, Denver, CO.

83 Watson, "Removing the Barricades," 109–112.

84 *Keyes v. School Dist. No. 1*, 303 F.Supp. 289 (D. Colo. 1969).

85 Ibid.

86 Ibid.

87 Robert T. Connery, "*Keyes v. School District No. 1*: A Personal Remembrance of Things Past and Present," *Denver University Law Review* 90, no. 5 (n.d.): 1083–1114.

88 *Keyes v. School District No. 1*, 90 S.Ct. 12.

89 Watson, "Removing the Barricades," 139–140.

90 "Chicano Liberation Day," Memo to FBI Director from SAC [special agent in charge] Denver, FBI File, Corky Gonzales Papers, Western History Collection, box 1, folder 61, Denver Public Library, Denver, CO.

91 Denver School Board Minutes, March 17, 1970.

92 The Denver Board of Education later upheld Hernandez's expulsion. See Denver School Board Minutes, May 21, 1970.

93 "Mexico Independence Day Celebrated; Hispano March Aims at School Needs," *Denver Post*, September 17, 1969, Corky Gonzales Papers, Western History Collection, box 5, folder 10, Denver Public Library, Denver, CO.

94 "Demonstration, Mexican American Students, North High School, Denver, Colorado, February 11, 1970," FBI File, Corky Gonzales Papers, Western History Collection, box 1, folder 61, Denver Public Library, Denver, CO.

95 Vigil, *The Crusade for Justice*, 118.

96 For a careful examination of the "racial minority" arguments made on behalf of Mexican American students, see Danielle R. Olden, "Becoming Minority: Mexican Americans, Race, and the Legal Struggle for Educational Equity in Denver, Colorado," *Western Historical Quarterly* 48, no. 1 (Spring 2017): 43–66.

97 *Sweatt v. Painter*, 339 U.S. 629 (1950); and *McLaurin v. Oklahoma*, 339 U.S. 637 (1950).

98 *Brown v. Board of Education*, 347 U.S. 483 (1954).

99   *Green v. County School Board of New Kent County*, 391 U.S. 430 (1968).

100 *Taylor v. Board of Education*, 195 F.Supp. 231 (S.D.N.Y. 1961).

101 *Bell v. School City of Gary, Indiana*, 324 F.2d 209 (7th Cir. 1963); *Downs v. Board of Education of Kansas City*, 336 F.2d 988 (10th Cir. 1964).

102 On the influence of J. Skelly Wright's decision in *Hobson v. Hansen*, see Connery, "*Keyes v. School District No. 1*," 1097–1098.

103 *Hobson v. Hansen*, 269 F.Supp. 401 (D.D.C. 1967).

104 See Robert L. Carter, "Law and Racial Equality in Education," *Journal of Negro Education* 37, no. 3 (Summer 1968): 205. The article was published just a few months before Carter resigned from the Legal Defense Fund in protest of the firing of Lewis M. Steel.

105 Ibid., 206.

106 Reporter's transcript, vol. I, pp. 10–11, February 2, 1970, *Keyes v. School District No. 1, Keyes* Collection, 1st accession, box 31, folder 2, Norlin Library Special Collections, University of Colorado at Boulder.

107 Ibid., pp. 6–7.

108 Ibid., p. 10.

109 *Keyes v. School Dist. No. 1*, 313 F.Supp. 61 (D. Colo. 1970).

110 When questioned directly by Judge Doyle, the lawyer agreed that his argument followed the logic of the contested "freedom of choice" plans offered by Southern districts. Reporter's Transcript, vol. I, pp. 16–17, February 2, 1970, *Keyes v. School District No. 1, Keyes* Collection, 1st accession, box 31, folder 2, Norlin Library Special Collections, University of Colorado at Boulder.

111 Testimony of Howard Johnson, reporter's transcript, vol. V, *Keyes v. School Dist. No. 1, Keyes* Collection, 1st accession, box 10, folder 1, Norlin Library Special Collections, University of Colorado at Boulder.

112 Testimony of Ethel Rollins, reporter's transcript, vol. II, *Keyes v. School Dist. No. 1, Keyes* Collection, 1st accession, box 31, folder 3, Norlin Library Special Collections, University of Colorado at Boulder.

113 Ibid.

114 Lawyers' notes for plaintiffs, *Keyes v. School Dist. No. 1, Keyes* Collection, 1st accession, box 1, folder 5, Norlin Library Special Collections, University of Colorado at Boulder.

115 *Keyes v. School Dist. No. 1*, 313 F.Supp. 61 (D. Colo. 1970).

116 Ibid.

117 James P. Coleman, *Equality of Educational Opportunity* (Washington, DC: Government Printing Office, 1966).

118 Watson, "Removing the Barricades," 157–161.

119 Ibid., 159–160. On the idea of "compensatory education" and its use in court-ordered remedies and federal legislation, see chap. 4, in this volume.

120 Watson, "Removing the Barricades," 164.

121 Denver School Board Minutes, October 15, 1970.

122 Watson, "Removing the Barricades," 167–168.

123 "Report of Meeting at Macedonia Baptist Church," September 28, 1970, Rachel Noel Papers, box 1, folder 7, Blair-Caldwell Research Library, Denver, CO.

124 Watson, "Removing the Barricades," 111.

125 Denver School Board Minutes, October 22, 1970. The school board minutes do not include the title of the study cited, but it was most likely a publication of the Senate Subcommittee on Juvenile Delinquency. See U.S. Senate, Subcommittee to Investigate Juvenile Delinquency, *Juvenile Delinquency* (Washington, DC: Government Printing Office, 1970).

126 Vigil, *The Crusade for Justice*, 160.

127 Juan Gómez-Quiñones and Irene Vásquez, *Making Aztlán: Ideology and Culture of the Chicana and Chicano Movement, 1966–1977* (Albuquerque: University of New Mexico Press, 2014), chap. 17.

128 On Septima Clark's role in developing the pedagogy for citizenship schools, see Katherine Mellen Charron, *Freedom's Teacher: The Life of Septima Clark* (Chapel Hill: University of North Carolina Press, 2009). On the Highlander Folk School, see John M. Glen, *Highlander: No Ordinary School* (Knoxville: University of Tennessee Press, 1996).

129 "First Draft Proposal to Establish a Viable Chicano Studies Program and the Development of the School of Tlatelolco" [ca. 1970], Corky Gonzales Papers, Western History Collection, box 3, folder 6, Denver Public Library, Denver, CO.

130 Reba Yépes, interview with author, July 27, 2016, Denver, CO.

131 Yearbook, La Escuela Tlatelolco [ca. 1971], Corky Gonzales Papers, Western History Collection, box 2, folder 46, Denver Public Library, Denver, CO.

132 Ibid. Gómez-Quiñones and Vásquez document other similar efforts in Texas, California, and New Mexico to develop alternative schools, but they were all short-lived in comparison to La Escuela Tlatelolco. See Gómez-Quiñones and Vásquez, *Making Aztlán*, 179–180.

133 "First Draft Proposal to Establish a Viable Chicano Studies Program and the Development of the School of Tlatelolco" [ca. 1970], Corky Gonzales Papers, Western History Collection, box 3, folder 6, Denver Public Library, Denver, CO.

134 Reba Yépes, interview with the author, July 27, 2016, Denver, Co.

135 *Keyes v. School District No. 1*, 445 F.2d 990 (1971).

136 Ibid.

137 John Herbers, "School Busing Becomes National Issue That May Affect '72 Presidential Race," *New York Times*, October 3, 1971. In Denver in 1966, 8,000 students were bused to and from school each day without protest. See Denver School Board Minutes, May 19, 1966.

138 Bill Kovach, "Boston's Schools Held Segregated," *New York Times*, December 1, 1971.

139 Ben A. Franklin, "A Decision That May be a Real Blockbuster: Busing," *New York Times*, January 16, 1972.

140 "Justices to Rule on Busing at Schools Outside the South," *New York Times*, January 18, 1972.

141 John Herbers, "Nixon Will Move to Offset Rulings for Pupil Busing," *New York Times*, February 15, 1972.

142 "Congress Gets Nixon's Plan for Moratorium on Busing," *New York Times*, March 17, 1972.

143 Robert B. Semple, "A Plan by Nixon That Will Test the Constitution: Busing," *New York Times*, March 19, 1972.

144 Oral argument, *Keyes v. School Dist. No. 1*, 413 U.S. 189 (1973).

145 Ibid.

146 Ibid.

147 Ibid.

148 Ibid.

149 William J. Brennan, Memorandum to the Conference, April 3, 1973, Thurgood Marshall Papers, Manuscripts Division, box 100, folder 8, Library of Congress, Washington, DC.

150 *Roberts v. City of Boston*, 59 Mass. (5 Cush.) 198 (1950).

151 Memo on *Keyes*, LAH [Larry Hammond] to Powell, *Keyes v. School District No. 1*, Supreme Court Case Files, Lewis Powell Papers, Washington and Lee School of Law, Lexington, VA.

152 *Keyes v. School Dist. No. 1*, 413 U.S. 189 (1973).

153 Michael A. Olivas, "From a 'Legal Organization of Militants' into a 'Law Firm for the Latino Community': MALDEF and the Purposive Cases of *Keyes, Rodriguez*, and *Plyler*," *Denver University Law Review* 90, no. 5 (n.d.): 1151–1208.

154 The three schools were Greenlee, Fairview, and Garden Place, all of which had a substantial majority of students of Mexican descent. See Intervenor's Objections to Court Consultant's Education Plan, US Dist. Ct. Colo., CA No. C-1499, April 3, 1974, *Keyes v. School Dist. No. 1* Pleading File, vol. I, Papers of the Mexican American Legal Defense Fund (hereafter MALDEF Papers), box 696, folder 1, RG 5, Special Collections and University Archives, Stanford University, Palo Alto, CA.

155 Ibid.

156 "Caution Urged in Bilingual Program," *Greeley Daily Tribune*, July 17, 1975.

157 "Guidelines Urged for Bilingual Act," *Greeley Daily Tribune*, July 21, 1975.

158 Sanford Rosen to José Cárdenas, November 26, 1973, MALDEF Papers, box 707, folder 8, RG 5, Special Collections and University Archives, Stanford University, Palo Alto, CA.

159 Congress of Hispanic Educators, "Addendum to the Intervenor's Education Plan for the Denver Public Schools," February 5, 1974, pp. 1–2, MALDEF Papers, box 703, folder 2, RG 5, Special Collections and University Archives, Stanford University, Palo Alto, CA.

160 José A. Cárdenas, "An Education Plan for the Denver Public Schools," January 21, 1974, p. 4, MALDEF Papers, box 703, folder 3, RG 5, Special Collections and University Archives, Stanford University, Palo Alto, CA.

161 Ibid.

162 Congress of Hispanic Educators, "Addendum to the Intervenor's Education Plan for the Denver Public Schools," February 5, 1974, pp. 3–4, MALDEF Papers, box 703, folder 2, RG 5, Special Collections and University Archives, Stanford University, Palo Alto, CA.

163 1975 Indochina Migration and Refugee Assistance Act, H.R. 6755, Pub.L. 94–23, 89 Stat. 87.

164 Deposition of Moises Martinez, March 25, 1982, vol. III, pp. 9, 17, MALDEF Papers, box 718, folder 7, RG 5, Special Collections and University Archives, Stanford University, Palo Alto, CA.

165 These children were classified as either "Lau A" or "Lau B," the two least-proficient categories of English-speaking. See ibid., p. 60.

166 *Keyes v. School Dist. No. 1*, 521 F.2d 465 (10th Cir. 1975).

167 Charles Zelden, "From Rights to Resources: The Southern Federal Courts and the Transformation of Civil Rights in Education, 1968–1974," *Akron Law Review* 32, no. 3 (1999): 472.

168 Oral argument, *Keyes v. School Dist. No. 1*, 413 U.S. 189 (1973).

169 "Twenty Worst Districts in the United States for Spanish-Surnamed Students," appendix B, table 6, "Suspensions in Denver Elementary Schools: Three Year Study," April 1980, MALDEF Papers, box 718, folder 4, RG 5, Special Collections and University Archives, Stanford University, Palo Alto, CA.

170 Ibid.

171 Denver Public Schools Division of Education, "Report to the Board of Education: Adoption-Adaptation of the Pass Program (Positive Alternatives to School Suspension)," February 1980, MALDEF Papers, box 718, folder 4, RG 5, Special Collections and University Archives, Stanford University, Palo Alto, CA.

172 "DPS Suspensions Spur Call for Talks with Judge," *Rocky Mountain News*, December 16, 1981, MALDEF Papers, box 717, folder 7, RG 5, Special Collections and University Archives, Stanford University, Palo Alto, CA.

CHAPTER 3. THE RIGHT TO DUE PROCESS

1 Deposition of Phillip F. Fulton, June 27, 1973, pp. 20–21, Civil Case #71-67, *Lopez v. Williams*, *Lopez v. Williams* case files, box 18, folder 2, National Archives and Records Administration Regional Facility, Chicago (hereafter NARA-Chicago).

2 *Lopez v. Williams*, 372 F.Supp. 1279 (S.D. Ohio 1974).

3 The sociologist Richard Arum has been the most vocal critic of *Goss* and other litigation involving school discipline, making the case that the intrusion of the courts into the internal affairs of schools has restrained the ability of school officials to establish moral authority and properly socialize students, leading to poorer outcomes for students in schools where conflict is endemic. See Richard Arum, *Judging School Discipline: The Crisis of Moral Authority* (Cambridge, MA: Harvard University Press, 2003).

4 See, generally, Gael Graham, *Young Activists: American High School Students in the Age of Protest* (DeKalb: Northern Illinois University Press, 2006).

5 Columbus's population in 1960 was roughly 471,000, and it gained nearly 70,000 residents between 1960 and 1970. Although population growth was slower than it had been in the 1950s, the city's growth remained steady throughout the late twentieth century. For a brief history of the economic development of Columbus in the mid-twentieth century, see Gregory Jacobs, *Getting around* Brown: *Desegregation, Development, and the Columbus Public Schools* (Columbus: Ohio State University Press, 1998), 66–76.

6 Ibid., 11.

7 See Barbee Durham, "Housing Discrimination," virtual exhibit at *Remembering the Act: Archival Reflections on Civil Rights*, University Libraries, The Ohio State University, www.osu.edu.

8 Champion Elementary School, built in 1910, was built in a historically black neighborhood, and by the 1930s, the city had three such segregated black schools. See Harold L. Carter, "Domestic Colonialism and Problems of Black Education with Special Reference to Columbus, Ohio" (MA thesis, Ohio State University, 1976), 163, 168–169.

9 Essie K. Payne, Cheryl Nowell, and Michelle Stolpa, "Student Perceptions: The Value of Desegregation," *Theory into Practice* 17, no. 2 (April 1978): 173.

10 In 1973, the Columbus school district would be the subject of a school desegregation case, *Columbus Board of Education v. Penick*, which reached the U.S. Supreme Court in 1979. In its decision, the Court found that the school board acted to create and perpetuate unconstitutional racial segregation in city schools, upholding a lower court order for system-wide desegregation. See *Board of Education v. Penick*, 443 U.S. 449 (1979). For early challenges to racial segregation that preceded the *Penick* case, see Jacobs, *Getting around* Brown, 20–26.

11 Jacobs, *Getting around* Brown, 24.

12 Payne et al., "Student Perceptions," 174.

13 Carter, "Domestic Colonialism," 177–180; and Jacobs, *Getting around* Brown, 20–21.

14 Carter, "Domestic Colonialism," 194–195.

15 Ibid., 200–201.

16 Ibid., 204.

17 Jacobs, *Getting around* Brown, 24.

18 Carter, "Domestic Colonialism," 210–211.

19 On the history of African American protest in the Columbus public schools and the eventual adoption of a district-wide desegregation plan, see Jacobs, *Getting around* Brown.

20 John Hope Franklin et al., "Black History Month: Serious Truth Telling or Triumph in Tokenism?" *Journal of Blacks in Higher Education*, no. 18 (Winter 1997–1998): 88.

21 "Racial Strife Hits Schools," *Columbus Evening Dispatch*, February 20, 1971.

22 Carter, "Domestic Colonialism," 211.

23 "School Officials Want Talks," *Columbus Evening Dispatch*, March 6, 1971.

24 "Racial Strife Hits Schools."

25 "School Principals Seek to End Student Clashes," *Columbus Evening Dispatch*, February 22, 1971.

26 "Racial Strife Hits Schools."

27 "Obituary: Clifford A. Tyree," *Columbus Dispatch*, August 10, 2011.

28 "Black History Week Held 'Token' Move," *Columbus Evening Dispatch*, March 4, 1971.

29 Minutes, Columbus Board of Education, March 2, 1971, Columbus Public Schools Administration Building, Columbus, OH.

30 "Black History Week Held 'Token' Move."

31 "Like a Hurricane, Blind Man Says," *Columbus Evening Dispatch*, March 9, 1971.

32 "Reopening of School Expected," *Columbus Dispatch*, April 27, 1971.

33 The number of students suspended at Central High differs between accounts. The superintendent at times claimed that fifty-five or fifty-eight students were suspended, but according to *Lopez v. Williams*, the number was seventy-five. The figure used here is from a newspaper report published the day after the disruptions at Central High. See "Central High Suspensions Follow Row," *Columbus Dispatch*, February 27, 1971; and "Eibling Replies to Blacks," *Columbus Dispatch*, March 8, 1971.

34 Initial complaint, April 1, 1971, *Lopez v. Williams*, Civil Action # 71-67, US Dist. Ct. Southern Division Ohio, Eastern District–Columbus, *Lopez v. Williams* case file, box 17, folder 1, NARA-Chicago.

35 *Lopez v. Williams*, 372 F.Supp. 1279 (S.D. Ohio 1974).

36 Ibid.

37 "Youth, Dad Arraigned in School Case," *Columbus Dispatch*, March 24, 1971.

38 Deposition of Philip F. Fulton, June 27, 1973, p. 53, Civil Case # 71-67, *Lopez v. Williams*, *Lopez v. Williams* case files, box 18, folder 2, NARA-Chicago.

39 *Lopez v. Williams*, 372 F.Supp. 1279 (S.D. Ohio 1974).

40 Deposition of Philip F. Fulton, June 27, 1973, p. 35, Civil Case # 71-67, *Lopez v. Williams*, *Lopez v. Williams* case files, box 18, folder 2, NARA-Chicago.

41 *Lopez v. Williams*, 372 F.Supp. 1279 (S.D. Ohio 1974).

42 "Policemen Keep Order at North High School," *Columbus Dispatch*, March 17, 1971.

43 "7 Students Arrested in School Disorder," *Columbus Dispatch*, March 18, 1971.

44 "White Parents Seek City Schools Order," *Columbus Dispatch*, March 31, 1971.

45 Dee Delaplane to the editor, *Columbus Dispatch*, March 29, 1971.

46 "Policemen Keep Order at North High School," *Columbus Dispatch*, March 17, 1971.

47 "Truancy Law Questioned," *Columbus Dispatch*, March 17, 1971.

48 "City Council Maintains Truancy Law Position," *Columbus Dispatch*, March 23, 1971.

49 "Student Repeat Protest of Curfew," *Columbus Dispatch*, April 13, 1971.

50 Carter, "Domestic Colonialism," 213–214.

51 "Minister to Head Task Force," *Columbus Dispatch*, March 26, 1971; and Carter, "Domestic Colonialism," 215–216.

52 Carter, "Domestic Colonialism," 217.

53 David Lore, "Legislators Silent on School Disturbances," *Columbus Dispatch*, April 4, 1971.

54 "Mayor Focuses on Schools," *Columbus Dispatch*, April 7, 1971.

55 In 1971, when the Columbus protests took place, the Supreme Court had not yet spoken on whether elementary and secondary school students had a constitutional right to an education. In 1973 the Court declared that the U.S. Constitution provided no such right in *San Antonio Independent School District v. Rodriguez*, 411 U.S. 1 (1973). This case is discussed at length in chapter 4, in this volume.

56 Simon Wittes, *People and Power: A Study of Crisis in Secondary Schools* (Ann Arbor: University of Michigan, 1970), 1.

57 "High School Arrest Rises, Alarming U.S. Educators," *New York Times*, May 9, 1969.

58 Ibid.

59 On the Columbia student protests of 1968, see Stefan M. Bradley, *Harlem vs. Columbia University: Black Student Power in the Late 1960s* (Urbana: University of Illinois Press, 2009).

60 "Teachers at Columbia Risk Violence as Mediators," *New York Times*, April 30, 1968.

61 "Moment of Truth," *New York Times*, May 10, 1968.

62 "Schools Hire Guards as Violence Rises Sharply," *New York Times*, January 12, 1970; "Schools Unrest Laid to Officials," *New York Times*, September 22, 1970; "Pupil Power: Disruptions Trouble Some U.S. High Schools as Youths Ask [for] 'Rights,'" *Wall Street Journal*, November 6, 1970; "High Schools Act to Defuse Protests," *Washington Post*, September 21, 1969; and "Rebels Made by High School Despots," *Guardian*, October 19, 1970.

63 Miguel A. Guajardo and Francisco J. Guajardo, "The Impact of *Brown* on the Brown of South Texas: A Micropolitical Perspective on the Education of Mexican Americans in a South Texas Community," *American Educational Research Journal* 41, no. 3 (Fall 2004): 506; and James B. Barrera, "The 1968 Edcouch-Elsa High School Walkout: Chicano Student Activism in a South Texas Community," *Aztlán: A Journal of Chicano Studies* 29, no. 2 (Fall 2004): 93.

64 Guajardo and Guajardo, "Impact of *Brown*," 520–521.

65 Guadalupe San Miguel, Jr., *"Let All of Them Take Heed": Mexican Americans and the Campaign for Educational Equality in Texas, 1910–1981* (Austin: University of Texas Press, 1987), 173.

66 One expert blamed Students for a Democratic Society for instigating unrest at high schools, citing a position paper written and circulated by high school students in Los Angeles. B. Frank Brown of I/D/E/A, an educational research organization, declared, "The current wave of organized high school revolt has its origin in a position paper prepared by a Los Angeles high school student for Students

for a Democratic Society in 1965." See "High School Arrest Rises, Alarming U.S. Educators."

67 Ibid.

68 Alan Westin, "Responding to Rebels with a Cause," in *The School and the Democratic Environment* (New York: Columbia University Press, 1970), 71.

69 Of 361 total protests, Westin counted 81 political protests, 71 against dress code regulations, 60 "against discipline," and 17 for educational reforms. See "High School Arrest Rises, Alarming U.S. Educators."

70 Stephen K. Bailey, *Disruption in Urban Public Secondary Schools* (Washington, DC: National Association of Secondary School Principals, 1970).

71 "Unrest in Urban Schools Linked to Race," *New York Times*, October 4, 1970.

72 Ibid.

73 Westin, "Responding to Rebels with a Cause," 77.

74 Mark G. Yudof, "Suspension and Expulsion of Black Students from the Public Schools: Academic Capital Punishment and the Constitution," *Law and Contemporary Problems* 39, no. 2 (Spring 1975): 380.

75 Philip W. Jackson, *Life in Classrooms* (New York: Holt, Reinhart & Winston, 1968), 33–34.

76 Ibid., 34.

77 Ivan Illich, *Deschooling Society* (New York: Harper & Row, 1971).

78 Postman and Weingartner borrowed the phrase "crap detecting" from an Ernest Hemingway interview, in which he declared that in order to be a "great writer," one "must have a built-in, shockproof crap detector." See Neil Postman and Charles Weingartner, *Teaching as a Subversive Activity* (New York: Delacorte Press, 1969), 3.

79 Ibid., 4.

80 Ibid., 120–121.

81 Peter Schrag, "Can the Traditional Classroom Survive in Today's School System?" *New York Times*, May 11, 1969.

82 Paulo Freire, *Pedagogy of the Oppressed*, 30th anniversary ed., trans. Myra Bergman Ramos (New York: Bloomsbury, 2000), 72, 75.

83 Ibid., 44.

84 Southern Regional Council and the Robert F. Kennedy Memorial Fund, *The Student Pushout: Victim of Continued Resistance to Desegregation* (Atlanta: Southern Regional Council, 1973), v.

85 Ibid., 2.

86 Ibid.

87 "Pushouts: New Outcasts from Public School," *Options on Education*, NPR, September 9, 1974.

88 "NAACP Plans Student Suit," *Columbus Evening Dispatch*, March 5, 1971.

89 Initial complaint, pp. 2–3, April 1, 1971, *Lopez v. Williams*, Civil Action # 71-67, US Dist. Ct. Southern Division Ohio, Eastern District–Columbus, *Lopez v. Williams* case file, box 17, folder 1, NARA-Chicago.

90 Memorandum in support of motion for temporary restraining order, class action, three-judge court, and preliminary injunction, p. 4, April 1, 1971, *Lopez v. Williams*, Civil Action # 71-67, US Dist. Ct. Southern Division Ohio, Eastern District–Columbus, *Lopez v. Williams* case file, box 17, folder 1, NARA-Chicago.

91 *Black Students, Etc., Ex Rel Shoemaker v. Williams*, 335 F.Supp. 820 (M.D. Fla. 1972). A federal district court later ruled that the automatic suspension rule was unconstitutional on its face.

92 Memorandum in support of motion for temporary restraining order, class action, three-judge court, and preliminary injunction, p. 5, April 1, 1971, *Lopez v. Williams*, Civil Action # 71-67, US Dist. Ct. Southern Division Ohio, Eastern District–Columbus, *Lopez v. Williams* case file, box 17, folder 1, NARA-Chicago.

93 Title 28, U.S.C. Sec. 2281.

94 *Lopez v. Williams*, 372 F.Supp. 1279 (S.D. Ohio 1974).

95 Ibid.

96 Brief for the National Association for the Advancement of Colored People and the Southern Christian Leadership Conference, footnote 2, *Goss v. Lopez*, 419 U.S. 565 (1975).

97 William Blackstone, *Commentaries on the Laws of England*, vol. 1, ed. William G. Hammond (San Francisco: Bancroft-Whitney Co., 1890), 441.

98 William G. Buss, "Procedural Due Process for School Discipline: Probing the Constitutional Outline," *University of Pennsylvania Law Review* 119, no. 4 (February 1971): 559–560.

99 Tracy Steffes, *School, Society, and State: A New Education to Govern Modern America, 1890–1940* (Chicago: University of Chicago Press, 2012), 126–127.

100 Bryant Simon, *A Fabric of Defeat: The Politics of South Carolina Millhands, 1910–1948* (Chapel Hill: University of North Carolina Press, 1998).

101 According to David Tyack, by 1885, only sixteen out of thirty-eight states had compulsory education laws, and they were seldom enforced. See David Tyack, *The One Best System: A History of American Urban Education* (Cambridge, MA: Harvard University Press, 1974), 71. Southern states were particularly reluctant to pass compulsory education laws, and Mississippi was the last state to do so. It later repealed the law in the wake of *Brown v. Board of Education*. See James D. Anderson, *The Education of Blacks in the South, 1860–1930* (Chapel Hill: University of North Carolina Press, 1988), 203.

102 Steffes, *School, Society, and State*, 119–121.

103 *Lucy v. Adams*, F.Supp. 235 (D.C.N.D. Ala. 1957).

104 Warren A. Seavey, "Dismissal of Students: 'Due Process,'" *Harvard Law Review* 70 (1957): 1407, quoted in *Dixon v. State Board of Education* 294 F.2d 150 (5th Cir. 1961) and in Children's Defense Fund, *Children out of School in America* (Washington, DC: Children's Defense Fund, 1974), 141.

105 On the origins of the student sit-in movement, see William Chafe, *Civility and Civil Rights: Greensboro, North Carolina, and the Black Struggle for Freedom* (New York: Oxford University Press, 1980).

106 *Dixon v. Alabama State Board of Education*, 294 F.2d 150 (5th Cir. 1961).

107 Ibid.

108 Ibid.

109 Ibid.

110 Dissent, *Dixon v. Alabama State Board of Education*, 294 F.2d 150 (1961).

111 *Knight v. State Board of Education*, 200 F.Supp. 174 (1961); and Bobby L. Levitt, *The Civil Rights Movement in Tennessee: A Narrative History* (Knoxville: University of Tennessee Press, 2015), 171–174. See also Raymond Arsenault, *Freedom Riders: 1961 and the Struggle for Racial Justice* (New York: Oxford University Press, 2007).

112 Michael Klarman, *From Jim Crow to Civil Rights: The Supreme Court and the Struggle for Racial Equality* (New York: Oxford University Press, 2004), 434.

113 Anne Emmanuel, *Elbert Parr Tuttle: Chief Jurist of the Civil Rights Revolution* (Athens: University of Georgia Press, 2011), 248–249.

114 The decision hinged upon the narrow question of whether or not the lower court's decision to reject a temporary restraining order could be appealed, and the ruling applied only to the board of education's decision to suspend and expel students who were arrested for parading without a license. The decision did not prohibit the board from punishing students for tardiness or truancy related to their participation in the marches. See *Woods v. Wright*, 334 F.2d 369 (5th Cir. 1964).

115 Ibid.

116 Tyler was one of twenty-six Texas school districts sued by the U.S. Justice Department in 1970 for failing to comply with *Brown v. Board of Education*. See "Texas Sued by U.S. on Desegregation," *New York Times*, August 8 1970.

117 *Dunn v. Tyler Ind. School Dist.*, 460 F.2d 137 (5th Cir. 1972).

118 *Murray v. West Baton Rouge Parish School Bd.*, 472 F.2d 438 (5th Cir. 1973).

119 *Pervis v. La Marque Ind. School Dist.*, 466 F.2d 1054 (5th Cir. 1972).

120 "Denver Hispano Beret Leader Is Convicted," *Greeley Tribune*, April 2, 1970.

121 *Hernandez v. School Dist. No. 1*, 315 F.Supp. 289 (D. Colo. 1970).

122 Minutes, May 21, 1970, archived at the Denver Public Schools Board of Education, Denver School Administration Building, Denver, CO.

123 *Goss v. Lopez*, 419 U.S. 565 (1975).

124 Brief for the National Association for the Advancement of Colored People and the Southern Christian Leadership Conference, footnote 2, *Goss v. Lopez*, 419 U.S. 565 (1975).

125 Ibid., p. 9.

126 Ibid., p. 13.

127 The brief cites Thomas Hobbes's *Leviathan*, vol. 3 of *The English Works of Thomas Hobbes of Malmesbury*, ed. Sir William Molesworth (London: Bohn, 1839), 257.

128 Brief for the Children's Defense Fund and American Friends Service Committee as Amicus Curiae, p. 10, *Goss v. Lopez*, 419 U.S. 565 (1975).

129 Ibid., p. 15.

130 *Tinker v. Des Moines*, 393 U.S. 503 (1969). For more on the *Tinker* case, see John W. Johnson, *The Struggle for Student Rights: Tinker v. Des Moines and the 1960s* (Lawrence: University of Kansas Press, 1997).

131 *Tinker v. Des Moines*, 393 U.S. 503 (1969).

132 U.S. Office of Education, *Civic Education in a Crisis Age: An Alternative to Repression and Revolution* (New York: Center for Research and Education in American Liberties, Teachers College, Columbia University, 1970).

133 Brief for the ACLU as Amicus Curiae, p. 3, *Goss v. Lopez*, 419 U.S. 565 (1975).

134 Reply Brief for Applicants, pp. 3–4, *Goss v. Lopez*, 419 U.S. 565 (1975).

135 *Goss v. Lopez*, 419 U.S. 565 (1975).

136 *Goldberg v. Kelly*, 397 U.S. 254 (1969).

137 The Supreme Court clearly stated this logic in another procedural due process case, *Board of Regents v. Roth*: "Property interests, of course, are not created by the Constitution. Rather, they are created and their dimensions are defined by existing rules or understandings that stem from an independent source such as state law—rules or understandings that secure certain benefits and that support claims of entitlement to those benefits." See *Board of Regents v. Roth*, 408 U.S. 564 (1972).

138 *Goss v. Lopez*, 419 U.S. 565 (1975). The *Rodriguez* decision is discussed at length in chapter 4, in this volume.

139 Dissent, *Goss v. Lopez*, 419 U.S. 565 (1975).

140 *Wood v. Strickland*, 420 U.S. 308 (1975); and *West Virginia v. Barnette*, 319 U.S. 624 (1943).

141 42 U.S.C. Sec. 1983.

142 *Wood v. Strickland*, 420 U.S. 308 (1975).

143 Ronald J. Anson, "The Educator's Response to *Goss* and *Wood*," *Phi Delta Kappan* 57, no. 1 (September 1975): 16.

144 Children's Defense Fund, *School Suspensions: Are They Helping Children?* (Washington, DC: Children's Defense Fund, 1975), 13.

145 Ibid., 18–19.

146 Ibid., 14.

147 Carter, "Domestic Colonialism," 223–225.

148 Ibid., 227–228.

149 *Columbus Board of Education v. Penick*, 443 U.S. 449 (1979).

150 Felix Frankfurter, Concurring Opinion, *Malinski v. New York*, 324 U.S. 401 (1945).

151 On the expansion of procedural rights during the Warren Court, see Mark Tushnet, ed., *The Warren Court in Historical and Political Perspective* (Charlottesville: University of Virginia Press, 1993); Michal Belknap, *The Supreme Court under Earl Warren, 1953–1969* (Columbia: University of South Carolina Press, 2005); and Harry N. Scheiber, *Earl Warren and the Warren Court: The Legacy in American and Foreign Law* (Lanham, MD: Lexington Books, 2007).

CHAPTER 4. A RIGHT TO EQUAL EDUCATION

1 For a detailed account of the motivations for and actions of high school student protesters in Topeka, see Beryl Ann New, "A Fire in the Sky: Student Activism in Topeka, Kansas and Lawrence, Kansas High Schools in 1969 and 1970" (MEd thesis, Washburn University 2007), chap. 3.

2 Ibid., 22.

3 A brief historical sketch and description of the Topeka High School protests can also be found in Amy Stuart Wells et al., *Both Sides Now: The Story of School Desegregation's Graduates* (Berkeley: University of California Press, 2009), 68–72.

4 Gerald Rosenberg, *The Hollow Hope: Can Courts Bring about Social Change?* (Chicago: University of Chicago Press, 1997).

5 The best known example is Boston, but violent resistance to desegregation occurred in places like Denver and Pontiac, Michigan, where individuals bombed school buses. See Ronald Formisano, *Boston against Busing: Race, Class, and Ethnicity in the 1960s and 1970s* (Chapel Hill: University of North Carolina Press, 1991). On Pontiac, see Joyce A. Baugh, *The Detroit School Busing Case:* Milliken v. Bradley *and the Controversy over Desegregation* (Lawrence: University Press of Kansas, 1971), 113; and on Denver, see chap. 2, in this volume.

6 See the *Civil Rights Cases*, 109 U.S. 3 (1883). On the history of the state action doctrine, see G. Sidney Buchanan, "A Conceptual History of the State Action Doctrine: The Search for Governmental Responsibility," *Houston Law Review* 34, no. 2 (Summer 1997): 333–424.

7 *Brown v. Board of Education of Topeka*, 349 U.S. 294 (1955).

8 Emphasis in original. See *Green v. County School Board of New Kent County*, 391 U.S. 430 (1968).

9 *Swann v. Charlotte-Mecklenburg Board of Education*, 402 U.S. 1 (1971).

10 Ibid.

11 Richard Nixon, "Special Message to the Congress on Equal Educational Opportunities and School Busing," March 17, 1972, posted at *The American Presidency Project*, University of California, Santa Barbara, www.ucsb.edu.

12 On urban renewal and racial segregation, see Arnold Hirsch, *Making the Second Ghetto: Race and Housing in Chicago, 1940–1960* (Cambridge: Cambridge University Press, 1983).

13 On redlining, see Thomas Sugrue, *Origins of the Urban Crisis: Race and Inequality in Postwar Detroit* (Princeton, NJ: Princeton University Press, 1996); and Richard Rothstein, *The Color of Law: A Forgotten History of How Our Government Segregated America* (New York: W. W. Norton, 2017).

14 See *Buchanan v. Warley*, 245 U.S. 60 (1917).

15 *Shelley v. Kraemer*, 334 U.S. 1 (1948).

16 Baugh, *Detroit School Busing Case*, 58–59.

17 Ibid., 60, 64.

18 See Sugrue, *Origins of the Urban Crisis*.

19 Baugh, *Detroit School Busing Case*, 68.

20 Ibid., 93.

21 Ibid., 96–97.

22 On Irene McCabe and opposition to busing in Pontiac, see David Riddle, "Race and Reaction in Warren, Michigan, 1971–1974: *Bradley v. Milliken* and the Cross-District Busing Controversy," *Michigan Historical Review* 26, no. 2 (Fall 2000): 1–49.

23 *Bradley v. Milliken*, 345 F.Supp. 914 (E.D. Mich. 1972); and Baugh, *Detroit School Busing Case*, 133.

24 *Milliken v. Bradley*, 418 U.S. 717 (1974).

25 Ibid.

26 Ibid.

27 Ibid.

28 "Busing Enemies Are Delighted, Advocates Disgusted but Hopeful," *Washington Post*, July 26, 1974.

29 "High Court Curbs Integration of Suburban and City Schools: Ban for Detroit Seems to Signal the End of an Era," *Los Angeles Times*, July 26, 1974.

30 Jack Greenberg's account of the LDF's efforts to combat racial inequality in the twentieth century ends with a discussion of *Keyes v. School Dist. No. 1* and *Milliken v. Bradley*. See Jack Greenberg, *Crusaders in the Courts: How a Dedicated Band of Lawyers Fought for the Civil Rights Revolution* (New York: Basic Books, 1994), 394. Michael Klarman's authoritative account of civil rights and the Supreme Court ends with *Green v. New Kent County* and *Swann v. Charlotte-Mecklenburg* without even mentioning *Milliken* in the text. See Michael Klarman, *From Jim Crow to Civil Rights: The Supreme Court and the Struggle for Racial Equality* (New York: Oxford University Press, 2004), 341–343.

31 Mark Tushnet, "The Supreme Court's Two Principles of Equality: From *Brown* to 2003," 340–360, and Davison M. Douglas, "*Brown v. Board of Education* and Its Impact on Black Education in America," 361–382, both in *From the Grassroots to the Supreme Court: Brown v. Board of Education and American Democracy*, ed. Peter F. Lau (Durham, NC: Duke University Press, 2004).

32 *Swann v. Charlotte-Mecklenburg Board of Education*, 402 U.S. 1 (1971), as quoted in *Milliken v. Bradley*, 418 U.S. 717 (1974).

33 Dissent, *Milliken v. Bradley*, 418 U.S. 717 (1974).

34 Quoted in U.S. Commission on Civil Rights, *The Unfinished Education: Outcomes for Minorities in the Five Southwestern States*, Mexican American Report Series, Report 2 (Washington, DC: Government Printing Office, 1971), 8–9.

35 U.S. Commission on Civil Rights, *Teachers and Students: Differences in Teacher Interaction with Mexican American and Anglo Students*, Report 5: Mexican American Education Study (Washington, DC: Government Printing Office, 1973), 22.

36 Guadalupe San Miguel, Jr., *"Let All of Them Take Heed": Mexican Americans and the Campaign for Educational Equality in Texas, 1910–1981* (Austin: University of Texas Press, 1987), 182–183.

37 "Intervenor's Memorandum with Respect to Minority Teacher Employment and Bilingual-Multicultural Education," April 4, 1974, *Keyes v. School District No. 1*, Papers of the Mexican American Legal Defense Fund (hereafter MALDEF Papers), box 696, folder 1, RG 5, Special Collections and University Archives, Stanford University, Palo Alto, CA.

38 *Keyes v. School Dist. No. 1*, 521 F.2d 465 (1975). The Cárdenas Plan is discussed in chapter 2, in this volume.

39 *Keyes v. School Dist. No. 1*, 521 F.2d 465 (1975).

40 The linkages between social science research and the conflation of race and culture go back at least to the 1930s. After academics abandoned biological explanations for racial difference, new strands of argument emerged that relied upon conceptions of "cultural deficiencies" rather than biological explanations in accounting for the gaps between everything from white and black education and workforce participation to rates of incarceration and out-of-wedlock births. See Nikhil Pal Singh, *Black Is a Country: Race and the Unfinished Struggle for Democracy* (Cambridge, MA: Harvard University Press, 2004); and Eduard Bonilla-Silva, *Racism without Racists: Color-Blind Racism and the Persistence of Racial Inequality in the United States* (Lanham, MD: Rowman & Littlefield, 2003).

41 On the history of social science research and poverty in the twentieth century, see Alice O'Connor, *Poverty Knowledge: Social Science, Social Policy and the Poor in Twentieth-Century U.S. History* (Princeton, NJ: Princeton University Press, 2001).

42 On the development of compensatory education programs in the late 1950s and early 1960s, see Peter Marris and Martin Rein, *Dilemmas of Social Reform: Poverty and Community Action in the United States* (New York: Atherton Press, 1967). The work of the sociologists Richard Cloward and Lloyd Ohlin was particularly influential in making linkages between "delinquency" and slum culture in the 1960s. See Richard Cloward and Lloyd Ohlin, *Delinquency and Opportunity: A Theory of Delinquent Gangs* (New York: Free Press, 1960). Policymakers often referred to the cultural roots of poverty, drawing on the work of the anthropologist Oscar Lewis. Lewis's first book on the "culture of poverty," which popularized the term, was published in 1959. See Oscar Lewis, *Five Families: Mexican Case Studies in the Culture of Poverty* (New York: Basic Books, 1959). Compensatory education as a solution to "cultural" problems found its fullest expression in the mid-1960s with the confluence of academic support and federal funding for such programs. See Benjamin S. Bloom, Allison Davis, and Robert D. Hess, *Compensatory Education for Cultural Deprivation* (New York: Holt, Rinehart & Winston, 1965).

43 Martha Minow calls this the "dilemma of difference," arguing that, depending on the context, such classifications of difference sometimes are used in the service of making education more equal while at other moments they operate against the interests of historically marginalized groups. Equal treatment can mean unequal treatment depending on the circumstance, or the reverse can be true. See Martha Minow, *Making All the Difference: Inclusion, Exclusion, and American Law* (Ithaca, NY: Cornell University Press, 1990).

44 Kishkunas testimony, trial transcript, vol. I., February 19, 1974, *Keyes v. School Dist. No. 1*, box 703, folder 4, MALDEF Papers.

45 Ibid.

46 Cárdenas testimony, trial transcript, February 25, 1974, *Keyes v. School Dist. No. 1*, box 705, folder 1, MALDEF Papers.

47 *United States v. Texas Education Agency*, 467 F.2d 848, 5th Cir. (1972).

48 Ibid.

49 See Clif Stratton, *Education for Empire: American Schools, Race, and the Paths of Good Citizenship* (Berkeley: University of California Press, 2016).

50 On the politics of bilingual education in California, see Mark Brilliant, *The Color of America Has Changed: How Racial Diversity Shaped Civil Rights Reform in California, 1941–1978* (New York: Oxford University Press, 2010), 227–256; and Natalia Mehlman Petrzela, *Classroom Wars: Language, Sex, and the Making of Modern Political Culture* (New York: Oxford University Press, 2015), 39–68.

51 Juan Gonzalez, *Harvest of Empire: A History of Latinos in America* (New York: Penguin Books, 2001), chap. 5.

52 Edward E. Telles and Vilma Ortiz, *Generations of Exclusion: Mexican Americans, Assimilation, and Race* (New York: Russell Sage, 2008), xxiii.

53 Carlos Kevin Blanton, *The Strange Career of Bilingual Education in Texas, 1836–1981* (College Station: Texas A&M Press, 2004); and Paul J. Ramsey, "In the Region of Babel: Public Bilingual Schooling in the Midwest, 1840s–1880s," *History of Education Quarterly* 49, no. 3 (August 2009): 270.

54 Based on data from a massive survey conducted by the U.S. Immigration Commission and published in 1908, more than half of the students in the schools of the nation's thirty-seven largest cities had parents who were born outside of the United States. See Sol Cohen, "Urban School Reform," *History of Education Quarterly* 9, no. 3 (Autumn 1969): 301. See also Michael R. Olneck and Marvin Lazerson, "The School Achievement of Immigrant Children: 1900–1930," *History of Education Quarterly* 14, no. 4 (Winter 1974): 453–482.

55 On the passage of the quota-setting 1924 Johnson-Reed Act, see Mae Ngai, *Impossible Subjects: Illegal Aliens and the Making of Modern America* (Princeton, NJ: Princeton University Press, 2004), chap. 1. See also William G. Ross, *Forging New Freedoms: Nativism, Education, and the Constitution, 1917–1927* (Lincoln: University of Nebraska Press, 1994).

56 On the development and passage of the 1968 Bilingual Education Act, see Guadalupe San Miguel, *Contested Policy: The Rise and Fall of Federal Bilingual Education in the United States, 1960–2001* (Denton: University of North Texas Press, 2004), chap. 1.

57 Ibid., 8.

58 See Peter D. Roos, "Bilingual Education: The Hispanic Response to Unequal Educational Opportunity," in "School Desegregation: Lessons of the First Twenty-Five Years," special issue, *Law and Contemporary Problems* 42, no. 2 (Autumn 1978): 111–140.

59 San Miguel, *Contested Policy*, 14–15.

60 Guadalupe San Miguel, "Conflict and Controversy in the Evolution of Bilingual Education in the United States—An Interpretation," *Social Science Quarterly* 65, no. 2 (June 1984): 506.

61 "President Will Seek Expanded Aid for Bilingual Schooling," *Los Angeles Times*, February 13, 1969.

62 Memo, J. Stanley Pottinger to School Districts with More than Five Percent National Origin-Minority Group Children, May 25, 1970, box 728, folder 3, RG 5, MALDEF Papers.

63 *Serna v. Portales*, 499 F.2d 1147 (10th Cir. 1974).

64 *Serna v. Portales*, 351 F.Supp. 1279 (D.N.M. 1972).

65 Ibid.

66 The 1964 Civil Rights Act prohibited discrimination on the basis of national origin, which is the rationale used by the Tenth Circuit despite the fact that no claim was made that the children were Mexican nationals. They were identified instead as "Spanish-surnamed" students. See *Serna v. Portales*, 499 F.2d 1147 (10th Cir. 1974).

67 Petitioners' Reply Memorandum, May 9, 1973, U.S. Supreme Court, October term, 1972, *Lau v. Nichols*, Case #72-6520, box 728, folder 4, RG 5, MALDEF Papers.

68 In 1872, the Democratic-controlled state legislature also passed a law that reinforced the segregation of black and Indian children from white children. See Charles Wollenberg, *All Deliberate Speed: Segregation and Exclusion in California Schools, 1855–1975* (Berkeley: University of California Press, 1976), 20, 33.

69 Ibid., 34.

70 Robert E. Jenkins, "Bilingual Education in the San Francisco Unified School District," November 21, 1967, box 728, folder 5, RG 5, MALDEF Papers.

71 *Lau v. Nichols*, 483 F.2d 791 (9th Cir. 1973).

72 Ibid.

73 Brief of the Mexican American Legal Defense Fund, the American GI Forum, the League of United Latin American Citizens, and the Association of Mexican American Educators, *Lau v. Nichols*, 414 U.S. 563 (1974).

74 *Lau v. Nichols*, 414 U.S. 563 (1974).

75 J. Stanley Pottinger, director of the Office of Civil Rights, "Memorandum to School Districts with More than Five Percent National Origin-Minority Group Children," May 25, 1970, box 728, folder 3, RG 5, MALDEF Papers.

76 *Guadalupe Organization, Inc. v. Tempe Elementary School Dist. No. 3*, 587 F.2d 1022 (1978).

77 *Heavy Runner v. Bremner*, 522 F.Supp. 162. (D. Mont. 1981).

78 Carlos Alcala, Beatriz Rivera, and Berta Thayer, "Legal Significance of *Lau v. Nichols*," p. 13, March 1, 1974, box 729, folder 5, RG 5, MALDEF Papers.

79 *Meyer v. Nebraska*, 262 U.S. 390 (1923).

80 *Griswold v. Connecticut*, 381 U.S. 479 (1965); *Loving v. Virginia*, 388 U.S. 1 (1967).

81 Camille Walsh, "Erasing Race, Dismissing Class: *San Antonio Independent School District v. Rodriguez*," *La Raza Law Journal* 21 (2011): 146.

82 *Brown v. Board of Education*, 347 U.S. 483 (1954).

83 *San Antonio Independent School District v. Rodriguez*, 411 U.S. 1 (1973).

84 "Pupils, Faculty Boycott Edgewood," *San Antonio Light*, May 16, 1968.

85 "Two S.A. Teachers Suspended," *San Antonio Light*, May 17, 1968.

86 "Edgewood Students Protest," *San Antonio Express*, May 17, 1968; and "400 March out of Classes," *San Antonio Light*, May 17, 1968.

87 "Two S.A. Teachers Suspended."

88 "Edgewood Rally Held," *San Antonio Light*, May 21, 1968.

89 Camille Walsh, *Racial Taxation: Schools, Segregation, and Taxpayer Citizenship, 1869–1973* (Chapel Hill: University of North Carolina Press, 2018), 142.

90 San Miguel, *"Let All of Them Take Heed,"* 171–172.

91 Walsh, "Erasing Race, Dismissing Class," 133–171.

92 Walsh, *Racial Taxation*, 142–143.

93 *San Antonio Independent School District v. Rodriguez*, 411 U.S. 1 (1973).

94 Walsh, "Erasing Race, Dismissing Class," 154.

95 *San Antonio Independent School District v. Rodriguez*, 411 U.S. 1 (1973).

96 Ibid.

97 "Students Can Join Protest," *San Antonio Express*, April 17, 1973.

98 "Stopgap School Aid Plan Announced," *San Antonio Express*, May 3, 1973.

99 "Edgewood Gets Additional Funds," *San Antonio Express*, June 11, 1975.

100 Richard Valencia, *Chicano Students in the Courts: The Mexican American Legal Struggle for Educational Equality* (New York: New York University Press, 2008), 84–89.

101 *Serrano v. Priest*, 5 Cal.3d 584 (1971).

102 *Edgewood Independent School District v. Kirby*, 777 S.W.2d 391 (1989).

103 Michael Rebell, *Kids and Courts: Pursuing Educational Equity through State Courts* (Chicago: University of Chicago Press, 2009), 16.

104 David Card and A. Abigail Payne, "School Finance Reform, the Distribution of School Spending, and the Distribution of Student Test Scores," *Journal of Public Economics* 83 (2002): 52–53.

105 Rebell, *Kids and Courts*, 2.

106 Children's Defense Fund, *School Suspensions: Are They Helping Children?* (Washington, DC: Children's Defense Fund, 1975), app. B, table 6, 165.

107 *Plyler v. Doe*, 457 U.S. 202 (1982).

108 Michael A. Olivas, *No Undocumented Child Left Behind*: Plyler v. Doe *and the Education of Undocumented Schoolchildren* (New York: New York University Press, 2012), 9.

109 In 2017, the tuition rate would be more than $4,000. See the CPI Inflation Calculator, Bureau of Labor Services, U.S. Department of Labor, www.bls.gov.

110 *Cooper v. Aaron*, 358 U.S. 1 (1958).

111 *Hall v. St. Helena Parish School Board*, 197 F.Supp. 649 (D.C.E.D.La. 1961).

112 *Griffin v. School Board*, 377 U.S. 218 (1964).

113 Olivas, *No Undocumented Child Left Behind*, 15.

114 *San Antonio Independent School District v. Rodriguez*, 411 U.S. 1 (1973).

115 *Plyler v. Doe*, 457 U.S. 202 (1982).

116 Josefine Almanza, letter to the editor, *Los Angeles Times*, July 17, 1977.

117 "Won't Settle for Second Best: Paralyzed Youth Faces Daily Dilemma: Getting to School," *Los Angeles Times*, January 20, 1969.

118 Ibid.

119 Children's Defense Fund, *Children out of School in America* (Washington, DC: Children's Defense Fund, 1974), 92. For a full list of the exemptions from compulsory attendance laws, see ibid., app. I.

120 "He Has Will—Friends Find Way: Quadriplegic Given Van to Get to School," *Los Angeles Times*, March 25, 1969.

121 "Students' Gift: Handicapped Boy Receives Van; 'A Dream Come True,'" *Los Angeles Times*, May 15, 1969.

122 "Paralyzed Youth Given Gift of Hope by Fellow Teenagers," *Los Angeles Times*, February 5, 1969.

123 "Funeral Rites Planned for Paralyzed Youth," *Los Angeles Times*, June 18, 1977.

124 Josefine Almanza, letter to the editor, *Los Angeles Times*.

125 Children's Defense Fund, *Children out of School in America*, 1.

126 On federal efforts to count and classify children out of school because of their status as disabled, see Donald W. Keim, "Legislative Notes: The Education for All Handicapped Children Act of 1975," *University of Michigan Journal of Law Reform* 10, no. 1 (Fall 1976): 110–152.

127 *PARC v. Commonwealth of Pennsylvania*, 343 F.Supp. 279 (1972).

128 *San Antonio Independent School District v. Rodriguez*, 411 U.S. 1 (1973).

129 *Mills v. Board of Education*, 348 F.Supp. 866 (1972).

130 "Suspension of Special Students Called 'Tragedy' by Judge Wright," *Washington Post*, July 27, 1971. For a discussion of *Hobson v. Hansen* and its effect on interpretations of the meaning of the right to equal educational opportunity, see chap. 2, in this volume.

131 *Mills v. Board of Education*, 348 F.Supp. 866 (1972).

132 "Special Education: A New Storm Center," *Washington Post*, May 29, 1973.

133 Jacqueline Vaughn Switzer, *Disabled Rights: American Disability Policy and the Fight for Equality* (Washington, DC: Georgetown University Press, 2003), 63.

134 The Education for All Handicapped Children Act became the Individuals with Disabilities Education Act in 1990. On the procedural guarantees provided by the act, see "Enforcing the Right to an 'Appropriate' Education: The Education for All Handicapped Children Act of 1975," *Harvard Law Review* 92, no. 5 (March 1979): 1103–1127.

135 *Stuart v. Nappi*, 443 F.Supp. 1235 (1978).

136 Rebell, *Kids and Courts*, 4.

137 Robert C. Smith, *The Case about Amy* (Philadelphia: Temple University Press, 1996), 2–3.

138 Ibid., 3.

139 For a detailed timeline of the case, see ibid.

140 *Rowley v. Bd. of Ed. of Hendrick Hudson Cent. SD*, 483 F.Supp. 528 (1980).

141 Ibid.

142 *Hendrick Hudson Central School District v. Rowley*, 458 U.S. 176 (1982).
143 Dissent, *Hendrick Hudson Central School District v. Rowley*, 458 U.S. 176 (1982).
144 See Margret Winzer, *From Integration to Inclusion: A History of Special Education in the Twentieth Century* (Washington, DC: Gallaudet University Press, 2009), chap. 4.
145 Ibid., 46.
146 Maris Vinovskis, *The Birth of Head Start: Preschool Education Policies in the Kennedy and Johnson Administrations* (Chicago: University of Chicago Press, 2005), 10.
147 *Larry P. v. Riles*, 495 F.Supp. 926 (1979).
148 Stanley O. Williford, "A Gadfly Exonerated," *Race Relations Reporter*, September 1974, box 728, folder 3, RG 5, MALDEF Papers.
149 "Suit Asks Release of 9 in Class for Retarded," *Los Angeles Times*, January 8, 1970.
150 "Sociologist Discovers: IQ Tests No Measure for Blacks," *Los Angeles Times*, July 29, 1971.
151 "IQ Test for Retardation Called Insufficient," *Los Angeles Times*, June 29, 1971.
152 *Larry P. v. Riles*, 495 F.Supp. 926 (1979).
153 "Parents Celebrate—with Caution—Education Victory," *Washington Post*, October 13, 1982.
154 Dissent, Thurgood Marshall, *San Antonio Independent School District v. Rodriguez*, 411 U.S. 1 (1973).

CHAPTER 5. *TINKER*'S TROUBLED LEGACY

1 "2 at Bronx School Accused of Paddling," *New York Times*, May 20, 1974.
2 "Two Deans in Paddling Case Removed," *New York Times*, May 22, 1974.
3 "Former J.H.S. Student Testifies to Being Paddled," *New York Times*, June 21, 1974.
4 "Two Deans in Paddling Case Removed," *New York Times*, May 22, 1974.
5 "School Board Votes to Discipline Three in Student Paddling," *New York Times*, June 18, 1974.
6 The sociologist Katherine Beckett attributes changing discourses about crime and punishment in the last third of the twentieth century to the behavior of political elites, arguing "that political elites have played a leading role in calling attention to crime-related problems, in defining these problems as the consequence of insufficient punishment and control, and in generating popular support for punitive anticrime policies." See Katherine Beckett, *Making Crime Pay: Law and Order in Contemporary American Politics* (New York: Oxford University Press, 1997), 8.
7 John F. Kennedy, "Remarks upon Signing the Juvenile Delinquency and Youth Offenses Control Act," September 22, 1961, posted at *The American Presidency Project*, University of California, Santa Barbara, www.ucsb.edu.
8 For young people in America, juvenile justice reforms in the postwar era varied by race. While whites were more likely to receive rehabilitative treatments, black and Latino teenagers were more likely to receive harsher punishments. See William S. Bush, *Who Gets a Childhood? Race and Juvenile Justice in Twentieth-Century Texas* (Athens: University of Georgia Press, 2010), chap. 4.

9 Beckett, *Making Crime Pay*, 31–33.

10 As historian Elizabeth Hinton demonstrates, the federal apparatus of funding and policy initiatives created for the War on Poverty "shifted even further from fighting poverty to controlling its violent symptoms" in the late 1960s, both at the behest of Lyndon Johnson's administration and, later, that of Richard Nixon. See Elizabeth Hinton, *From the War on Poverty to the War on Crime* (Cambridge, MA: Harvard University Press, 2016), 21.

11 Heather Ann Thompson, "Why Mass Incarceration Matters: Rethinking Crisis, Decline, and Transformation in Postwar American History," *Journal of American History* 97, no. 3 (December 2010): 707.

12 On preemptive attempts to forestall crime by targeting young black men, see Hinton, *From the War on Poverty to the War on Crime*, 22–25.

13 Risa Goluboff, *The Lost Promise of Civil Rights* (Cambridge, MA: Harvard University Press, 2010); and Douglas Blackmon, *Slavery by Another Name: The Re-enslavement of Black Americans from the Civil War to World War II* (New York: Anchor Books, 2009).

14 Khalil Gibran Muhammad, *The Criminalization of Blackness: Race, Crime, and the Making of Modern Urban America* (Cambridge, MA: Harvard University Press, 2010).

15 Edward J. Escobar, *Race, Police, and the Making of a Political Identity: Mexican Americans and the Los Angeles Police Department, 1900–1945* (Berkeley: University of California Press, 1999); and Lilia Fernández, *Brown in the Windy City: Mexicans and Puerto Ricans in Postwar Chicago* (Chicago: University of Chicago Press, 2012).

16 See Bush, *Who Gets a Childhood?*; and Laura Pulido, *Black, Brown, Yellow, and Left: Radical Activism in Los Angeles* (Berkeley: University of California Press, 2006).

17 Ian Haney López, *Racism on Trial: The Chicano Fight for Justice* (Cambridge, MA: Belknap, 2003), 8.

18 Historians disagree about the meaning of the Moynihan Report itself and the heated debates sparked among contemporaries by its arguments. Daniel Geary has argued persuasively that the inconsistencies in ideas and argumentation in the Moynihan Report, the complicated relationship between how Americans thought about race and class, and tensions inherent in Cold War liberalism led to its conflicted reception. See Daniel P. Moynihan, *The Negro Family: The Case for National Action* (hereafter the Moynihan Report; Washington, DC: Office of Policy Planning and Research, 1965); Daniel Geary, *Beyond Civil Rights: The Moynihan Report and Its Legacy* (Philadelphia: University of Pennsylvania Press, 2015); and James T. Patterson, *Freedom Is Not Enough: The Moynihan Report and America's Struggle over Black Family Life—From LBJ to Obama* (New York: Basic Books, 2010).

19 The Moynihan Report, 31.

20 Ibid., 29–30.

21 *Report of the National Advisory Commission on Civil Disorders* (hereafter the Kerner Commission Report; New York: Bantam, 1968), 114. Although he previously demonstrated a reluctance to embrace "law and order" politics, in his acceptance speech at the 1968 Republican National Convention, Nixon began by referencing "cities enveloped in smoke and flame." See Rick Perlstein, *Nixonland: The Rise of a President and the Fracturing of America* (New York: Scribner, 2008), 304.

22 According to the historian Michael Flamm, "Law and order thus became the vehicle by which urban whites transmitted their antipathy to neighborhood integration and fear of racial violence from the municipal to the presidential arena." Michael Flamm, *Law and Order: Street Crime, Civil Unrest, and the Crisis of Liberalism in the 1960s* (New York: Columbia University Press, 2005), 9.

23 The Kerner Commission Report, 114.

24 William M. Tuttle, *Race Riot: Chicago in the Red Summer of 1919* (New York: Antheneum, 1970); David F. Krugler, *1919, the Year of Racial Violence: How African Americans Fought Back* (New York: Cambridge University Press, 2014); and Glenda Gilmore, *Gender and Jim Crow: Women and the Politics of White Supremacy in North Carolina* (Chapel Hill: University of North Carolina Press, 1996).

25 See Paul Gilje, *Rioting in America* (Bloomington: Indiana University Press, 1996).

26 Matthew Lassiter, *The Silent Majority: Suburban Politics in the Sunbelt South* (Princeton, NJ: Princeton University Press, 2006), 24.

27 See Clive Webb, ed., *Massive Resistance: Southern Opposition to the Second Reconstruction* (New York: Oxford University Press, 2005).

28 Tomiko Brown-Nagin, *Courage to Dissent: Atlanta and the Long History of the Civil Rights Movement* (New York: Oxford University Press, 2011), 136–137.

29 Arnold Hirsch coined this term in *Making the Second Ghetto: Race and Housing in Chicago, 1940–1960* (Cambridge: Cambridge University Press, 1983).

30 Scholars disagree about the precise roots of the rise of mass incarceration. On this debate, see Hinton, *From the War on Poverty to the War on Crime*; Thompson, "Why Mass Incarceration Matters"; and Michelle Alexander, *The New Jim Crow: Mass Incarceration in the Age of Colorblindness* (New York: New Press, 2012).

31 Robert Brink, "States Tighten Anti-riot Laws," *Washington Post*, December 5, 1968.

32 For examples, see Marian Wright Edelman, "Time to Stop 'Stop and Frisk,'" *San Francisco Sun-Reporter*, May 31, 2012; and Benjamin Todd Jealous, "'Stop and Frisk'—Unconstitutional Racial Profiling," *New York Beacon*, August 22, 2013.

33 *Terry v. Ohio*, 392 U.S. 1 (1968).

34 Brink, "States Tighten Anti-riot Laws."

35 Marjorie Hunter, "Riot Curb Added to Bill on Rights by Senate, 82–13," *New York Times*, March 6, 1968.

36 "Negro Violence Hits U.S. Cities in Wake of Dr. King Slaying," *Chicago Tribune*, April 5, 1968; "12 Are Arrested Here: Sporadic Violence Erupts in Harlem," *New York Times*, April 5, 1968.

37 "President Signs Civil Rights Bill; Pleads for Calm," *New York Times*, April 12, 1968.
38 The Kerner Commission Report, 5.
39 Ibid., 9, 24.
40 Ibid., 25.
41 Michael Javen Fortner, *The Black Silent Majority: The Rockefeller Drug Laws and the Politics of Punishment* (Cambridge, MA: Harvard University Press, 2015).
42 James Forman, Jr., *Locking Up Our Own: Crime and Punishment in Black America* (New York: Farrar, Straus & Giroux, 2017), 11.
43 "2 at Bronx School Accused of Paddling."
44 See Jerald E. Podair, *The Strike That Changed New York: Blacks, Whites, and the Ocean Hill–Brownsville Crisis* (New Haven, CT: Yale University Press, 2004).
45 "Discontent High in Gallup Poll," *Los Angeles Times*, October 2, 1977.
46 "Discipline: Schools are Stuck with a Parent Problem," *Washington Post*, January 26, 1976.
47 "School Crime a National Problem," *Chicago Tribune*, April 15, 1975.
48 "Discontent High in Gallup Poll."
49 "About Education: A Warning on Discipline," *New York Times*, October 30, 1979.
50 U.S. Department of Health, Education and Welfare, "Violent Schools—Safe Schools: The Safe School Study Report to the Congress" (Washington, DC: U.S. Department of Health, Education, and Welfare, 1978), "Executive Summary," 1.
51 Ibid., 9.
52 "Problems of Discipline and Violence in Schools," *Atlanta Daily World*, April 14, 1977.
53 "Casualties in the Classrooms," *New York Times*, December 10, 1978.
54 Children's Defense Fund, *Children out of School in America* (Washington, DC: Children's Defense Fund, 1974), 130.
55 Ibid., 5.
56 Children's Defense Fund, *School Suspensions: Are They Helping Children?* (Washington, DC: Children's Defense Fund, 1975).
57 Ibid., 9.
58 Ibid.
59 Ibid.
60 Ibid., 69.
61 Ibid., 68.
62 Ibid., 13; emphasis in original.
63 The Civil Rights Act of 1964 included language authorizing the Department of Justice to bring lawsuits against school districts on behalf of black children in segregated schools.
64 *United States v. Wilcox County Board of Ed.*, 494 F.2d 575 (1974).
65 Felicia Kornbluh, *The Battle for Welfare Rights: Politics and Poverty in Modern America* (Philadelphia: University of Pennsylvania Press, 2007), 18.
66 The Kerner Commission Report, 158–159; and "Blacks Upstate Voice Pessimism," *New York Times*, June 16, 1971.

67 "Calm Returns to Troubled Newburgh," *New York Times*, October 8, 1972.

68 "600 Walk out of 3 Schools in Newburgh Demonstration," *New York Times*, April 1, 1969.

69 "Newburgh Students Stage Pro-busing Boycott," *Chicago Daily Defender*, April 4, 1969.

70 "Blacks Upstate Voice Pessimism."

71 *Ross v. Saltmarsh*, 500 F.Supp. 935 (1980).

72 Ibid.

73 *Tillman v. Dade County School Board*, 327 F.Supp. 930 (S.D. Fla. 1971).

74 *Rhyne v. Childs*, 359 F.Supp. 1085 (N.D. Fla. 1973).

75 *Sweet v. Childs*, 518 F.2d 320 (1975).

76 Title VI of the 1965 Elementary and Secondary Act, which prohibited discrimination on the basis of race, color, or religion, eventually became Title VIII after a series of amendments to the law. See the Elementary and Secondary Education Act of 1965, 20 U.S.C. 7914, Sec. 8534.

77 *Griggs v. Duke Power Co.*, 401 U.S. 424 (1971).

78 *Alexander v. Sandoval*, 532 U.S. 275 (2001).

79 Catherine Y. Kim, Daniel J. Losen, and Damon T. Hewitt, *The School-to-Prison Pipeline: Structuring Legal Reform* (New York: New York University Press, 2010), 39–40.

80 Doris Ann Samples, "Disciplining Students on a Racial Basis," *New York Times*, December 29, 1974.

81 *Hawkins v. Coleman*, 376 F.Supp. 1330 (N.D. Tex. 1974).

82 Samples, "Disciplining Students on a Racial Basis."

83 "Overrepresentation of Minorities in Suspensions," July, 18, 1979, box 718, folder 4, RG 5, MALDEF Papers.

84 *Sims v. Waln*, 388 F.Supp. 543 (S.D. Ohio 1974).

85 *Gonyaw v. Gray*, 361 F.Supp. 366 (D. Vt. 1973).

86 *Ware v. Estes*, 328 F.Supp. 657 (N.D. Tex. 1971).

87 *Sims v. Waln*, 388 F.Supp. 543 (S.D. Ohio 1974); *Gonyaw v. Gray*, 361 F.Supp. 366 (D. Vt. 1973).

88 Anne-Marie Cusac, *Cruel and Unusual: The Culture of Punishment in America* (New Haven, CT: Yale University Press, 2009), 78.

89 Robert G. Caldwell, "The Deterrent Influence of Corporal Punishment upon Prisoners Who Have Been Whipped," *American Sociological Review* 9, no. 2 (April 1944): 171–177.

90 On convict leasing, see David M. Oshinsky, *Worse than Slavery: Parchman Farm and the Ordeal of Jim Crow Justice* (New York: Free Press, 1996); and Blackmon, *Slavery by Another Name*.

91 *Robinson v. California*, 370 U.S. 660 (1962).

92 The Thirteenth Amendment was ratified in December 1865. See *Jackson v. Bishop*, 268 F.Supp. 804 (E.D. Ark. 1967).

93 *Jackson v. Bishop*, 404 F.2d 571 (1968).

94 *Commonwealth v. Fell*, 11 Haz. Reg. 179 (Pa. Com. Pl. 1833).

95 *State v. Pendergrass*, 19 N.C. 365 (1837).
96 The exact legal meaning of "*in loco parentis*" as used by the courts has occasionally been unclear. A particular issue is who stands "in the place of the parent" and can therefore discipline children. In the nineteenth and early twentieth centuries, it was assumed that teachers had such powers. Whether or not superintendents and principals also stood *in loco parentis* was a point of controversy, and in one case from the late nineteenth century, a judge found that a superintendent did not have the right to corporally punish students. By the midtwentieth century, with the bureaucratization of the schools, school officials other than teachers—usually assistant principals—were explicitly given the role of disciplinarian and therefore had the right to use corporal punishment. See E. C. Bolmeier, "The Law Governing the Corporal Punishment of Students," *Elementary School Journal* 33, no. 7 (March 1933): 528. Such was the case in *Ingraham v. Wright*, and the majority opinion alludes to (citing it as being legal under the common law) but does not name *in loco parentis* as a source of this authority.
97 *State v. Pendergrass*, 19 N.C. 365 (1837).
98 Anders Walker, "Blackboard Jungle: Delinquency, Desegregation, and the Cultural Politics of *Brown*," *Columbia Law Review* 110 (2010): 1942.
99 "Physical Cruelty in Schools: A Painstaking Look at Discipline," *Chicago Tribune*, May 8, 1972.
100 "It's the Idea Teachers Want, Not Literal Job of Spanking," *Washington Post*, April 7, 1963.
101 "Corporal Punishment Ban in Schools Sought," *New York Times*, May 8, 1972; "No Spanking for Unruly Students," *Norfolk (VA) New Journal and Guide*, February 6, 1971.
102 "School Discipline," *Berkshire (MA) Eagle*, March 16, 1972.
103 On the case where a teacher ripped the earring from the earlobe of a teenaged girl, *Murphy v. Kerrigan*, see Peter S. Aron and Martin L. Katz, "Corporal Punishment in the Public Schools," *Harvard Civil Rights–Civil Liberties Law Review* 6 (1971): 583–594.
104 "'Thou Shalt Beat Him with the Rod and Shalt Deliver His Soul from Hell': The Corporal Punishment Debate, Updated," *New York Times*, October 6, 1974.
105 "Pupil-Paddling Defended in Dallas," *Washington Post*, November 23, 1972.
106 "Report of the Task Force on Corporal Punishment" (Washington, DC: National Education Association, 1972), 3.
107 Ibid., 13.
108 Ibid.
109 "Corporal Punishment Ban in Schools Sought," *New York Times*, May 8, 1972.
110 "Report of the Task Force on Corporal Punishment," 7.
111 Jerry L. Patterson, "How Popular Is the Paddle?" *Phi Delta Kappan* 55, no. 10 (June 1974): 707.
112 "Spanking: All Sides Take Swats at Issue," *Los Angeles Times*, October 19, 1978.

113 "Demands for a Return to Spanking in Schools Stir Heated Disputes," *Wall Street Journal*, June 16, 1970.

114 *Ingraham v. Wright*, 498 F.2d 248, 5th Cir. (1974).

115 Ibid.

116 Ibid.

117 *Ingraham v. Wright*, 430 U.S. 651 (1977).

118 Ibid.

119 *Ingraham v. Wright*, 498 F.2d 248, 5th Cir. (1974).

120 Ibid.

121 Ellen Goodman, "A Spanking Bad Decision," *Washington Post*, April 30, 1977.

122 *Ingraham v. Wright*, 498 F.2d 248, 5th Cir. (1974).

123 *Baker v. Owen*, 395 F.Supp. 294 (M.D.N.C. 1975).

124 For a detailed critique of the majority's logic on whether or not the Eighth Amendment was limited to criminal rather than civil law, see Irene Merker Rosenberg, "*Ingraham v. Wright*: The Supreme Court's Whipping Boy," *Columbia Law Review* 78, no. 1 (January 1978): 75–110.

125 *Ingraham v. Wright*, 430 U.S. 651 (1977).

126 Dissent, *Ingraham v. Wright*, 430 U.S. 651 (1977).

127 On developments in substantive due process protections for students subjected to corporal punishment, see Courtney Mitchell, "Corporal Punishment in Public Schools: An Analysis of Federal Constitutional Claims," in "Corporal Punishment of Children," special issue, *Law and Contemporary Problems* 73, no. 2 (Spring 2010): 321–341.

128 Perry A. Zirkel, "You Bruise, You Lose," *Phi Delta Kappan* 71, no. 5 (January 1990): 410–411.

129 *West Virginia v. Barnette*, 319 U.S. 624 (1943).

130 The Sentencing Project, *How Tough on Crime Became Tough on Kids: Prosecuting Teenage Drug Charges in Adult Courts* (Washington, DC: The Sentencing Project, 2016).

131 *New Jersey v. T.L.O.*, 469 U.S. 325 (1985).

132 N.J. Stat. Ann. tit. 24 Secs. 24-1 to 45 (1971).

133 "Broad Authority for Teachers to Search Students Urged," *Los Angeles Times*, October 3, 1984.

134 Ibid.

135 *New Jersey v. T.L.O.*, 469 U.S. 325 (1985).

136 Ibid.

137 Dissent, Marshall, *New Jersey v. T.L.O.*, 469 U.S. 325 (1985).

138 Ibid., footnote 4.

139 On the rise of zero-tolerance policies in American public education, see Judith Kafka, *The History of "Zero Tolerance" in American Public Schooling* (New York: Palgrave Macmillan, 2016).

140 Aaron H. Caplan, "The Human Rights of Students in Public Schools: Principles and Trends," *Human Rights* 32, no. 4 (Fall 2005): 9.

141 *Safford Unified School Dist. No. 1 v. Redding*, 557 U.S. 364 (2009).
142 Dissent, *Safford Unified School Dist. No. 1 v. Redding*, 557 U.S. 364 (2009).
143 The National Commission on Excellence in Education, *A Nation at Risk: The Imperative for Educational Reform* (Washington, DC: Government Printing Office, 1983).
144 Ibid.
145 David C. Berliner and Bruce J. Biddle, *The Manufactured Crisis: Myths, Fraud, and the Attack on America's Public Schools* (Reading, MA: Addison-Wesley, 1995).
146 Anna McFadden et al., "A Study of Race and Gender Bias in the Punishment of School Children," *Education and Treatment of Children* 15, no. 2 (May 1992): 140–146.
147 Ibid., 144.
148 Ibid., 142, table 1.
149 Ibid., 144.
150 John R. Slate et al., "Corporal Punishment: Used in a Discriminatory Manner?" *Clearing House* 64, no. 6 (July–August 1991): 362.
151 The figure for black children was 5.22 percent, while for white children it was 2.28 and for Hispanic children, 2.06. See ibid., 363.
152 Ibid., 363.
153 Daniel J. Losen and Tia Elena Martinez, "Out of School and Off Track: The Overuse of Suspensions in American Middle and High Schools," *The Civil Rights Project/Proyecto Derechos Civiles*, University of California, Los Angeles, April 8, 2013, www.ucla.edu.

EPILOGUE

1 UN General Assembly, *Convention on the Rights of the Child*, resolution adopted November 20, 1989 (UN Treaty Series 1577:3), entered into force September 2, 1990. The resolution was adopted on the thirtieth anniversary of the adoption of the *Declaration of the Rights of the Child*, November 20, 1959, UN General Assembly, Resolution 1386 (XIV), posted at *UN Documents: Gathering a Body of Global Agreements*, www.un-documents.net.
2 "Long Talks Bring Child Rights Charter to UN," *New York Times*, October 29, 1989.
3 Barbara Bennett Woodhouse, *Hidden in Plain Sight: The Tragedy of Children's Rights from Ben Franklin to Lionel Tate* (Princeton, NJ: Princeton University Press, 2008), 33–34.
4 William Martin, "The Christian Right and American Foreign Policy," *Foreign Policy*, no. 114 (Spring 1999): 66–80.
5 "U.S. to Sign U.N. Pact on Child Rights," *Washington Post*, February 11, 1995.
6 *Gary B. v. Snyder*, Civil Action #16-CV-13292 (E.D. Mich.).
7 Michael Jackman, "How Detroit Students Made a Federal Case out of the City's Broken Schools," *Detroit (MI) Metro Times*, September 6, 2017, www.metrotimes.com.
8 *San Antonio Independent School District v. Rodriguez*, 411 U.S. 1 (1973).

9   "ACLU: State Fails HP Youth," *Michigan Citizen*, July 22, 2012.

10 "Court Rules Michigan Has No Responsibility to Provide Quality Education," *San Francisco Sun-Reporter*, November 20, 2014.

11 Victor M. Rios, *Punished: Policing the Lives of Black and Latino Boys* (New York: New York University Press, 2011), 5.

12 Aaron Kupchik, *Homeroom Security: School Discipline in an Age of Fear* (New York: New York University Press, 2010).

13 Ibid., 44.

14 Fenit Nirappil, "The Story Behind 11Year-Old Naomi Wadler and Her March for Our Lives Speech," *Washington Post*, March 25, 2018.

15 John Woodrow Cox and Stephen Rich, "Scarred by School Shootings," *Washington Post*, March 25, 2018.

16 Woodhouse, *Hidden in Plain Sight*, 44.

INDEX

adolescents, 4–5, 14. *See also* youth

affirmative action, 189

African Americans: black student activism, 11–14, 19–20, 30–34, 65, 68, 92–93, 97–100, 108; in Columbus, Ohio, 94; and corporal punishment, 171–173; and crime, 174–176, 180–181; and disproportionate rates of suspension and expulsion, 184–189, 206–208; educational outcomes, 139, 142; and IQ testing, 167–168; as school administrators, 12–13, 20–21, 34–35, 43–44; school attendance, 230n121; support for school desegregation litigation in Denver, 53; as teachers, 75–76

administrators: disciplinary authority, 1, 23–25, 43–44, 94, 115, 119–121, 124–125; and discriminatory treatment of students, 104, 112; relationship to Black Freedom Movement, 12, 20–21, 33; student demands, 65; and student searches, 200–202; and tenure, 34

age of majority, 4

Alabama State Board of Education, 118

Alabama State College, 117–118

Alcala, Carlos, 151

Alexander v. Holmes County, 46

Alexander v. Sandoval, 188

Almanza, Josefine, 161

American Civil Liberties Union, 122–124, 194–195, 211, 219n3

American Friends Service Committee, 122–123

American GI Forum, 150

American Indians, 139, 151, 236n24, 256n68

Amesse, John, 61–62, 78–79

Andrews, Irving, 60

Andrews, Roosevelt, 196

Anson, Ronald, 127–128

Aronson, Henry, 22, 26–27, 38, 42

assimilation, 88, 146. *See also* bilingual education

Association of Mexican American Educators, 150

Bailey, Stephen, 107

Barnes, Soloman, 196–197

Barnett, O. H., 19–20

Bayh, Birch, 183

Bell, Terrel H., 181–182, 204–205

Benton, Edgar, 61, 64, 79

Berkeley Free Speech Movement, 3

bilingual-bicultural education: in Denver, 86, 88; and legislation, 144–145; and litigation, 140–141, 143, 147–148, 150

bilingual education: and the Chicano Movement, 66, 68, 71; and Colorado law, 86; and federal law, 88, 144–147; and litigation, 139–141, 144, 147–151

Bilingual Education Act (1968), 145–146

Billings, Montana, 106

Birmingham Campaign, 120

Black Berets, 66–67, 71

Black, Hugo, 48–49

black history: Black History Week, 92–93, 96–99, 115; and the freedom schools, 14–15; and student demands, 65, 68

Black Panther Party, 65, 68, 238n60, 240n81

Black Power, 93–94, 97–98, 101

Blackstone, William, 23

Blackwell, Jeremiah, Jr., 35

Blackwell, Unita, 29–30, 35–36, 39, 47

Blackwell v. Issaquena County: desegregation suit, 38–39, 45–47; district court ruling, 39–40; Fifth Circuit ruling, 41–46; initial filing, 34–38; as precedent, 48, 50; and student protests, 29–34

blockbusting, 53, 94

Boston, 193–194

Bradley, Edmund, 167

Brennan, William, 70, 84–85, 125, 134, 158, 166

Bridges, Ruby, 177

Briscoe, Dolph, 155

Broderick, Vincent, 165–166

Bronx paddling scandal, 171–172, 181, 190–191, 196

Broward County, Florida, 190

Brown, Joyce, 30

Brown, Linda, 131

Brown, Oliver, 131

Brown v. Board of Education, 1–2, 118, 131–132; and compulsory education, 37; and corporal punishment, 193; "damage" thesis, 150; and equal educational opportunity, 117; implementation, 11–12, 20, 34, 39; and pedagogical reform, 109; protests at Topeka High School, 131; the right to education, 152; and school closures, 157; and school desegregation lawsuits, 38, 70, 72, 74, 133–135; and student protests, 13; and white violence, 60, 113, 177

Brown v. Board of Education II, 133–134

Burger, Warren, 7, 137

Burger Court, 7–8, 132, 156, 169

Burnside, Canzetta, 11–13, 18–19, 25–26, 223n1

Burnside, Margaret, 21–22

Burnside, Martha, 11–12, 18, 21–22, 25

Burnside v. Byars: district court hearing, 25–29; Fifth Circuit ruling, 41–44; initial filing, 22, 37–38; as precedent, 48, 50, 120; and student protests, 11–12, 18–22

Bush, George H. W., 209

busing: in Denver, 69–71, 77–78; as national issue, 82–83, 132; public opposition, 69; and Supreme Court rulings, 89, 134–138

Cameron, Benjamin Franklin, 119

Cárdenas, José, 86–87, 143

Cárdenas Plan, 87–88, 140, 148

Carter, Jimmy, 204

Carter, Robert L., 74, 237n41

Center for Research and Education in American Liberties, 105

Chaney, James, 12, 18, 21, 30

Chicano Movement, 9; and bilingual-bicultural education, 144–146; Chicano freedom schools, 79–80; in Denver, 51, 53, 64–65; East L.A. "blowouts," 3, 65; and educational reform, 79–81, 86; and racial identity, 3; student protest, 51, 65–66, 69–71, 106–107, 121; in Topeka, Kansas, 131

Chicano Youth Association, 147

Children out of School in America, 161–162, 183–184

Children's Crusade, 120

Children's Defense Fund: amicus brief in Goss v. Lopez, 122–123; and children excluded from school, 161–162, 183–184; and student suspensions, 128–129, 156, 183–187, 207, 212; and students with disabilities, 163, 166. See also Children out of School in America

children's rights, 4–8, 122, 209–210. See also students' rights

Chinese Americans, 148–150

Citizens' Councils, 60, 111, 237n44

civil disorder. See riots

Civil Obedience Act (1968), 179

Civil Rights Act (1964): and bilingual education, 148, 150, 256n66; and racial discrimination in education, 187–188; and school desegregation, 6, 262n63; and students with disabilities, 163, 168
Civil Rights Act (1968), 178–179
Civil Rights Project, 207–208
Clark, Septima, 79
Clinton, Bill, 209
Cobb, Charles, 15–17
Coleman, James, 77
college preparatory education, 57, 84, 141, 147, 160
Columbia University student protests, 105
Columbine High School massacre, 213
Columbus Board of Education v. Penick, 129, 245n10
Columbus, Ohio, 94: city council, 102; population growth, 245n5; school desegregation suit, 129; and school segregation, 95–96, 245n8; and student protests, 100
Columbus, Ohio, public schools; Central High School, 98–100; Eastmoor High School, 97, 103; Franklin Junior High School, 97; Hilltonia Junior High School, 99, 102; Linden-McKinley, 98; Marion-Franklin High School, 92, 100–101, 123; McGuffey Junior High School, 100, 102; Mohawk Junior High School, 99; North High School, 102; West High School, 97
common law, 23, 119, 152, 198
common schools. *See* public education
community control of schools: in Columbus, 96–97; in Denver, 65–66, 68; in New York City, 181
compensatory education: and bilingual education, 146–147; and cultural deprivation theory, 142, 254n42; and desegregation, 77
compulsory education laws: and bilingual education, 148; and enforcement,

249n101; exemptions for disabled students, 160–164; and *in loco parentis*, 23–24, 116, 202; in Mississippi, 36–37, 161, 231n126; and the right to education, 104, 125, 227n54
Congress: busing legislation, 82–83; and Southeast Asian refugees, 88
Connor, Bull, 120
conservatives, 209, 211
constitutional law. *See* corporal punishment; due process; equal protection; right to privacy; school desegregation
Convention on the Rights of the Child, 209–210
convict leasing, 174, 192
Coolidge v. New Hampshire, 203
Cooper, Susan, 101
corporal punishment, 9, 47, 190; constitutionality of, 197–199; illegal use of, 171–173, 181; as punishment for crime, 191–192; and racial disparities, 189, 190–191, 205–207; state laws governing, 193, 196, 199; and student protest, 33–34, 71
Council of Federated Organizations: and the freedom schools, 15–16, 49; in Issaquena County, 29–32; in Neshoba County, 18–20, 22, 26–29, 46; and student protests, 17–20, 26–28, 32; and voter registration, 12, 14
Cox, Harold, 38–40, 46, 49
Craig, Marian, 96–97, 114
Crain, Virginia, 126
crime, 173–174, 178, 180, 259n6
Crome, Betty, 100
cruel and unusual punishment. *See* corporal punishment; Eighth Amendment
Crusade for Justice, 53, 65, 67–68, 71, 80, 240n81. *See also* La Escuela Tlatelolco
cultural deprivation theory: and bilingual-bicultural education, 141–143; and pedagogical reform, 109; and school desegregation litigation, 84

curricular reform: and bilingual-bicultural education, 140–143, 145, 148; and black student protest, 65, 68, 107; and the Chicano Movement, 80; and Mexican American history, 86–87; as student demand, 98, 131

Dade County, Florida, 190, 196
Dallas, Texas, public schools, 113, 189, 191, 194
Davis v. County School Board of Prince Edward County, 3
Dean, James, 173
democracy, and education reform, 106, 124
Democratic National Convention of 1964, 14
Denver, Colorado: Commission on Community Relations, 61; Community Education Council, 90; police department, 67; population growth, 52, 234n5; residential segregation, 52–54, 61–62
Denver neighborhoods, 56; Five Points, 54–55, 58, 65; North Denver, 54, 57; Park Hill, 54, 58, 60–62, 64, 77
Denver public schools, 56–58; Abraham Lincoln High School, 55–56; attendance zones, 58; Barrett Elementary School, 57–58, 76, 81; Cole Junior High School, 58, 65; Del Pueblo Elementary School, 86, 88; East High School, 55–58, 64, 68–69, 76; George Washington High School, 55–56, 77–79; John F. Kennedy High School, 55; Manual High School, 55–58, 77, 84, 68–69, 76; and mobile classrooms, 57–58, 81, 236n32; North High School, 55–56, 58, 71, 121; racial composition of student population, 90; school discipline, 90; segregation, 56–58; Smiley Junior High School, 65; South High School, 55–56, 58; Sted-

man Elementary School, 60, 76–77; Thomas Jefferson High School, 55–56, 58; West High School, 55–56, 58, 66–69, 76, 78
Denver School Board: and the Chicano Movement, 66; elections, 69; and equal educational opportunity, 58–60; and Noel Resolution, 64, 69; role in school segregation, 54–55, 57–58, 70, 74; and student protest, 71
desegregation: of bus terminals, 13; of lunch counters, 14; of places of public accommodation, 17. *See also* school desegregation
Detroit public schools, 135–138, 210–211
Devine, Annie, 29
Diggs, Bernice, 32
direct action protests, 15, 17
disability: "educable mentally retarded" classification, 45, 167–168; exclusion of disabled children from public schools, 160–163; legislation, 163; and school segregation, 167–168, 233n156; special education, 163; and students' rights, 164–166
Disabled and Incapacitated Students of Santa Ana College, 161
disparate impact, 188–189
disruption principle, 48, 50
Dixon v. Alabama State Board of Education, 117–120
Douglas, William O., 85, 125
Doyle, William, 69–71, 76–77, 81, 85
due process: and corporal punishment, 198; and the rights of college students, 118; and the right to education, 125, 151–152, 251n137; and school discipline, 40, 93, 115, 120–124, 130; and students with disabilities, 162
drug use, 200–202, 214

East Los Angeles "blowouts," 3, 65–66
Eckhard, Christopher, 48

Edcouch, Texas, 106

Edelman, Marian Wright, 38, 40–41, 128, 183–184

Edgewood, Texas, school district, 152–153, 155–156

Edgewood Independent School District v. Kirby, 156

Education for All Handicapped Children Act, 163–164, 168, 258n134

Eighth Amendment, 190–192, 195–199, 205

Elementary and Secondary Education Act (1965), 145, 188, 263n76

Enforcement Act (1871), 127

English, Neva Louise, 11–13, 19, 25–26

English-only policies, 144, 148–149

equal educational opportunity: and adequate education, 164; and bilingual-bicultural education, 140–141, 145, 147–151; and bilingual education, 150–151; and court-ordered remedies, 77, 79, 90; and Denver School Board policy, 59–60; and disability, 163, 166–167; and the Fourteenth Amendment, 9; and *Keyes v. School Dist. No. 1*, 69–70, 72, 76–77, 82, 89; and school desegregation, 73–74, 79, 83, 138–139; and school discipline, 113

Equal Educational Opportunities Act, 82

equal protection: and bilingual-bicultural education, 143, 148–151; and bilingual education, 140, 144, 149–151; and educational equity, 169, 210–211; and educational quality, 74–75, 81–82, 85, 90; and immigration status, 158–159; and school segregation, 72, 74, 81, 132–133, 139; and socioeconomic status, 153–154; and student discipline, 91, 120; and students with disabilities, 162, 165. *See also* equal educational opportunity

Estes, Nolan, 113–114, 189, 194

Evers, Charles, 29

Evers, Medgar, 29

Fair Housing Act, 54, 178–179

Fanon, Frantz, 111

Featherstone, Ralph, 19, 22

Federal Bureau of Investigation, 68

Federal Housing Administration, 53, 136. *See also* redlining

Fifth Amendment, 130

Fifth Circuit Court of Appeals: rulings on corporal punishment, 196–199; rulings on school discipline, 118–121, 189; rulings on student speech, 27, 29, 40–44, 48, 50; rulings on undocumented students, 158

Finch, Robert H., 105, 146

Finger, John, 86

Finger Plan, 86

First Amendment. *See* free speech

flag salute cases, 24–25

Ford, Gerald, 205

Fourteenth Amendment: and bilingual-bicultural education, 143, 147–148; and bilingual education, 139, 144, 149–151; and corporal punishment, 190–191, 205; and disability, 162; and educational equity, 169, 210–211; and immigration status, 158; and racial classifications, 45; and the rights of college students, 118; and the right to literacy, 210–211; and school discipline, 91, 93, 114–115, 124–125, 130; and school finance litigation, 153–156; and school segregation, 52, 70, 72–74, 77, 81, 83–85, 89, 129, 135–138; and the state action doctrine, 132–133, 136–140. *See also* equal protection; due process

Fourth Amendment, 200–204

Fox, Deborah, 101

Frankfurter, Felix, 24

freedom buttons, 20, 32–34: and free speech, 11–12, 25–27, 38, 40–43; and student discipline, 36, 41 freedom of choice plans: constitutionality of, 73, 133; in Mississippi, 39, 46; and resistance to *Brown v. Board of Education*, 75

Freedom Rides, 3, 13, 26, 35, 117, 119

freedom schools: Chicano freedom schools, 79–80; in Columbus, 96; and curriculum, 16; and Freedom Summer, 15–17; in Hattiesburg, 16–17; in the Mississippi Delta, 30; and the Mississippi Student Union, 32; and proposed school boycott, 17; and punishment of students, 17

freedom schools convention, 30

Freedom Summer, 12, 14–16, 19, 22, 30, 38, 40, 47, 49

free speech: as fundamental right, 155; in public schools, 1–2, 8, 22–25, 29, 34, 38, 41–44; and school discipline, 11–12, 29, 40, 114, 121–122, 186–187; and the Supreme Court, 47–49

Freire, Paulo, 111

Fromm, Erich, 111

Fulton, Philip, 123

fundamental rights, 124, 151–156, 158, 162

Gary B. v. Snyder, 210–211

Gilberts, Harry, 68

Gochman, Arthur, 153

Goldwater, Barry, 174

Gonzales, Rodolfo (Corky), 65–68, 70, 80

Goodman, Andrew, 12, 18, 21

Goss v. Lopez: and administrators' authority, 200; amicus briefs, 122–124; and *in loco parentis*, 115, 202; as precedent, 164, 198; precedents to, 119–120; and racial disparities in school discipline, 128–130, 206; and student protest, 95–97, 99–101; Supreme Court dissent, 125–126; Supreme Court ruling, 93, 124–125

Great Society, 155

Greenberg, Jack, 38, 45

Green v. New Kent County, 133–134, 138

Green, William E., 181

Grenier, Gordon, 69, 74, 83

Griffin v. School Board, 158

Griggs v. Duke Power Co., 188

Griswold v. Connecticut, 152

Guadalupe Organization, Inc. v. Tempe Elementary School District No. 1, 151

Hammond, Larry, 84–85

Harris, Bruce, 101

Harris, Carl, 101

Hart-Celler Act (1965), 149

Hawkins v. Coleman, 189

Hendrick Hudson Central School District v. Rowley, 166

Hernandez, Manuel, 70–71, 121–122

hidden curriculum, 109, 111

Highlander Folk School, 79

Hilgen, Janie, 153

Hillsborough County, Florida, 190

Hilltop Civic Council, 103

Hobson v. Hansen, 73–74, 162

Home Owners Loan Corporation, 135

Horace Mann School, 14

housing discrimination: in Columbus, 94–95; in Denver, 63–64

Houston, Charles Hamilton, 163

Hughes, Sarah, 189

Illich, Ivan, 110

immigrants: and bilingual education, 144, 149; education of undocumented children, 157; and IQ testing, 167; Mexican migration, 145; and public education, 89–90

Individuals with Disabilities Education Act, 163–166

Indochinese Refugee Transition Act, 88

Ingraham, James, 195–196

Ingraham v. Wright: corporal punishment after *Ingraham*, 205–206, 208;

facts of the case, 195–197; Fifth Circuit ruling, 196–197; Supreme Court dissent, 198–199; Supreme Court ruling, 198, 200

in loco parentis: and authority of school officials, 115–116, 264n96; challenges to, 119, 130; common law origins, 23; and corporal punishment, 192–193, 197; and student searches, 201–202, 204

In re Gault, 7

IQ testing, 167–168

Issaquena County, Mississippi, 29–30, 32, 35–37, 44, 47

Jackson, Philip, 109

Jackson, William, 192

Jehovah's Witnesses, 24

Johnson, Lyndon B., 46, 113, 174, 179

Jordan, Linda, 26

Jordan, Orsmond E., 32–36, 42–43

juvenile courts, 7, 13–14, 102–103, 114, 200–201

juvenile delinquency, 29, 173–174, 201; Senate Subcommittee on Juvenile Delinquency, 182–183

Juvenile Delinquency Act (1961), 173

Kennedy, John F., 38, 120, 173

Kerner Commission, 62, 176, 179–181

Keyes v. School Dist. No. 1: and bilingual-bicultural education, 140–143, 147–148; and de jure segregation, 76; district court hearing, 71–72, 74–76; and educational quality, 52, 76, 83; and employment discrimination, 75–76; initial filing, 69–70; litigation strategy, 73–74; as precedent, 129; remedial order, 77; Supreme Court oral arguments, 153; Supreme Court ruling, 82–85, 89

King, Martin Luther, Jr., 3, 51, 62, 64, 179

Kishkunas, Louis, 142–143

Ku Klux Klan, 13, 18–19, 127

La Escuela Tlatelolco, 79–80, 88

La Raza Unida, 153

Larry P. v. Riles, 168

Latinos, 206–208. *See also* Mexican Americans; Mexicans; Puerto Ricans

Lausche, Frank, 178–179

Lau v. Nichols, 148–151

law and order politics, 176–181

lawyers: in Mississippi, 7, 40–41; in Denver, 60, 69

League of United Latin American Citizens, 150

Lee, Herbert, 13

Lewis, Ike, 13

Little Rock, Arkansas, 113, 157, 177

Lopez, Dwight, 99–101

Loving v. Virginia, 152

Lucy, Autherine, 116–117

Lucy v. Adams, 117

March for Our Lives, 213

March on Washington, 30

Mars, Florence, 18

Marshall, St. Clair, 172

Marshall, Thurgood: appointment to federal judiciary, 38; dissent in *Milliken*, 138; dissent in *New Jersey v. T.L.O.*, 202–203; dissent in *Rodriguez*, 170; and rights of disabled students, 166; and students' due process rights, 125; and teacher pay equalization suits, 189

Martinez, Baltazar, 71

mass incarceration, 178, 211–212

Massive Resistance campaign, 113, 177

McCabe, Irene, 136

McComb, Mississippi, 19; Burgland High School, 13; student protests, 13–14

McLaurin v. Oklahoma, 72, 74

Mercer, Jane, 168

Meridian, Mississippi, 13

Metcalfe, George, 39

Mexican American Legal Defense Fund, 7: and bilingual education, 140, 150–151; and Chicano student protests, 106; and the color line, 174–175; critique of desegregation, 87–88; and educational achievement, 139, 147; exclusion of undocumented students, 158; and *Keyes*, 85–86; school finance litigation, 156

Mexican Americans: in Denver, 52, 88; and disproportionate rates of suspension and expulsion, 184, 206–208; and educational outcomes, 53, 59, 139, 141–142, 146, 150; and IQ testing, 167–168; as racial minorities, 85, 221n12, 234n6; and school finance litigation, 153–156; and school segregation, 52, 55, 85–86, 140, 143; and student protest, 65–66; as teachers, 76, 86–87

Mexicans, 174–175

Meyer v. Nebraska, 152

Miami, Florida, public schools, 190, 195–197

Milliken v. Bradley, 135–138

Mills v. Board of Education of the District of Columbia, 163

Minersville v. Gobitis, 24

Mississippi. *See* Freedom Summer; Issaquena County; McComb; Sharkey County

Mississippi Freedom Democratic Party, 14

Mississippi Project, 14, 21. *See also* Freedom Summer

Mississippi Student Union, 30, 32, 229n95

Mize, Sidney, 25, 28–29, 37

Moore, Montgomery, 20–22, 26–28, 42

Morris, Ajatha, 18, 21, 46

Morris, Ola, 21–22, 46

Moses, Robert, 14, 30

Motley, Constance Baker, 120

Moynihan Report, 175–176, 260n18

multicultural education, 87

NAACP (National Association for the Advancement of Colored People): Columbus branch, 96, 103, 114–115, 129; Denver branch, 60; Detroit branch, 136; in Mississippi, 13, 29, 35, 39; Youth Councils, 13

NAACP Legal Defense Fund: amicus briefs, 122; and bilingual education, 150; and free speech litigation, 22, 25–26, 29, 38, 40–42, 45; Jackson office, 7, 22, 40–41; and school desegregation litigation, 6, 34, 74, 86, 138; and school discipline litigation, 120, 130, 187; teacher pay equalization cases, 36

Nabrit, James, III, 83, 89

National Association of Secondary School Principals, 104–105

National Committee for Citizens in Education, 122

National Education Association, 122, 194–195

National Institute of Education, 127

A Nation at Risk, 205

natural rights, 23–24, 116

Neshoba County: and civil rights activism, 21; murders of civil rights workers, 18–19, 28; and school desegregation, 46. *See also* Philadelphia, Mississippi

Newburgh, New York, 186

New Jersey v. T.L.O., 200–203, 208

New Left, 3

New York State Board of Regents, 107

Ninth Circuit Court of Appeals, 149

Nixon, Richard, 4, 46, 105, 205: and bilingual education, 146–147; and busing, 82–84, 135; and crime, 174, 176

Nodes, Allan, 201

Noel, Rachel, 60–62, 64, 68–69, 78–79, 90

Noel Resolution: implementation of, 66; passage of, 62–64; reinstatement of, 70; repeal of, 69–72

Nonviolent High, 14

Obledo, Mario, 139
Ocean Hill-Brownsville experiment, 65, 181
Ohio Avenue School Ad Hoc Committee, 96
Ohio state legislature, 103–104
open enrollment, 58–59

Paddling. *See* corporal punishment
parents: rights of, 197, 200, 202, 226n54; and student protesters, 14. See also *in loco parentis*
Park Hill Action Committee, 54, 60
Parkland, Florida, 213
Patterson, John M., 118
pedagogy, 5, 17–18; and cultural deprivation theory, 142; and reform efforts, 108–112
Pemberton, Mack, 104
penal reform, 191–192
Pennsylvania Association for Retarded Children, 162
Philadelphia, Mississippi: and free speech lawsuit, 11; murders of civil rights workers, 12, 18; school segregation, 11–12; student protests, 19–20
Philadelphia, Mississippi, public schools: Booker T. Washington High School, 18–19; Philadelphia High School, 46
Pledge of Allegiance. *See* flag salute cases
Plessy v. Ferguson, 72, 74, 84–85
Plyler v. Doe, 158–159
police brutality: and civil rights protest, 13–14; in Denver, 65, 67, 239n71; and "shock the conscience" standard, 199
police officers: and arrests of protesting students, 99–101, 107–108; in schools, 71, 78–79, 92, 97, 102, 203, 214
politics of respectability, 44, 232n148
Pontiac, Michigan, 136
Poor People's Campaign, 51
Port Allen, Louisiana, 121
Postman, Neil, 110

Pottinger, J. Stanley, 146
poverty: school breakfast programs, 87; and school finance, 152–156; and student achievement, 82–84
Powell, Lewis, 84–85, 125–126, 154
Prince Edward County, Virginia, 3, 157–158
private schools, 157
Progressive Era, 23, 116
Puerto Rican Legal Defense Fund, 7, 150
Puerto Ricans, 111, 146, 174–175; and corporal punishment, 171–173; and disproportionate rates of suspension and expulsion, 183, 186, 206–208
Public Counsel, 210
public education: and capitalism, 159; and citizenship, 202; and civic virtue, 23, 124; development of, 23, 116; as entitlement, 125; in Mississippi, 36; and state constitutions, 23
punishment. *See* corporal punishment; school discipline; suspensions and expulsions
pushouts, 112–113, 122, 183

racial discrimination: and corporal punishment, 190–191, 194; and IQ testing, 167; in public education, 134, 210–212; in suspensions and expulsions, 112–113, 122–123, 126, 183–189. *See also* real estate; school segregation
Rainey, Lee, 19–21
Randolph, A. Philip, 30
Reagan, Ronald, 144, 170, 201, 204–205
real estate: laws prohibiting discrimination, 54; and racial discrimination, 53–54, 135–136; racially restrictive housing covenants, 53, 136; schools and property values, 152. *See also* Fair Housing Act
Reconstruction, 23
redlining, 53, 135
Rehabilitation Act (1973), 163, 165, 168

Rehnquist, William, 85, 166

Resurrection City, 51

right to education: and compulsory education, 104; and the Convention on the Rights of the Child, 209–211; and due process, 124; fundamental rights argument, 151–152, 154–155; in Mississippi, 37; and state constitutions, 155–156, 164; and the Supreme Court, 155, 158, 247n55

right to literacy, 210–211

right to privacy, 108, 200–203

riots: and the Civil Rights Act (1968), 178–179; in Denver, 61–62, 64; and Kerner Commission Report, 176, 179–180; and law and order politics, 177–178; and the Martin Luther King, Jr., assassination, 179; and Moynihan Report, 175–176; in Newburgh, New York, 186; and student protest, 68–69; Thanksgiving Day Riot, 193; Watts Riots, 16, 175–176, 237n48

Ris, William, 84

Rivera, Victor, 159–161

Rives, Richard, 118

Robert F. Kennedy Memorial Fund, 112

Robert Russa Moton High School, 3

Rollins, Ethel, 75–76

Roosevelt, Franklin Delano, 30

Roth, Stephen, 137

Rowley, Amy, 164–166

Rowley, Clifford, 165

Rowley, Nancy, 165

San Antonio v. Rodriguez, 125, 152–158, 162, 170, 211

Sandrof, Irving, 171–172

Santa Ana, California: Carl Harvey School, 160; Santa Ana Valley High School, 159–161

school crime, 182–184, 200, 208, 212, 214

school desegregation: and bilingual education programs, 144; of colleges and universities, 117; in Columbus, 95, 128–129; and corporal punishment, 194; critiques by Chicano activists, 66, 87; in Denver, 52–53, 62, 64, 69; as legal remedy, 77, 81, 86, 89; litigation, 52–53, 69–70, 73–74, 132–139; in Mississippi, 35–36, 38–39, 43, 46–47; and pedagogical reform, 109; resistance by state legislatures, 158; and student conflict, 95, 107–108, 121; and student discipline, 113, 122, 126, 130, 185, 189; and the Supreme Court, 85, 132–135, 137–138, 158; and violent resistance, 177; and white retaliation, 46, 231n133. See also busing

school discipline: disparate rates in Denver, 90–91; and due process, 93, 125; and free speech, 33, 40; and public opinion, 181–183; and racial discrimination, 114–115, 120, 122–123, 207; and racial disparities, 108, 206–208; and school disorders, 92–94, 99–100; and school officials' authority, 23; and student protest, 1–2, 13, 37, 71, 153; and students' rights, 219n3. See also corporal punishment; suspensions and expulsions

school finance litigation, 153–156

school segregation: attendance zones, 73; in Columbus, 94–95; de facto/de jure divide, 60, 70, 72–74, 83–85, 133, 134; in Denver, 55–58, 69, 72; and Mexican Americans, 55, 72; in Mississippi, 12, 15, 21, 36–38, 46; as prima facie case, 85; and residential segregation, 53–54, 135–137; and unequal education, 52–53, 58, 81–83, 96, 230n125

school shootings, 213–214

school-to-prison pipeline, 211–212

Schrag, Peter, 111

Schwerner, Michael, 12, 18, 21, 40

Seavey, Warren A., 117

Second Circuit Court of Appeals, 166

segregation academies, 47

Sensenbrenner, Jack, 104

Serna v. Portales, 148, 256n66

Serrano v. Priest, 155–156

Shafer, Harry, 66–68

Sharkey County, Mississippi: Henry Weathers High School, 29–30, 32–34, 43–44; school boycotts, 34–36, 41; and school desegregation, 44, 47; and school funding, 37; and school segregation, 34–35

Shelley v. Kraemer, 135

"shock the conscience" standard, 199

Shorter, Toni, 103

Shuttlesworth, Fred, 177

Shuttlesworth, Ruby, 177

Sias, Henry, 35

Sims, Leatha Benita, 191

Sims v. Waln, 191

sit-in movement, 3, 14, 117, 119

Sixteenth Street Baptist Church, 120

Sixth Circuit Court of Appeals, 129, 137

SNCC buttons. *See* freedom buttons

Southern Christian Leadership Council, 120, 122

Southern Regional Council, 112–113, 122, 126, 130, 212

Southwest Action Center, 51

Spanish language bans, 106

state constitutions, 23, 155–156

State v. Pendergrass, 192–193, 197

Stewart, Potter, 84, 125, 203

Stone, Harlan Fiske, 24

stop and frisk laws, 178

Strickland, Peggy, 126

Stuart v. Nappi, 164

student boycotts: and Chicano activism, 3; in Columbus, 96–98, 102; in Denver, 62, 65, 69–70; in Edgewood, Texas, 152–153; and Freedom Summer, 17, 30; in Mississippi, 14, 34, 36, 38, 47; in Tyler, Texas, 121. *See also* student protests

Student Nonviolent Coordinating Committee (SNCC), 11–15, 26–27, 30

student protests: of administrators' authority, 17; and the Black Freedom Movement, 219n1; and the Columbus city council, 103; in Columbus schools, 92–93, 97–101; and demands for minority teachers, 78, 99; in Denver schools, 65–70; frequency of, 105, 248n69; in Mississippi schools, 13, 28–29, 33, 37; in Ohio, 103–104; and public opinion, 105; and racial conflict, 107–108; and school discipline, 13, 17, 33–34, 79, 99–101, 186–187. *See also* student boycotts; walkouts

Students' Afro-American Society, 105

Students for a Democratic Society, 105–106, 247n66

students' rights, 7–10; to bilingual education, 150; and corporal punishment, 198; to due process of law, 124–125; to equal educational opportunity, 90; to free expression, 42–44, 47–49; and *in loco parentis*, 22–25; to privacy, 202; and racial disparities in school discipline, 207–208; and students with disabilities, 166

suspensions and expulsions: and the Children's Crusade, 120; and disruptive students, 97–99; litigation over, 114–120; as punishment for protest, 17, 20, 97, 107, 115, 118, 120–121; and racial disparities, 104, 112–113, 122, 126, 183–189, 206–208, 212; and state laws, 104, 115, 121–122, 125; and students' rights, 125–126, 198, 200

Sutton, Rudolph, 101

Swann v. Charlotte-Mecklenburg, 134–136, 138

Sweatt v. Painter, 72, 74, 83

Tasby v. Estes, 189

teacher pay equalization litigation, 36, 189

teachers: authority to search students, 200–203; disciplinary authority, 23, 115–116, 192–193, 264n96; and discriminatory treatment of students, 112, 122–123; employment discrimination, 75–76; student demands in relation to hiring, 65, 99; support for corporal punishment, 195; support for student protest, 153

Tennessee A & I State University, 119

Tennessee Board of Education, 119

Tenth Circuit Court of Appeals: appeal of *Keyes v. School Dist. No. 1*, 70, 77, 81–82, 85; and bilingual-bicultural education, 140, 148; response to Cárdenas Plan, 88; and school discipline, 122

Terry v. Ohio, 178

Thirteenth Amendment, 187, 192

Thomas, Clarence, 5, 204

Thurmond, Strom, 178

Tinker, John, 48

Tinker, Mary Beth, 48

Tinker v. Des Moines: critique by Lewis Powell, 125; disruption test, 48, 50, 173; as precedent, 127, 198, 200, 202; and the right to education, 152; and school discipline, 115, 123; and student protest, 120; and students' rights, 2, 7; Supreme Court ruling, 47–50

Topeka, Kansas, 131

Tougaloo College, 14, 30, 32

tracking, 147, 162

Travis, Brenda, 13

truancy, 102–103, 120, 184, 206. *See also* compulsory education laws

Tyler, Texas, 121, 157–158

Tyree, Clifford, 98–99

United Nations, 209

U.S. Commission on Civil Rights, 61, 122, 139

U.S. Department of Education, 170, 204–205

U.S. Department of Health, Education, and Welfare: bilingual education policy, 146, 150; data on school suspensions, 115, 128, 187; and educational quality, 204–205; Office of Civil Rights, 128, 146, 184–185, 190; and school crime, 182–183; and school desegregation, 47, 82; and student protest, 105

U.S. Department of Justice, 46

U.S. Supreme Court: and corporal punishment, 195, 198–199; and cruel and unusual punishment, 192; ruling in *Goss v. Lopez*, 124–125; ruling in *Keyes v. School Dist. No. 1*, 82–85, 89–90; ruling in *Lau v. Nichols*, 150–151; and school desegregation, 52, 70, 72–73, 133–138; and school finance litigation, 154–156; and student searches, 201–204; and students with disabilities, 166; and undocumented students, 158

University of Alabama, 116–117

Urban League, 96

vagrancy laws, 174

Velasquez, Willie, 153

Vietnam War: refugee resettlement, 88; student protests, 47, 93, 105

violence, retaliation by whites, 13

"Violent Schools, Safe Schools," 182–183, 201–202

vocational education, 56–57

Voorhees, James, 78

voter registration, 11–13, 15

voting rights, 25

Voting Rights Act, 14

Waddy, Joseph C., 163

Wadler, Naomi, 213

walkouts: in Denver, 67–69; in Edcouch, Texas, 106; in Edgewood, Texas, 152–153; and free speech litigation, 187; in Los Angeles, 3, 65; and the March for

Our Lives, 213; in Mississippi, 13–14, 17; in Topeka, Kansas, 131
War on Crime, 174, 200, 208
War on Drugs, 203
War on Poverty, 51, 146, 174, 260n10
Warren Court, 7
Washington, Tyrone, 92–93, 100
Watson, Lauren, 65, 238n60
Watts Riots. *See* riots
Weingartner, Charles, 110
Wells, Will S., 26
Western Caravan, 51
West High School "blowouts," 67–68
Westin, Alan, 105–106
West Virginia v. Barnette, 25, 127, 226n54
White, Byron: dissent in *Ingraham v. Wright*, 198–199; dissent in *Rowley v. Board of Education*, 166; opinion in *Goss v. Lopez*, 125; opinion in *Wood v. Strickland*, 127

White, Eugene, 32
White, Roosevelt, 32
white flight, 54
Wilcox County, Alabama, 185
Woods, Calvin, 120
Woods, Linda Cal, 120
Woodson, Carter, 97
Wood v. Strickland, 126–128
Wright, J. Skelly, 73, 162, 237n41

Yarborough, Ralph, 146
Yépes, Reba, 51–52, 80–81
Young, Gene, 14
youth: and social movements, 12, 16; political participation 4–7, 12. *See also* adolescents; students' rights
Yudof, Mark, 109

Zarr, Melvyn, 38, 40–41
zero tolerance policies, 203–204, 214

ABOUT THE AUTHOR

Kathryn Schumaker is Edith Kinney Gaylord Presidential Professor and Assistant Professor of Classics and Letters at the University of Oklahoma.

Lightning Source UK Ltd.
Milton Keynes UK
UKHW010914031222
413248UK00004B/173